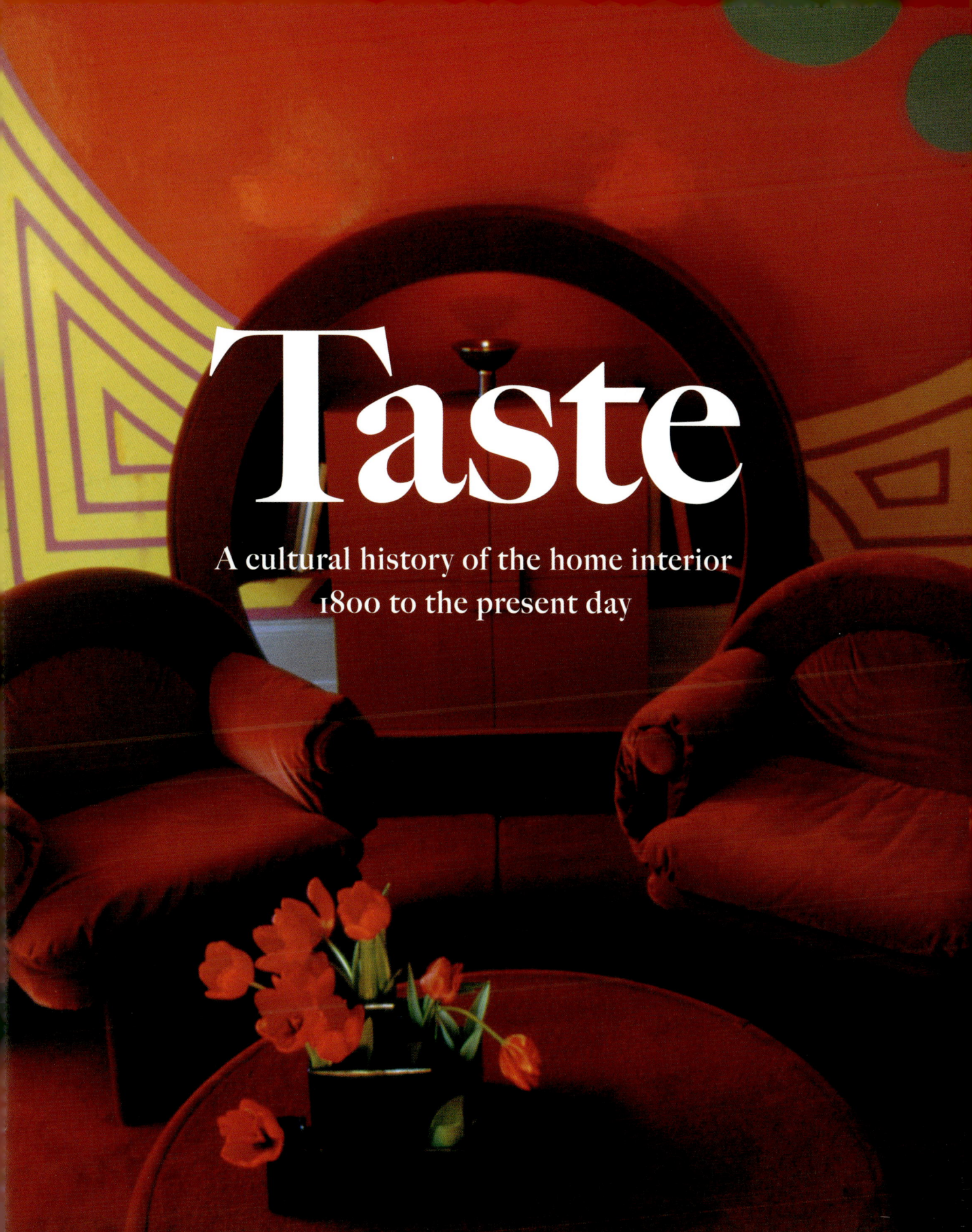

Taste

A cultural history of the home interior
1800 to the present day

*For my father who built our house, my mother who made it a home
and Lindsay Taylor who taught me the importance of decoration.*

*I thank Susannah Lear who saw merit in the subject and shaped the book
and those at RIBA Publishing who brought it to a peaceful conclusion.*

© RIBA Publishing, 2020

Published by RIBA Publishing, 66 Portland Place, London, W1B 1AD

ISBN 978-1-85946-925-5

The rights of Drew Plunkett to be identified as the Author of this Work has been asserted in accordance with the Copyright, Designs and Patents Act 1988 sections 77 and 78.

All rights reserved. No part of this publication may be reproduced, stored in a retrieval system, or transmitted, in any form or by any means, electronic, mechanical, photocopying, recording or otherwise, without prior permission of the copyright owner.

British Library Cataloguing-in-Publication Data

A catalogue record for this book is available from the British Library.

Commissioning Editor: Elizabeth Webster

Assistant Editor: Clare Holloway

Production: Jane Rogers

Designed and typeset by John Round

Printed and bound in Italy by L.E.G.O. Spa

Cover image: Getty Images

While every effort has been made to check the accuracy and quality of the information given in this publication, neither the Author nor the Publisher accept any responsibility for the subsequent use of this information, for any errors or omissions that it may contain, or for any misunderstandings arising from it.

www.ribapublishing.com

Taste

A cultural history of the home interior
1800 to the present day

Drew Plunkett

RIBA Publishing

Contents

Prologue
VI

1:
New Money,
Old Ideas
1

2:
Disapproving
Dilletantes
23

6:
1951 and All That
109

7:
The Empire
Strikes Back
129

8:
Carrying on
Regardless
149

3:
New Century,
New Style
43

4:
The People
Decorate
69

5:
Post-War Populism
91

9:
Back to the Future
165

10:
Having it and
Having it More
Abundantly
187

Epilogue
204

Notes 207
Index 211
Image Credits 215

Prologue

'Taste is one of the weaker words in our language. It means a little less than something, a little more than nothing … It expresses a familiarity with what is *au courant* among persons of so-called culture, of so-called good form.'

Louis Sullivan, *Kindergarten Chats*, 1892[1]

Taste is personal but never unique and it's dangerous to think that it doesn't matter. It is how we describe ourselves to the world. We first declare it when we decide how we'll dress and so demonstrate the tribe to which we are condemned, by circumstances or inclination, to belong. We hope it will demonstrate that we're at the top of our particular pile and, perhaps, that we're ready to move to the next level. It's about aspiration and therefore about imitation and conforming; even individualism has its own look. From clothes we then move to homes and we also fashion those in our own images.

Home is intriguing because it encompasses the gamut of human activity. Of all the buildings we spend time in, it is the one we can tune to suit our practical and impractical needs, the one on which we can most impose our taste.

Taste is not timeless. Its bare bones, if they exist, are so fleshed out by changing times and circumstances that they are lost under the weight of whim and fancy that reflects the circumstances and psyches of individuals, families and nations.

It's never static and few are immune to its changes, major and minor. One might suspect that it is capricious. There are a few who initiate change, there are a few more who take raw new ideas and tune them, but most absorb change at their own pace and don't notice their metamorphosis.

Taste is visceral but it can be selectively bred. Architects and designers are caught at an impressionable age and taught to be iconoclastic. Untaught taste, that of everyone not inducted into professional mysteries, is subjective and stubbornly sceptical of anything radical and the innocent perversions of the untaught offer critiques of professional indulgences. These aberrations need to be sympathetically examined.

And to examine the taste(s) that shape homes it seems appropriate to make a case study. Britain, over the last 200 years, is a good place and time to start. It was becoming the most powerful country in the world 200 years ago, with the biggest most diverse empire, and it had pioneered the Industrial Revolution that would change first Europe and then the rest of the world. Its industry and its empire brought it wealth and systemic change. It moved from being a rural society to an urban one, from a hierarchical social structure to something distinctly more egalitarian. All that brought new ways of living and new perceptions of taste. Then, 100 years ago, it began its slippage from dominant power to something more modest. Its former little colony had grown to become the United States of America and to usurp its place as the richest, most militarily powerful, most culturally influential country in the world. Britain now lacks hard power but continues to be adept at the softer version. Like every other country she now borrows ideas from the USA, tweaks them and respectfully offers them back.

We all hope and are inclined to presume that our taste is impeccable for to be accused of having poor taste is disturbing. This book will presume that there is no such a thing as a definitive good taste (unless evidence emerges to the contrary). It will assume that there's no need to be judgemental but authorial prejudices will be plain to see. One person's *sine qua non* is, after all, another's *infra dig*.

CHAPTER 1

New Money, Old Ideas

'In the 19th century taste was a weapon in the war between the new mercantile middle and the old gentry.'

Simon Heffer, *High Minds: The Victorians and the Birth of Modern Britain*, 2013[1]

The late 18th century had a taste for revolution. The American Revolutionary War set the stage for the French Revolution which, in turn, inspired a century and more of unrest across Europe. Less violent but every bit as seismic and systemic was Britain's Industrial Revolution, which changed the country's economic and social templates and gave the rest of the world a model for a post-agrarian society.

In the early 19th century Britain ruled the waves and its collection of colonies and trading quangos provided the raw materials and the markets that underpinned its economic and political pre-eminence. That supremacy would not be challenged until the modest coastal strip, wrested from it by tax-phobic colonial rebels, grew to become the United States of America and to dominate the 20th century.

The French Revolution worried Britain's ruling classes. A few idealists, like William Wordsworth, pursued the chimera of liberty, equality and fraternity and visited the new French utopia, only to retreat before the brutalities of the revolutionaries' reign of terror. In 1799 Napoleon Bonaparte dispatched the revolutionary rump, established the First Empire and, having awarded himself the title of Emperor, embarked, with his *grand armée* on his *grand projet*, on the conquest of Europe. Britain dispatched Wellington and Nelson to deal with him and their victories encouraged her presumption that she ruled the world.

France's revolution had been partly precipitated by taxes levied on the peasantry but in Britain the relative prosperity of those deserting the uncertainties of agricultural labour for the meagre but reliable subsistence of factory work diffused the likelihood of rebellion. The last of Britain's Hanoverian monarchs, 'mad' George III and the foppish Prince Regent (later George IV), were considered too absurd to be worth the trouble of hanging.

As more immediate Georgian heirs died without legitimate issue in 1837 the 18-year-old Princess Victoria ascended to the throne. Her youth and gender perhaps suggested a new beginning and her overt piety and enthusiasm for domestic bliss matched a change in the national mood. Her name came to embody the mores that defined the 19th century in Britain and, perhaps curiously given its blossoming republicanism, in the United States. With the virtues of hindsight, the period is castigated as a time when the poor were mercilessly exploited but Simon Heffer offers a more nuanced perception: *Although poverty, disease, ignorance, squalor and injustice were far from eliminated, they were beaten back more in those 40 years or so years [1840–1880] than at any time in the previous history of Britain, a nation that might have been overwhelmed by industrial change, rapid expansion and social upheaval instead saw the challenges of modernism and embraced them.*[2] While Britain's creative entrepreneurs – like Isambard Kingdom Brunel who built railways and ships, bridges and tunnels and Joseph Bazalgette who designed and built the sewage system that rescued London from its own effluent – set about shaping the country's future, her architects and artists were more inclined to shy away from unedifying modernity and to take refuge in the principles and practices of an idealised Middle Ages.

The Georgian Neo-Classicism of the late 18th century was beginning to look a little too continental for the island race. France was happy to find architectural inspiration in the pagan models of Classical Greece and Rome but Britain turned to something Christian that might, just, be considered indigenous. Gothic architecture might have originated in 12th-century France but England, in its Late Medieval churches and cathedrals, had evolved its own structurally and decoratively complex Gothic traditions which could and would be adapted to serve a diversity of secular functions that were exclusively of the 19th century.

The ascension of the new queen encouraged an extraordinary enthusiasm for religious debate and practice. It was generally assumed that the success of the country, and its empire, was built on Christian values. In his painting *The Secret of England's Greatness*, Thomas Jones Barker depicted Victoria handing a bible – the handbook for virtuous and civilised behaviour and the prosperity that would follow it – to a kneeling African. Anglicanism remained the state religion but in its internal doctrinal disputes a significant faction of its adherents veered towards more austere personal conduct while paradoxically advocating the more flamboyant ceremonial trappings that were closer to Roman Catholic practices. The Church of England acted as the arbiter of national mores but its primacy was challenged. As industry brought wealth and comparative prosperity to the provincial strongholds of non-conformity, a more proscriptive morality asserted itself, every bit as austere in matters of personal conduct but with a decidedly Protestant suspicion of ceremony. While bishops debated the origins of humankind with Darwin and his acolytes, itinerant evangelists were drawing enormous and excited audiences across the country to rallies that were catalysts for the conversion of huge swathes of the population to a benign fundamentalism. Charismatic preachers expounded the finer points of doctrine, but they were also non-violent revolutionaries who condemned social injustices.

Churches were the nuclei of social life. Governments, anxious about revolution amongst workers crammed into brutal factories and foul slums, financed the building and refurbishment of 2859 Anglican churches between 1841 and 1870 to strengthen the restraining hand of religion. Not attending church risked social exclusion at higher social levels and the chances of employment at the lowest. It could be a vicious circle: in his *London Labour and the London Poor* Henry Mayhew cited a slum-dwelling labourer who said 'my wife and children can go to chapel at certain times, when work is pretty good and our things are not in pawn'.[3]

Piety needed displays of decency and, for everyone other than the very poor, home furnishings represented tangible evidence of decency. In *Turning Houses Into Homes* Clive Edwards wrote: 'The home is both an idea and a reality … a symbolic environment representing one's identity through the things therein.'[4] If Christian doctrine is lukewarm about ostentation, even of hard work ('… consider the lilies of the fields; how they grow; they toil not …'[5]) its followers were increasingly inclined to see conspicuous consumption as proof of piety and propriety. Sudden wealth, however modest, and the extravaganza of factory-produced ornaments that might crowd the mantelpieces and whatnots of homes great and small was too much for all but the stoutest spirits. The perfectly human instinct for virtuous prettification was too strong for all but the most abstemious anchorites.

Edwards also suggested that 'as people moved from cottage industries to working in factories and offices, their homes became places of rest and recreation…'[6] but he considers it ironic that it was the brutalities of manufacturing and commerce that provided the glut of objects that the Victorian householder found irresistible. The home he said was a place where an individual or a family could, through their interiors and their contents, make public expressions of their identity, expressions that also served to 'remind the owners of themselves and their position'.[7] The furniture designer and maker Thomas Sheraton however advised upholsterers to discourage customers from aiming above their station, because to try too hard or to fall too short would bring ridicule.[8] The exercise of taste is a delicate matter.

The architectural historian Mark Girouard saw the accumulation of ornaments as a national psychosis because there was more money in more pockets – the surfeit was being spent on what were, strictly speaking, non-essentials. However, the appetite for ornament might suggest that, when shelter and food are secured, ornament becomes a necessity and the relentless churning out of inexpensive, mass-produced decorative objects puts temptation in householders' way. He concluded that 'collecting something or other became a nineteenth century craze, not just one confined to the dilettanti'.[9] The nature of objects accumulated was presumed to confirm that one was serious about one's taste: the more one accumulated, in emulation of the myriad monkeys who might type a Shakespearean phrase or two, the more likely one was by default to offer some evidence of deserving one's place in the social order.

Change of ownership

Opposite
The stuccoed terraces and streets of Pimlico in 1973.

With industrial progress and an expanding Empire during the 19th century there was a partial but still distinct shift of power and influence from the upper classes to the middle classes.

The old rich, the aristocracy, were put out by the entrepreneurial middle class who bought the houses and land they could no longer afford. The gentry absorbed the flourishes of manners and the grace notes of taste with their wet nurses' milk instinctively and they weaponised those enigmas against the upstarts who could never quite convince – even themselves – that they had mastered the finer points of social interaction. The arrivistes could send their sons to the best schools and on to university but they 'did so with imperfect manners and taste'.[10] The crudely benevolent, essentially feudal, interdependence of landowners and their workers limped on for another century but industrialists and their managers were less inclined to sense a symbiotic connection with the lumpen masses who were too many, too anonymous and little more than functionaries of the machines they attended.

As inhabitants of country, village and small town followed the opportunities offered in the manufacturing and trading cities to become wealthy, well-off or modestly prosperous they installed themselves in terraced houses, of varying degrees of grandeur, offered by the speculative builders who were subsuming the fields and villages that surrounded ancient civic cores. An example was the Pimlico area on the periphery of central London where market gardens that had served the Georgian city were developed for housing by the Cubitt Brothers. The Cubitts were responsible for a number of major bouts of housebuilding across early 19th-century London.

The increasingly popular but complex Neo-Gothic detail was inevitably more expensive

to build than flat Georgian facades and geometric decorative motifs. The speculators who were providing dwellings for the representatives of every social strata congregating in the centres of towns and cities continued to favour exteriors that were decidedly more Georgian, and therefore cheaper to build, over Neo-Gothic. If exteriors, grand and not so grand, remained expediently Georgian, the interiors, despite a light dusting of what were essentially Classical mouldings, offered householders empty spaces in which to indulge their penchants for Gothic furniture and fittings. Appetites for ornament might be satisfied in interiors where the economics of mass production made intricately worked Gothic artefacts affordable.

In 2008 Clive Aslet, an architectural writer and broadcaster, described his own terraced house in Pimlico built in 1851: *The front door opens into a narrow hallway, from the side of the hallway rises the staircase; there are two rooms to each floor, a precipitous (open) area (at basement level) and an umbrageous yard at the back. Each house front along Tachbrook Street is about the same as the next. But not quite … The interiors are broadly similar but not identical; quirky details make each house slightly different from its neighbour. This is how the English like their houses: individuality keeps bubbling to the surface.*[11] Despite that paean to independent thinking, Aslet conceded: 'Our house belongs to a standard London type.'[12] And it does but it is little different from the medium-sized spec-built houses that were appearing in flourishing cities and towns throughout the country.

Detailing might have been 'quirky' but not too quirky – much housing remained Georgian in essence. Developers offered minor variations on a base template that would speak to and tweak the aspirations of buyers. The furnishings and fittings with which householders itched to pack their empty rooms would be distinctly similar to those of their neighbours. Even if they were itching to express risky individuality, choice was limited. Retailers determined what artefacts were available and were as keen as builders to offer a common denominator that would appeal to the broadest cross-section of customers. The upwardly mobile were keen to show that they belonged to the tribe – in Pimlico, or wherever they found themselves. If they had the good fortune to move up to Belgravia they would take care to acquire the trappings that would mark them as suitable for its more prestigious streets and squares.

Speculative housing development brought compromise. In Pimlico the consequences of hastily laid brickwork were concealed behind stucco, a fine render that also lends itself to making simple mouldings around doors and windows. The same material, which could be painted to suggest stonework, was used in the grander town houses, intended for the various strata of the aristocracy in Belgravia, and borrowed their superiority. Pimlico was for the middle classes and was less intimidating. In Anthony Trollope's novel, *The Small House at Allington* Lady Alexandrina de Courcy 'had beauty according to law rather than beauty according to taste'.[13] Trollope would appear to be of the opinion that beauty cannot be appreciated according to definitive rules of taste but is recognised only by something in the eye of the beholder, that is visceral rather than intellectual and that divergence from the prescribed ideal adds irresistible piquancy.

Lady Alexandrina had been obliged to marry a relatively senior clerk in the Post Office for whom Pimlico was a desirable address but her friend pleaded 'For heaven's sake my dear, don't let him take you anywhere beyond Eccleston Square.'[14] Eccleston Square was on the

Left
The Neo-Gothic decoration of the Royal Gallery in Pugin's House of Lords, 1858.

Below
Pugin: Houses of Parliament, 1844, designs for floor tiles.

wrong side of the railway tracks into Victoria Station. The Belgravian friend was no doubt concerned about 'knowing' a resident of Pimlico, especially one who might live on a street. Matters of domestic status are powerful themes in Victorian novels, and addresses remain so in our own not particularly egalitarian times. The richest still congregate in Belgravia.

Belgravia was thoroughly stuccoed but grand enough and rich enough to avoid mockery; yet modest little Pimlico was labelled 'Stuccoville' and high-minded architects condemned the deception that gave expedient brickwork the appearance of nobler stone. However, no matter how magisterially they might pontificate, hints of corruption, including suspicions about a prodigious overspend on remodelling Buckingham Palace and Windsor Castle, had left public opinion disenchanted with the architectural establishment and its Classical regurgitations. There was popular acclaim when the competition for the redesign of the Houses of Parliament, destroyed by fire in 1834, was won by the promiscuously eclectic Sir Charles Barry with a Neo-Gothic proposal which suggested that change, even if only stylistic, was in the air. Novelty tends to find an appreciative audience.

Augustus Pugin, an architect, designer and artist, made the drawings for Barry's winning competition entry. He was subsequently given responsibility for the interiors. Taking cues from the early 16th-century perpendicular Gothic Lady Chapel, which survived the fire, he comprehensively decorated every surface with pattern and colour, topped every opening with a pointed arch and had timbers carved with period convolutions.

Above
An armchair in the Gothic Revival style designed by Pugin in 1830 when he was 18 years old.

Pugin, whose French architect father had fled from the terrors of post-revolutionary Paris, was born in 1812. He was bizarrely precocious. As a teenager, he designed silverware for the royal goldsmiths and furniture for Windsor Castle but he was a brief, very bright, candle and died in 1852, shortly after designing the tower in which hangs Big Ben. Like many of the earnest young men of his time, he engaged in the Church of England's internal wrangling about doctrine and liturgy and, like a number of them, converted to full-blown Roman Catholicism in 1835. He poured out Gothic-esque artefacts; furniture, ceramics, metalwork, wallpapers, stained glass and embroideries, some for his own buildings and some for manufacturers. He was also, as far as he could squeeze it into his cerebral preoccupations, a man of action. He owned a fishing boat and salvaged sailors and cargoes from ships wrecked on Goodwin Sands in Kent, which he could see from his cliff-top home.

Pugin was a one-man practice but profusely prolific, as perhaps only a Victorian motivated by high-minded certainties could be. He brought Gothic intensity of decoration to the 40 churches and six cathedrals he designed in England, Wales and Ireland. The houses he designed were more restrained, but became models for the homes of the prosperous middle class: people like himself with enough money to build well in the grander suburbs of provincial towns and cities. He built several houses for himself; The Grange, on the cliffs above Ramsgate, was the last and the most complete realisation of his thoughts. He organised his plan so that rooms abutted and connected rationally but organically, and this pragmatism generated picturesque agglomerations of steeply pitched roofs over irregular brick volumes, punctured by irregularly spaced windows that were sized to meet the needs of the rooms they served. It was the antithesis of the mathematically rational Georgian elevations which offered the street flat brick screens, punctuated by regularly sized and regularly spaced windows, which in turn imposed a formal organisation of rooms behind them. His wide-reaching influence on 19th and 20th-century design is clear, from the grand scale in the country houses of Charles Voysey and Lutyens to the semi-detached villas of 20th-century suburbia.

Pugin had his own private chapel in The Grange but, keen as always to proselytise on behalf of his religion and his architecture, he also built a small Neo-Gothic church for public worship on half of his site. If the house paid tribute to the pragmatic good sense of the English vernacular, the church was a manifesto of his architectural and moral principles, in its style, its symbols and its materials.

Pugin led by examples: an astonishing number of them given that he died when he was 40, but ultimately as much significance is attached to his publications, which argued for society's, and architects', moral obligation to relieve the brutalities that were being visited on factory workers, those emigrants from country to conurbations who had not found their way to prosperity.

Above
Pugin's own house in Ramsgate next to the church he designed, built and donated to the town.

Below
The Red House by Philip Webb, showing the influence of Pugin's rationally informal planning, Bexleyheath, London, 1860.

He had the energy of the most driven of his entrepreneurial contemporaries but directed it to right the wrongs for which he implied they were responsible. In 1836, aged 24, he published what has been described as the first architectural manifesto. While earlier treatises, by Vitruvius, Palladio and British dilettantes returning from their Grand Tours, had set out rules for aesthetics and construction, he concentrated on social matters, arguing that architecture was best placed to eliminate the moral and social problems that were the by-products of industrialisation. He proposed that the answer to the dark satanic mills and workhouses that constituted the sordid lives of factory workers lay in the past, with the model of medieval communities clustered around Gothic abbeys, in receipt of charitable physical sustenance

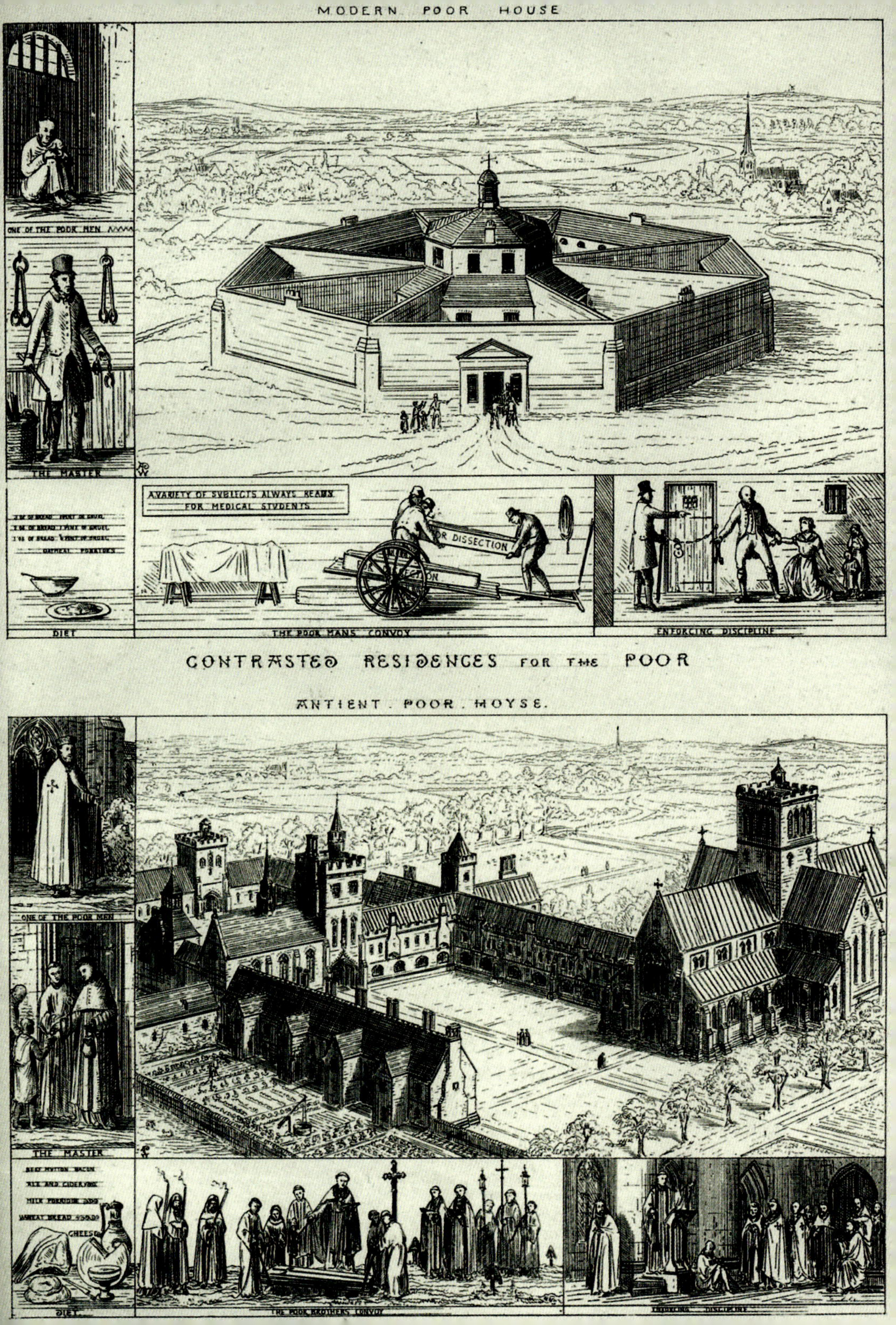
MODERN POOR HOUSE
ONE OF THE POOR MEN
THE MASTER
A VARIETY OF SUBJECTS ALWAYS READY FOR MEDICAL STUDENTS
FOR DISSECTION
DIET
THE POOR MANS CONVOY
ENFORCING DISCIPLINE
CONTRASTED RESIDENCES FOR THE POOR
ANTIENT . POOR . HOYSE .
ONE OF THE POOR MEN
THE MASTER
BEEF MUTTON BACON
MILK PORRIDGE
CHEESE
DIET
THE POOR BROTHERS CONVOY
ENFORCING DISCIPLINE

and moral enrichment. His argument was summed up by a pair of drawings, *Contrasted Residences of the Poor,* published in 1841, in which examples of 19th-century urban building types are contrasted, most unfavourably, with their distinctly more florid 15th-century equivalents. In one, an image of a 19th-century workhouse, obviously planned on authoritarian panopticon principles, is bordered by secondary images of poorly clad paupers, of menacing cudgel-bearing overseers, of families broken up and housed in comfortless cells, fed gruel and, when dead, delivered for dissection before their mutilated remains are thrown into unmarked graves. In the second drawing a Gothic abbey replaces the workhouse and factories, the poor have adequate and rather elegant clothes, gentle monks and abbots explain uplifting Christian values to them, they eat and drink well and are buried, intact, with the dignities of Christian ritual. The principles were elaborated on in his publication of 1841, *The True Principles of Christian or Pointed Architecture*, in which he wrote 'Let then the Beautiful and the True be our watchword.'[15] Beautiful and true are unfortunately open to interpretation and they or their synonyms are prey to the priorities of every theorist.

Although some were motivated to undertake what were ostensibly good works in the cause of eliminating potential causes of civil unrest or of creating a more effective industrial model, 19th-century philanthropists and reformers largely shared Pugin's ambition to eliminate the extremes of misery, objectively recorded by Henry Mayhew and in lachrymose prose by Charles Dickens. Simon Heffer writes that 'a sense of earnest, disinterested moral purpose distinguished many politicians, intellectuals and citizens …'[16] But even the high-minded were inclined to be paternalistic.

Thomas Carlyle, the 'Sage of Chelsea', was one such. Disillusioned by the failure of his early democratic experiments but concerned for the material and intellectual welfare of those locked into subsistence existences, he agreed with Pugin that medieval feudalism was more likely to offer the lower social echelons spiritual and corporal redemption.

John Ruskin, the pre-eminent Victorian authority on art and architecture, believed that an appreciation of art and beauty would ennoble lives, particularly, but not only, of the poor. It is a presumption shared by all advocates for the arts. Ruskin was particularly enthusiastic about Gothic ornament, which he presumed to embody somehow the pleasurable fulfilment of the artisan who had made it. He championed the Pre-Raphaelite painters, both pious and profane, whose pretty pictures of medieval myth helped feed the growing national obsession with the Gothic; that its artefacts were factory-made did not greatly inhibit popular pleasure in its pretty complexities. One might wonder if the intellectuals who promoted the Gothic Revival were no more immune to shifts of taste than anyone else. They might have taken as their model of social perfection the democracy of ancient Athens as enthusiastically, had the chronology been reversed.

Neo-Gothic houses were not unprecedented. Horace Walpole's Strawberry Hill, begun in 1749, is generally given credit for launching the Gothic Revival. Its exterior and interiors were particularly innovative because they were conceived from scratch, without being additions to or taking inspiration from extant medieval fragments. Walpole was extremely rich and to an extent indulging himself but Strawberry Hill showed that a new Gothic architecture was feasible; it was for others to presume that social salvation lay in medieval structures.

Opposite
Pugin's drawings 'Contrasted residences for the poor', unfavourably comparing care for the poor in the 19th century with its medieval equivalent, 1841.

Above
Horace Walpole's Strawberry Hill: the first Neo-Gothic structure, London, 1763.

Right
Walpole's Strawberry Hill: the Long Gallery with newly built Gothic fan vaulting, London, 1763.

TASTE

Left
Strawberry Hill: the ante-room in the Waldegrave additions of 1862.

Above
Strawberry Hill: the ceiling of the ante-room in the Waldegrave additions.

Walpole's literary activities further romanticised the Gothic. He claimed that Strawberry Hill, and particularly its interiors, inspired the gloomy and sinister rooms in his book of 1764, *The Castle of Otranto*, which is usually recognised as the first 'Gothic' novel. He sowed a seed, put the Gothic vocabulary on the architectural agenda and whetted appetites for it amongst his readers. His literary innovation was supplemented by a flotilla of 19th-century authors. A genre evolved that added to the mystique and romance of the Gothic, bookended by Mary Shelley's *Frankenstein* in 1818 and Bram Stoker's *Dracula* in 1897 while, in the United States, Edgar Allan Poe and Henry James turned the Gothic screw.

After Walpole's death in 1797 Strawberry Hill was rather neglected by his heirs and its contents were auctioned in 1844. The house then passed to the wealthy society hostess, Frances Lady Waldegrave who extended it in a mid 19th-century Gothic fashion. She introduced contemporary manufacturing techniques to apply Gothic decorative detail to cast iron balustrades and radiators. She might be seen, on a very grand scale, as one of the Victorian women whose responsibility was to manage their households, which included ordering the decoration of their homes.

In *High Minds* Simon Heffer devotes a chapter to recording the fracas that broke out amongst professionals about the comparative virtues of Gothic sub-styles for major public buildings and demonstrates that the outcomes had more to do with the manipulative abilities and political connections of architects than with philosophical rectitude. Amateurs did not worry about finer points of aesthetics, they just liked ornament, and wanted lots of it. Nor, it seems, could architects resist Neo-Gothic excess and their acceptance of ornament and elaboration was happily in tune with popular taste.

Letting them have it

Writing in 1852 Richard Redgrave, headmaster of the Government School of Design, said 'The desire evinced by the rudest as well as the most civilised nations for the decoration of their buildings, utensils and clothing almost raises ornament into a natural want and must render its proper application of the utmost consequence to the manufacturer'.[17]

Pugin considered ornament essential and integral to architecture and its *raison d'être* to be the transmission of awe, leavened with the aesthetic pleasures, to point medieval peasants to higher things and he held that ornament which borrowed lavishly from that romantic past had the same capacity to appeal to popular taste in the 19th century.

The wealth of entrepreneurial innovators and industrialists outstripped that of the hereditary landowners unlucky enough not to be collecting ground rents from swathes of the more fashionable inner cities. Cash-strapped aristocrats were obliged to affect indifference to the new and to flaunt the old and worn. They were forfeiting their roles as taste-makers to the newly moneyed – and new money liked Neo-Gothic. Mark Girouard offers another perspective and suggests that there was a degeneration of the upper class taste: *The almost total lack of visual discrimination, which the arrangement of [objects in] all these rooms shows, demonstrates how whole heartedly the aristocracy and the Royal family were addicted to what some might think of as middle class tastelessness. Any sense of style is completely absent.*[18] Or perhaps the Gothic spirit was simply the spirit of that age, to the taste of all, transcending class and wealth and not to be critically assessed 100 years on. Simon Heffer, more concerned with society at large than the particularities of taste, proposes that 'the Gothic revival defined a new contemporary style. It was about show paid for by a prosperous country … The majority of architects built in that style because of public demand: they would have been short of work had they not'.[19]

It was also a time of conciliation between amateur and professional. Complex ornament, whether two- or three-dimensional, was integral to Gothic design. Professionals can and probably should worry about doctrinal niceties but amateurs do not care, and the opportunity to regurgitate ornament by the former and to feast on it by the latter led to the extremes of Victorian interior decoration.

Machine production could make complex decorative objects of varying degrees of intricacy that were within the means of a broad swathe of society. As the public sweet tooth for ornament grew, no surface, flat or curved, was spared the application of colour and pattern, however incongruous. Ornament was what amateur taste demanded but for a moralising aesthete like Pugin there had to be rules about its application, regardless of how life-enhancing the uninitiated might find it: no one could be allowed to indulge base instincts. In 1841 he uttered his 'two great rules of design', which were his reaction to what was shaping up to be the gratuitous and ill-informed application of Gothicisms.[20] The first rule was that 'there should be no features about a building that are not necessary for convenience, construction or propriety' and the second was that 'all ornament should consist of enrichment of the essential construction of the building'. To Modernist professionals for whom the very word ornament is unsettling and its implementation considered a crime, these rules are barely comprehensible. Pugin's argument was that the functional bare bones, the columns and arches that carried loads, the lintels that spanned openings and the cills that cast off water, all the necessities that made buildings sound and habitable were the only elements that should make up any structure and that ornamentation should be confined to the enrichment of these essentials. It was an argument against the addition of non-essential elements or ornamental elements for their own sake but, logically, if the first rule was respected every part of every surface, which would be essential, was fair game for applied ornament. Modernist professionals would happily subscribe to the first rule but be disturbed by slathering structural elements beneath a layer of what they would perceive as gratuitous ornament.

Ever willing to offer enlightenment and manipulate taste, Pugin was one of several prominent designers who took it upon themselves to offer pattern books of ornament for the inspiration of manufacturers and the instruction of their less-informed designers, to steer both away from the excess that brought their profits. Always keen to lay down doctrine, he decreed that ornament 'must possess appropriate meaning and be introduced with an intelligent purpose and on reasonable grounds'.[21] In his *Symbolism of Art in Society* he repeated the decree that legitimate ornament should only be used to enrich elements that were essential to the construction or operation of the building and offered as an example a decorated weathervane. He also decreed that every ornament should have meaning that was appropriate to the function of the building and that its introduction should appear logical and justified. For his decorative devices he turned like many to nature for inspiration, a strategy justified by Ruskin: *the function of ornament is to make you happy ... Now in what are you rightly happy? Not in thinking about what you have done yourself ... but in looking at God; watching what he does ... then the proper material of ornament will be whatever God has created.*[22] Pugin was not alone in publishing pattern books. In 1836, Owen Jones produced his first volume of drawings of the Alhambra in Granada, and his second of

Below left
Owen Jones, *The Grammar of Ornament*, 1856: Egyptian ornament no. 2: ornamentation for head-dresses, fans, vases and boat oars.

Below centre
Owen Jones, *The Grammar of Ornament*, 1856: Pompeiian ornament no. 2: painted decoration of pilasters and friezes.

Below right
Owen Jones, *The Grammar of Ornament*, 1856: Chinese ornament no. 4: flowers and fruit decoration painted on porcelain.

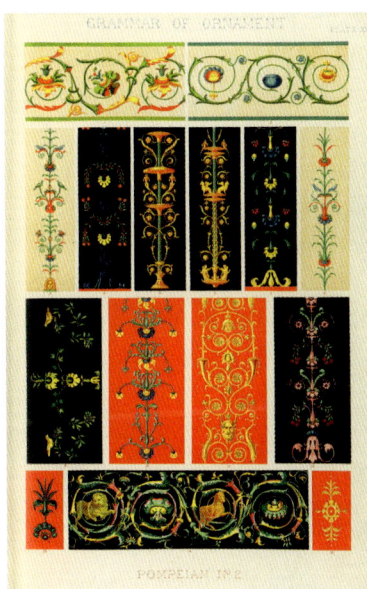

1845 was entirely devoted to the building's ornament. In 1839 George Phillips published his *Rudiments of Curvilinear Design*, in which he catalogued Classical, Renaissance, Elizabethan and Oriental forms of ornament. In 1856 Jones published *Grammar of Ornament*, a compendium of decorative motifs from across the world, tidied up for the convenience of any manufacturers who cared to use them. In it he pronounced that ornament 'must necessarily increase with all peoples in the ratio of the progress of civilisation'.[23] This would be contradicted 60 years later by Adolf Loos who declared, to the gratification of the Modernists who rallied behind him, that the more civilised individuals became the less need they would have for ornament. Perhaps Loos could have argued equally strongly that the more people were educated the more they were likely to lose contact with essentials. But before Loos would lay down his law and in response to industrialisation of the European mainland, Albert Racinet published ten volumes in France between 1869 and 1873 of *L'Ornement Polychrome* and in 1889 Heinrich Dolmetsch published *Der Ornamentenschatz in Germany*. All were intended to inspire and improve the decorative arts that were seen everywhere as a staple of commerce.

Seal of approval

Prince Albert of Saxe-Coburg and Gotha married his first cousin Queen Victoria in 1840. He found his role frustratingly peripheral but her infatuated respect ensured that he had considerable influence behind the scenes and more overt involvement in areas considered not to be of significant political importance. One of those safe areas was design and in that he made his views well known and lent his celebrity to those whose principles agreed with his. As post-industrialisation social changes were being comprehensively embedded, the proliferating strata of middle classes were confident and enthusiastic about recycling their new wealth. Factories churned out products and what was not exported was happily consumed on home soil. If popular taste wanted things that made aesthetes queasy, factory owners were uninhibited by aesthetic abstractions and happy to supply the market.

Prince Albert had no animosity towards anything being tricked out in Gothic devices but he aligned himself with those who were concerned that frivolities were not for the common good. He regretted that 'the taste of the public is not what it now ought to be and that the taste of the artists themselves could do with refinement through further study'.[24] He suggested that artists could do better if they spent time in Munich, Florence and Rome, which might have been a partisan perspective or an obvious ploy to polish his own credentials.

If one were to doubt the importance of taste as a cultural phenomenon it is only necessary to reflect on the dedication that is brought to the propagation of 'good' taste, which is frequently, and in the face of evidence to the contrary, offered as a commercial panacea: to paraphrase H. L. Mencken, nobody ever went broke underestimating popular taste. Influential persons not involved in commerce feel the need to advocate a definitive taste: *their* taste. Denied a statesman's role, Prince Albert consoled himself by setting about refining popular taste. It requires an authoritarian mindset to presume to shape the visceral responses of humankind but *noblesse oblige*.

Early in the course of grappling with lapses in public taste, Prince Albert developed a relationship with Henry Cole, a civil servant with a bureaucratic impulse to regulate public taste. A typical eminent Victorian, Cole was inclined to step confidently outside the parameters of his obvious area of expertise and, under the pseudonym Felix Summerly, operated with obdurate diversity as an industrial designer and author of children's books. In his official governmental role he is credited with having designed the world's first postage stamp, while assisting in the setting up of the Penny Post and the invention of the Christmas card in 1843, which helped sell stamps. The latter innovation may have done something to consolidate his relationship with Albert who introduced the Christmas rituals of Germany into the royal household, which encouraged a loyal and ornamentally inclined public to deck their halls with seasonal knick-knacks.

Albert and Henry's greatest achievements were 1851's *Great Exhibition of the Works of Industry of All Nations* and the national institutions they created in its wake. The Great Exhibition, as it was more concisely and commonly known, confirmed, certainly to British visitors, the superiority of British industry. Evidence was offered by spectacles of the latest industrial machines operating at full throttle and displays of the highly decorated products they produced. Celebration of the relentlessly expanding Empire was provided by artisans brought from India who demonstrated the making of the intricately wrought ornamental pieces that brought exoticism to Victorian homes. No mention was made of the Indian opium that was traded for the porcelain and silks of China. With refreshing symmetry both India and China offered alternative teas for the afternoon parties that provided English ladies with the opportunity to display their *objets d'arts*.

After vigorous debates about possible sites for Exhibition buildings and in the face of opposition from eminent Victorian tree-huggers, a site was chosen in Hyde Park. Joseph Paxton, a young and innovative designer of monumental cast iron and glass conservatories for municipalities and aristocrats, was given the task. His building, which was bolted together and easily demountable, was 1851 ft (or 555 m) long and high enough to accommodate those trees that trespassed on its footprint. Its industrial aesthetic did not meet the expectations of patriots who expected England's greatness to be celebrated with a more conventional, and solid, building. The modest mouldings on the metal components seem extravagantly ornamental today but in the middle of the 19th century they were downright utilitarian. The spectacle of the enormous enclosed volume coupled with the exoticism of the products it displayed won over those who entered it and aesthetic and environmental concerns were ameliorated when it became known that it was demountable. When the exhibition ended there was popular support for its retention but the behemoth was dismantled as prescribed by Paxton and reconstructed in an outer London suburb, which was renamed Crystal Palace in recognition of its considerable presence. Ultimately, size is everything. Considerations of taste are irrelevant.

The Exhibition ran for only five and a half summer months but six million people visited – the equivalent of a third of the British population. It delivered a profit of £186,000, which was enough to fund the next phase of Prince Albert and Henry Cole's campaign;

Top right
Crystal Palace: view across the Serpentine, 1851.

———————

Below right
Crystal Palace: the opening ceremony, 1851.

to make the cultural and educational activities of the Exhibition permanent. The money was used to buy land in South Kensington, then on the periphery of the city. On this land Cole, with the active support of Prince Albert, who brought with him the support of the Queen, began building three major museums for design, science and natural history. Cole was appointed the first General Superintendent of the Department of Practical Art and given the job of improving design education so that it could make a more appropriate contribution to industry. He set up the National Art Training School which became the Royal College of Art, The Royal College of Music and Imperial College, the school for science. The mechanisms to spread official good taste throughout the kingdom were in place. Only the predilections of unenlightened consumers could thwart them – but – there were a lot of the unenlightened eager to consume. With its agglomeration of museums and educational establishments, the area became Albertopolis. Its northern boundary would be marked in 1872 by the Neo-Gothic megastructure that was the Albert Memorial in which a monstrous gilded effigy of the dead consort leafs thoughtfully through the Great Exhibition catalogue.

Cole selected examples of good design and bad and displayed them in his new museum, which would grow to become the Victoria and Albert Museum. In that more deferential age, people were anxious to conform. Good taste was being gradually institutionalised and a series of bodies appointed by successive governments became national arbiters of acceptable taste.

In education, Cole was consolidating beginnings made by William Dyce a decade earlier. As the first head of the newly established Government School of Design, Dyce, appointed in 1838, had laid solid foundations for art education after visits to France and Germany to observe their provisions. He was particularly impressed by the Prussian system, which required artisans to be introduced to art and artist/designers to be familiarised with details of production processes so that each could appreciate, and contribute productively to, the work of the other. This philosophy would be borrowed 50 years later by the Arts and Crafts movement. Dyce shared Prince Albert's feeling that Britain could learn from Germany, and was likely to have found a rapport with Albert had he not, in 1843, deserted his educational role to return to painting. His professional connections were excellent but he lacked Cole's experience of, and appetite for, bureaucratic wrangling.

Cole was the man to build on Dyce's foundations. While the importance of specialised education was recognised, training was centred on drawing – not drawing as a means of exploring and testing radical ideas but as a way of copying precedents and respectfully adapting them to contemporary needs. This lack of initiative was perhaps justified, since consumers were content with what they knew. Or it may have been that, in a world of technological turmoil, artists did not know where to go, or how to get there. With little to offer, artists retreated to live off past glories. The role of designer for industry had not previously existed and the process of copying the works of the Masters was at the core of fine art education so it was assumed that imitation should be the essential activity. If artist/designers were unequipped or unable to offer consumers something fresh it would be unreasonable to criticise consumers' taste.

Pugin had, predictably, objections to the Exhibition building's sheer un-Gothicness and called it the 'glass monster'. This did not stop him designing the Medieval Court area that offered Gothic visions and included many objects that he had designed himself. Presumably he saw an opportunity to proselytise that would have been remiss to refuse. He may have concluded that the contrast between the building's industrial aesthetic – although he might not have considered 'aesthetic' to be the *mot juste* – could only flatter his opulent visions. And no doubt he was right. In 1851 the overwhelming majority of visitors, while cautiously appreciating the engineering skill and audacity of Paxton's work, would not have

seen in it a pointer to an alternative aesthetic. Speculation since about the incongruity of retrospective exhibits in scientific and industrial Britain misses the point: it was science and it was industry that made the production of elaborate and historicist objects possible on a scale that made them accessible to a vast and eager customer base. Pugin himself had never been averse to taking advantage of engineering and manufacturing innovations: many of the artefacts he created for his churches were assembled, in various configurations, from a kit of components produced for him by his preferred metalwork fabricators.

Complex ornament, whether two- or three-dimensional, was integral to the Gothic. Professionals can and probably should worry about doctrinal niceties but amateurs do not care and wallowed in the opportunity to feast on regurgitated ornament.

The cartoonist and architectural critic, Osbert Lancaster (1908–1982) published *Homes Sweet Homes*, his droll perspective on the English interior, from the Normans up to 1939, the date of its publication and the outbreak of war. Lancaster was distinctly upper middle class and had grown up amongst remnants of Victorian and Edwardian domesticity. He knew at first hand some of the people and the interiors they had lived in; his descriptions are concise and illuminating.

In the early Victorian era Lancaster regrets the erosion of 'the elegance of the Georgian and the vitality of the Regency'. He concedes that, although proportions were good, 'lines are heavier, the decoration coarser' but that there was 'a general atmosphere of solidity and comfort'. He offers a comprehensive overview: *Painted walls now vanish, not to reappear for nearly a century, beneath a variety of patterned papers, striped, spotted and flowered. Mahogany reigns almost supreme as the popular wood for furniture, though both birch and rosewood maintain a certain vogue. Carpets are either elaborately floral in pink and white or severely patterned in billiard-cloth green or scarlet. Fireplaces are comparatively plain in marble.*[25] As Lancaster suggests, the early Victorians very quickly found their sense of style which was distinctly different from the delicacies of the Regency period. Popular taste was led by, but by no means unsympathetic to, architects' sudden switch from Classical to Gothic sources of inspiration to make a style that tangibly linked the secular – whether a railway station or a parliament building – to the spiritual. The 'Secret of England's Greatness' was not just the Bible, but the Victorian interpretation of it that conjoined rectitude and prosperity.

Whatever their social pretentions, those made prosperous (to varying degrees) by the Industrial Revolution and the spoils of Empire understood that they were something other, and decidedly more numerous, than the landowners and their tenants. They needed to find a way to live with style, appropriate to their status, in the terraces of mushrooming towns. The Neo-Classical restraint that had styled the rooms housing Georgian turpitudes was superseded by the gaudy Neo-Gothic fancies that accommodated sober Victorian public and private formalities. If louche Georgians indulged their sensual appetites in couth interiors, morally upstanding Victorians let off steam with uncouth decorative intemperance: interior style seemed to counterbalance lifestyle. One might wonder how much the Victorians enjoyed their excesses.

Opposite
Pugin, the Medieval Court at the Great Exhibition, 1851.

CHAPTER 2

Disapproving Dilettantes

'In everything we are too elaborate, a city warehouse in the Gothic style must have the marbles and enrichments of a cathedral presbytery: even a village church is not allowed the dignity of simplicity.'

The Quarterly Review July 1867[1]

During the 19th century architecture had been infatuated with everything Gothic. Architects were delighted to supply industry with the ideas it needed to turn its machinery. The Great Exhibition officially sanctioned decorative excess, and specialist manufacturers and retailers supplied the goods that householders needed to fill their interiors to the brim.

The architect William Burges, born in 1827, served Gothic Revival neat. He designed two projects for the 3rd Marquess of Bute, who had become immensely wealthy from ownership of the port of Cardiff which shipped coal from Welsh mines. Bute also owned the mines. A controversial Catholic convert, he enthusiastically accepted Gothicism and was delighted to underwrite two of Burges's most extravagant creations: Cardiff Castle and, a few miles outside the city, Castell Coch, a romantic summer house perched in wooded landscape. Both were built on the remains of modest Norman forts. They were demonstrably Gothic, yet filtered through 19th-century perceptions and processes. They had a diversity of detail that was not locked into a particular time and place, but was yet clearly of their own time. Both buildings spanned the breadth of the medieval period, but there were some compromises: Thomas Nicholls, who carved the abundance of three-dimensional decoration, was too accomplished a sculptor to allow medieval precedents to shape his heraldic beasts unduly and Horatio Lonsdale's murals look distinctly of their time.

By the middle of the century mongrelised medievalism had the wind in its sails. The Pre-Raphaelite Brotherhood, founded in 1848, chose to imitate painters of the Italian Quattrocento, but looked even further back for its subject matter. Delving into medieval myths and trappings, its predilections chimed with Pugin's but its agenda was aesthetic rather than social. However anti-establishment the Brotherhood might have aspired to be, their pretty images were fully in tune with the sentiments that were shaping the High Victorian domestic interior.

Left
William Burges, The Winter Smoking Room, Cardiff Castle, 1873.

Right
William Burges, Summer Smoking Room, Cardiff Castle, 1873.

Throughout the century London was comfortably the largest city and continued to grow, but provincial cities were growing faster as country people flocked to take advantage of the opportunities offered by the burgeoning industries. A more sophisticated system of shops had evolved to cope with the increasingly specialist demands that followed, increasing prosperity in all but the lowest social orders. The newly prosperous were ready to consume in the cause of prettification and they were no longer satisfied with the limited stock of small shops serving small towns or by what itinerant pedlars could carry on their backs door to door. The ability to buy non-essentials offered reassurance to middle-class householders and skilled workers that they could do more than survive and might consider climbing the social ladder. Easier access to better stocked shops allowed householders to acquire objects – practical and impractical – that demonstrated that they were people of appropriate taste, in tune with that of their neighbours. For the upwardly mobile making decisions about decorating could be stressful, and a sensibility that passed muster at one level might not cut the mustard at the next.

Above
William Burges, Tower House, dining room, Kensington, London, 1878.

Fledgling mail order catered for those beyond easy the reach of shops and hire purchase systems helped those short of ready cash. Both those with and without disposable income were no longer content with bare necessities. Clive Edwards explains that 'One of the major developments in consumer behaviour was the change from being "users of things" to "consumers of commodities"'.[2] But there were social hazards attached: 'taste' became an important part of an individual's moral character. This clearly gave support to the opposite 'vice' of being 'in the fashion'. Indeed, a lack of virtue could be expressed by failing to show the correct judgement in matters of taste; objects that demonstrated good taste also indicated respectability.[3]

Extravagant consumption was – and is still – considered to be in bad taste, and there is a persistent prejudice against fashion and what are assumed to be its whims, but this is matched by a persistent anxiety that following the wrong trend can lead to one's looking foolish. Shifts in fashion, and taste, were, and are, most immediately obvious in cuts of clothes and personal adornments. Then, in 1727, Daniel Defoe noticed that fashion was moving beyond the body: 'the fashions alter now in the more durable kind of things, such as Furniture of houses, Equipages, Coaches, nay even of Houses themselves'.[4] In 1759 Adam Smith noted that clothes were out of date in a year, and furniture fashions were superseded every five or six years.[5] It is simple economics. Clothes cost less and mistakes are readily rectified. Furnishings cost more and the consequences of a lapse of taste must be endured for longer. The impulse to keep up with fashions in clothing, which particularly afflicts the young, is of course likely to evolve into a similar concern for the styling of one's home. Taste may, theoretically, transcend fashion but is in reality a fashion victim.

The blank canvas

In the middle classes, responsibility for dressing interiors tended to devolve to women who were no longer obliged to work to make their family's ends meet. Men of business were generally not interested in fine-tuning their interiors and, in all likelihood, considered the activity downright unmanly. In 1834, John Arkwright explained the philosophy behind his rebuilding of his 17th-century Herefordshire house: 'Comfort is the only consideration that has induced me to make any changes whatever and, that obtained I care as far as my own taste is concerned but little for the rest.'[6]

The principal rooms of any middle-class house were neutral ground, reserved for receiving and entertaining guests. During the day, they were the preserve of women who, with servants to perform domestic duties, could practice the rituals: of taking tea, reading novels and needlework. They had many empty hours to decorate every surface, regardless of the desirability of their house. The writer Augustus Hare remembered an 'ugly brick villa' in which a fine of a penny was extracted from anyone leaning on the mantelpiece 'as they might injure the ornaments'.[7]

Furnishings in men's domains were chosen to suggest that they were men of business and importance. Grander households had a library in which shelves held more volumes than there were knick-knacks in women's quarters, but books were presumed to be serious: a desk and well-padded chair suggested a place of work. A billiards room reminded everyone that men were warriors, ready to demonstrate their physical prowess, and not inclined to worry about subtler details of soft furnishings. While the head of the house was out bread-winning, the library could be appropriated by women and children. In her novel of 1849, *The Diamond and the Pearl*, Mrs Catherine Gore wrote that the family spent their mornings in the library with 'half a dozen work-tables and writing-tables being in play in various nooks of the room, with a praiseworthy activity of small-talk'.[8] At the opposite end of the financial and social scale the head of a more modest household could signify his status with exclusive use of the best chair. The dining room was common ground but presided over by the head of the household in accordance with 'precision of etiquette and observance of precedence'.

The impulse to decorate was shared across classes but expression was curtailed by the intricacies of social strata. There were distinct gradations within working-class dwellings. The Artisans', Labourers' and General Dwelling Estate in Hornsey in London in 1833 all had small gardens at the front, but inside were various permutations of two rooms on the ground floor, one of which might be a parlour and one a kitchen, or both might be parlours with a kitchen added to the back. All had two bedrooms upstairs and a back yard with an outside lavatory.[9] Social nuances were consolidated, or subverted, by demonstrations of taste. Those higher in the order were keen to justify their station, those lower were keen to demonstrate their suitability for progression. It would be accurate to say that instincts for interior enhancement were shared across social strata, and objects that had no function but to demonstrate taste were near necessities for all, apart from the very poorest in society.

Enthusiasm amongst the less well-off for excesses of applied ornament encouraged divergent thinking. Affordable factory-made furniture and ornaments were common to all and the ability to assemble a tasteful collection provided proof of one's having the right stuff. Prevailing taste was, and is, broadly shared across the classes but choice and quality are determined by wealth. In 1858 the White and Parlby company patented a method of recreating plaster, wood and stone ornaments from papier mâché.[10]

John Ruskin pronounced that good design could not be produced by machines. It was the sort of judgement that independently wealthy cultural patriarchs were inclined to make throughout the 19th century. Nevertheless, inventions such as machine-made wallpaper became a relatively cheap way of transforming any wall, a boon to the deserving poor. The rich, should they wish, could persist with expensive handmade offerings but there were rules. Taste dictated that flock papers were appropriate for drawing rooms, sitting rooms, dining rooms and libraries; marble patterns with a gloss finish were correct for halls, staircases and corridors; moire, suggesting watered silks, or flocks with small scaled patterns, typically coloured red, green or blue, were considered correct for bedrooms.[11] There were other subtleties of received taste: Charles Voysey, perhaps the best of the Arts and Crafts designers, created wallpapers, carpets and rugs, tiles and textiles prolifically, yet favoured 'flatness' for wallpapers, explaining: 'An additional reason for aiming at flatness in wall coverings is that found in the fact that an attempt at realism provokes comparison with the subtleties of nature.'[12]

As the market for interior furnishings grew, retailers, who in the early years of the 19th century were also often manufacturers, realised that to attract customers they had to offer something that was distinctively their own. In *The Complete Cabinetmaker and Upholsterers Guide* J. Stokes wrote, in 1829: 'In a business where change and caprice rule with unbounded sway – in that the fashion of today may become obsolete tomorrow – an inventive genius and discriminating judgment are certainly essential qualifications.'[13]

Competition encouraged chicanery. A writer in *Fraser's* magazine of 1853 worried that 'the whole domain of decorative art and of furniture [had fallen under the control of] a parcel of dealers, who make their market out of the foolish vanity of that large section of the public which is stimulated to extravagance.'[14] Despite such suspicions interior retailing sold itself as a panacea and would have welcomed a saccharine tribute to the home from Ruskin who in 1864 in *Sesame and Lillies* declared: 'it is the place of Peace, the shelter, not only from all injury, but from all terror, doubt and division … So far as it is a sacred place, a vestal temple of the hearth, watched over by Household Gods'.[15]

But Ruskin also condemned retailers who, he believed, deceived customers into buying aesthetically inferior items. The accusation was repeated by Charles Eastlake in his *Hints On Household Taste* of 1872: 'At the furniture warehouse they (the public) are in the upholsterer's hands; at the china shop they are as easily taken over by the obsequious vendor of glasses and dinner plates, the carpet merchant leads them by the nose …'[16] Ruskin and Eastlake were brazenly foisting their own standards on a public who, they presumed, would be dazzled by their reputations as arbiters of refinement. They might be chastened to learn that those reputations have not stood the tests of time.

Ruskin felt particularly strongly about pollution of his 'sacred place' by commercial priorities and, with the certainty of a very wealthy man given to imagining socialist utopias, suggested in 1867 'making all retail dealers merely salaried officers in the employ of trade guilds', or dispensers of state taste.[17]

Retailers persisted in thinking that they offered sound products and valuable advice. The business was competitive and customers' preferences could not be ignored: new lines attracted new customers and what customers liked they bought, a stubbornly democratic alternative to Ruskinian totalitarianism. A Darwinian process that weeded out the unpopular while the popular, however meretricious, evolved. Under Ruskin's 'salaried officers', following Ruskin's diktats, choices would have been fewer and aesthetically convergent with no obligation to accommodate a popular consensus. As the Industrial Revolution raged about him Adam Smith had been objective. In *The Wealth of Nations*, he declared: 'consumption is the sole end and purpose of all production'.[18]

Shops and shoppers

'... the public wants a thing, therefore it is supplied with it; or the public is supplied with a thing, therefore it wants it.'
W. M. Thackeray, *Punch* magazine, 1848

The time when makers might barter had gone; untenable when customers made money rather than things. There were enough city dwellers to support a wide range of shops but these still had to be strategic. Options of ways for customers to pay became factors in their decision-making, particularly for the 'lower and middling classes' who felt comfortable with fixed prices and cash payments.[19]

It was a fine old aristocratic tradition to command goods from traders and postpone repayment inordinately: consider the trail of exploited tradesmen Becky Sharp and Rawdon Crawley left behind them in William Thackeray's novel *Vanity Fair*. On the other hand, many newly prosperous 19th-century commoners craved respectability too much to renege on debts but, as long as 'good taste' indicated probity, failing households were obliged to sail closer to the financial wind to keep up appearances.

Hire purchase began in the 18th century and was streamlined in the 19th.[20] Finance companies emerged to bridge gulfs between customers' ambitions and resources, relieving retailers of the need to chase debts. It is perhaps unnecessary to record that women, who were seldom breadwinners but principally responsible for making decisions about decorating, had difficulty getting credit.

Ease of borrowing is credited with the proliferation of upright pianos in already over-furnished parlours.[21] Their owners might not have the space or money for a baby grand but a piano of sorts signalled musical taste, which could be added to the total of a household's taste tally. And an upright's flat top offered another surface for more knick-knacks.

Clive Edwards has identified six categories of retailers. Department stores were beginning to emerge, so customers making small purchases could browse in furniture departments, mulling over major purchases and payment strategies. The first was *Le Bon Marche* which opened in Paris in 1838 selling lace, ribbons, sheets, mattresses, buttons and other modest household goods. It introduced fixed prices, guarantees, exchanges and refunds. Its spectacular interior provided customers with an 'experience' of towering voids and ornamental ironwork. It provided entertainments for children and a reading room for husbands who preferred to leave routine shopping to their wives while remaining on hand to make decisions about major purchases. The *Bon Marche* name was borrowed by imitators of various degrees of sophistication across Britain. Others borrowed the idea of spectacle. In 1855 Wylie and Lochhead offered Glaswegians a hall, 60 m long and 21 m high, which was so popular that they issued (free) tickets to control Saturday crowds. In London, Whiteleys had a nave 90 m long. When it opened in 1875, Liberty and Co. grouped its sales areas around a generous Tudor-esque central void.

Specialist furnishers catered for more niche markets. Gillows, to polish its credentials, claimed to be more of an educational experience than a museum with examples of furniture from every significant historical period. For those not partial to the Gothic, in its workshop it could reproduce designs from the pattern books of distinguished predecessors like Chippendale, Hepplewhite and Sheraton. It became a byword for quality and attained a degree of glamour, mentioned in novels by Jane Austen, William Thackeray and in a Gilbert and Sullivan opera. Shopping at Gillows validated your taste.

Those whom Edwards calls 'artistic furnishers' produced bespoke pieces or whole housefuls of furniture and fittings: 'customers' became 'clients',[16] and matters of taste were firmly on the agenda. The presentation, of varying degrees of theatricality – but always tastefully – massaged clients' decision-making. And help was welcomed; customers wanted to get

Below left
Magasins du Bon Marche: atrium, Paris, 1876.

Below right
Whiteleys: main staircase, London, 1912.

it right. Retailers offered advice but they did not, could not, stray too far from customers' comfort zones.

(Gazing in the windows of expensive shops could be educational. In Thomas Mann's novel *Felix Krull, Confidence Man* the young Krull studies goods on display to learn the details of taste that would ease his access to superior social echelons.)

The *House Furnisher* magazine suggested in 1873 'your true upholsterer is a man of the most varied and important qualifications, and is often as necessary and as trusted an agent in many homes as are the family lawyer and doctor.'[22] The adjective 'true' suggests that the magazine doubted the abilities and, perhaps, the integrity, of some of its readers.

Shops and showrooms were learning how to signal their exclusivity. The sparser the window display, the more tasteful the shop was presumed to be. Even the most knick-knack prone Victorian seemed to sense that less in a shop window implied more quality. Mid-range shops offered room layouts, the lower level offered lower prices.[23]

It was easier for aristocrats who – should they be too hard up to change their interiors – could affect contempt for the *nouveau riche*'s buying of new furniture. Conversely, the *nouveaux* understood that old pieces had kudos that only age could confer. The demarcation persists: in the 1990s the cabinet minister Michael Heseltine was denounced as the sort of self-made man who had to buy his own furniture. He had had the temerity to build himself a Neo-Classical pile and filled it with antiques of appropriate vintage. The attack, prompted by political differences, confirmed that taste can always be a weapon.

A market for second-hand furniture appeared in the 18th century and grew throughout the 19th. Conservative taste tends to find contemporary fads distasteful. When Gothic inspired pieces were fashionable 'Elizabethan' relics were a curmudgeonly alternative. They suggested something ancestral while 'Louis XIV' pieces offered decorative delicacies. The French had a reputation for knowing about these things. In 1812, in the middle of the Napoleonic Wars Maria Edgeworth published a satire suggesting that her fictional retailer, Mr Soho, understood the 'value of a French name'.[24] Soho was the centre of 'artistic' reproduction and 'Wardour Street English' became a label for pieces of questionable provenance. Enthusiasm for the second-hand and the quasi-old was enough to prompt a retailer of new furniture, Oetzmann & Co. to pronounce that 'for modern houses, we would prefer the comfort and elegance of modern furniture to antique and for drawing rooms, antique furniture is simply inadmissible.'[25]

Department stores also opened antique departments: for those with more money, Harrods had a gallery for antique and second-hand contemporary furniture. Heal & Son, who were to become a byword for progressive good taste in the 20th century, had an antique furniture department with a stock of complementary fabrics. New could be old and interiors could tell fanciful stories.

Furniture shops for the lower orders usually put price before artistry and offered credit without security. One company published a range of prices offering to furnish a modest four bedroom house for £27 and a grander eight bedroom house for £655.23p. Another would furnish a room for £5 with a 50p deposit and weekly repayments of 10p.[26] Room sets became a selling strategy and offered prototypes for customer consideration.

Tottenham Court Road in London became both the centre of furnishing retail and a byword for poor design and quality. Its infamy spread beyond London. In 1927 Le Corbusier, perhaps through the medium of his English translator, pronounced 'the existing plan of the dwelling house takes no account of man and is conceived as a furniture store. This scheme of things, favourable enough to the trade of Tottenham Court Road, is of ill omen for society'.[27] But 'society' at large never had much sympathy for Corbusier's opinions.

The social reformer Henry Mayhew, in *Life and Labours of the London Poor* (1889, 1891) complained that at the lowest end of the market 'every art and trick that scheming can devise or avarice suggest' was used to dupe the financially precarious. He also plumbed another depth of house furnishing to which no retailers would cater: 'a few sacks were thrown over an old palliasse, a blanket seemed to be used for a quilt; there were no fire irons or fender, no cooking utensils. Beside the bed was an old chest, serving for a chair, while a board resting on a trestle did duty for a table'.[28] It was an existence only bearable because the workhouse was worse. But aspirations still moved the destitute to treasure whatever scrap of ornament they might forage.

Beyond the industrial cities, life for the lower social strata could be less immediately grim and workers of limited means could accumulate some luxuries. *In the parlour [of a cottage at Merthyr Tydfil iron works] there was a good four-post bedstead, a French-polished chest of drawers, covered with a profusion of glass and other articles ... In a corner was a glass fronted cupboard, filled with china and glass and displaying ostentatiously silver sugar tongs and set of spoons There was also a mahogany table with a bright copper tea-kettle reposing on it.*[29] And in a cottage in Northumberland pit village: 'As a general rule the furniture is decidedly good; some articles even costly' and not 'out of place in a house of some pretentions.'[sic][30]

Chroniclers and critics

Osbert Lancaster had disapproved of early Victorian domestic interiors and he approved less of what followed as the number of artefacts increased precipitately and offered a comprehensive catalogue of the excesses: *it is not so much the quality of the individual furnishings that has altered but the quantity. Now for the first time the part tends to become more important than the whole and the room assumes the function of a museum of objets d'art. The mantelpiece is transformed into a parade ground for the perpetual marshalling of rows of Bristol glass candlesticks, Sèvres vases, Bohemian lustres around the glass-protected focal point of a massively allegorical clock. For the better display of whole cavalry divisions of plunging bronze equestrians, Covent Gardens of wax fruit, bales of Berlin woolwork, the drawing room, the library and the boudoir are forced to accommodate innumerable cupboards, consoles and occasional tables. The large family portrait loses none of its popularity but the fashion for miniatures and silhouettes enables the range of visible reminders of the importance of family ties to be extended to the third and fourth generations of uncles, aunts and cousins of every degree.*[31] He suggested that the Victorian 'passion for tangible evidence of past emotions' added to the clutter and suggested that, to avoid giving offence or prioritising affections it was necessary to accommodate 'such a surrealist variety of objects as a sand-filled paperweight from Alum Bay, a lock of little Willy's hair and dear Fido, stuffed and mounted'. He also suggested that the sentimental collection could, with increasing prosperity, become a demonstration of raw wealth complemented with 'lavishly gilded Louis Quinze furniture'. He credited the tendency with having 'the courage of its opulent convictions'.[32]

Mark Girouard, speaking in particular of the end of the century's Aesthetic movement, agreed: 'Most Victorians were incurable nest makers; but their equivalents of twigs, straws and leaves were Japanese fans, vases, photographs, bronze statues and clocks which they wove together into a richly indistinguishable fuzz.'[33]

He complained that for the mid-Victorians 'gloom was romantic' and kept daylight out while 'the early and late Victorians let it in …' – first as part of the Regency legacy and the second as taste moved away from Gothic theatricality.[34]

Lancaster singled out the dining room as the one place that changed little across the 19th century. Other, perhaps less facetious, commentators have also seen it as a room apart: stolidly male, where the master of the house and its fortune sat at the head of the table and controlled proceedings, a place where other males could be impressed and, when ladies withdrew to the decorative delicacies and conversational frivolities in the (with)drawing room, could talk about matters of import. *The Gentleman's House* of 1865 advised: 'the dining room should have an air of "masculine importance" and the drawing room should be "entirely ladylike"'.[35] In his novel *Conings* by Benjamin Disraeli went further, perhaps to supplement his strategic schmoozing of Queen Victoria: 'Woman alone can organise a drawing room; man succeeds sometimes in a library.'[36]

Writing in a catalogue, c.1880, for the retailers William Wallace and Company, a Mrs Panton observed that: 'in our dining room we are frankly all we pretend to be'.[37] It was a place where a family could rehearse and perform their self-mythologies.

Lancaster suggested that the dining room was close to sacred ground, shielded from the whims of fashionable interior taste but dedicated to the constants of gustatory taste and, as has been frequently chronicled, the Victorians ate enormously. He described the elements of the room: *The table, sideboard and chairs were invariably of mahogany and of a sufficiently massive construction safely to support the respective weights of the serried ranks of decanters and side dishes, the monumental epergnes and the diners themselves. The wall-paper was always dark and nine times out of ten of a self-patterned crimson design; that colour being considered, quite rightly, as stimulating to the appetite. The carpet was invariably a fine Turkey.*[38] Lancaster also identified criteria for pictures. They should be still-lives of raw foods, animal and vegetable, piled high, storms at sea, Highland cattle or gloomy forests. Pictures with a connection to religion were tolerated, the Holy land at sunset perhaps or 'carousing Cardinals … the only alternative to oil-paintings … were steel engravings … of sacred subjects'.[39]

Lancaster's description of the dining room is confirmed with added detail by the first-hand memories of the novelist E. F. Benson, creator of Mapp and Lucia, those fictional martyrs to vagaries of taste. Benson recalled as a child in the early 1870s: *the monstrous round-backed mahogany chairs of the period that lined the elongated dining-room table. Upon it stood a pair of branched candlesticks and other lesser lights, and for a centre-piece there was a wondrous silver epergne. Upon the ornamented base of it reclined a camel with a turbaned*

Arab driver: he leaned against the trunk of a tall palm-tree that soared upwards straight and bare for a full eighteen inches. At the top of this majestic stem there spread out all around the feathery fronds of its foliage, and resting on them (though in reality firmly screwed into the top of the palm-trunk) stood a bowl of cut glass filled with moist sand. In this was planted a bower of roses and honeysuckle which trailed over the silver leaves of the palm-tree and completed the oasis for the Arab and his camel.[40] The factories of industrial England could produce absurdly confected ornaments that were enough to satisfy the average householder's aesthetic sweet tooth but to conceive and execute pieces on the scale and complexity of the Arab and his camel required medieval skills and medieval mindsets.

Radical chic

As the spoils of prosperity flooded in throughout the 19th century, those who were amongst the greatest beneficiaries began to imagine they could see benefits in a simple life. The Arts and Crafts movement evolved directly from the Gothic Revival. M. T. Saler called it 'Medieval Modernism'.[41] Gentlemen artists and social reformers, Ruskin and William Morris in particular, promoted a return to craft production, organised and monitored by equivalents of medieval guilds as a strategy to improve the aesthetic standards of the products churned out. Its advocates had benevolent intentions, but were not immune to Victorian condescension. They sought to improve the squalid working and living conditions of factory workers, but their motivation was as much aesthetic as fellow feeling for the unfortunates. Their paternalistic presumption was that factory-made artefacts concocted to appeal to householders' untutored taste could only corrupt it further.

Arts and Crafts output was easy to like; it eschewed excessive ornament but the quality of its making was plain to see and as good as decoration. It provided the artefacts needed to live a life of exquisite, socially responsible, leisure but in the end could only distance further those rich enough to pay for days of craft skills from those of average incomes obliged to make do with the factory-made.

Pugin accepted industrial scale production to give him the ornament for his churches and trusted Christian principles rather than conditions of employment to enhance the lives of workers. Arts and Crafts ignored religious principles, as far as any Victorian institute could. It had a secular social agenda. It valued hand-forged, hand-beaten metals, hardwoods selected for their grain and assembled with traditional joints so perfectly made that they could only delight the eye.

Morris was the driving force of the Arts and Crafts movement and a poet, a novelist, a translator of Icelandic sagas and a socialist activist. A typical young Victorian of independent means, he had no inclination to join the family firm and presumed himself to be better suited to artistic activities. Born in 1834, he became embroiled in the religious debates of his day and, while at Oxford, inspired by its medieval buildings, took a stance against industrialisation. Although he would become an atheist, he was influenced by Christian Socialist writings, particularly those of Ruskin.

Right
William Morris, The Red House entrance hallway, 1860.

Below
William Morris, The Red House living room, 1860.

At Oxford he met the future Pre-Raphaelite painter Edward Burne-Jones. They thought of taking holy orders, founding a monastery and living a life of chastity and artistic activity. They abandoned the monastery and chastity but remained friends and artistic collaborators.

Morris apprenticed himself to an architect while Burne-Jones opted for painting and attached himself to the Pre-Raphaelite Dante Gabriel Rossetti. Bored by the technical grind of architecture, Morris joined them but, with no aptitude for painting, concentrated on designing illuminated manuscripts and embroideries to complement his poetry. He had Philip Webb, an acquaintance from his architectural days, design the Pugin-esque Red House in Kent for him and designed the interior himself. The very twee Burne-Jones called it the 'beautifullest place on earth'.

In 1861, Morris formed a decorative arts company with three Pre-Raphaelites, Ford Maddox Ford, Burne-Jones and Dante Gabriel Rossetti, who were unlikely businessmen, an academic, Charles Faulkner, an engineer, Peter Paul Marshall and the architect Philip Webb. They called themselves 'the Firm'.

A client, Lady Mount-Temple, wrote of her home before and after the 'Firm' got to it: *You remember our dear little house in Curzon Street; when we furnished it, nothing would please me but watered paper on the walls, garlands of roses tied with blue bows! Glazed chintzes with bunches of roses, so natural they looked, I thought, as if they had been gathered (between you and me I still think it was very pretty), and most lovely ornaments we had in perfect harmony, gilt pelicans or swans as candlesticks.*[42] She recalled how, at a dinner in the house, Rossetti suggested its decor was vile and its contents should be burnt. Extraordinarily, she asked the Firm to redecorate the staircase and described the result: 'A Morris paper was hung on the walls, and a lovely little bit of glass by Burne-Jones filled the staircase window.' 'Now,' she reported 'our taste was attacked on the other side, and all our candid relations and friends intimated that they thought we had made our pretty little house hideous!' She purported 'to like it more and more' and suggested that: *nearly all people confess that they owe a deep debt to the Morris & Co firm, for having saved them from trampling roses under foot, and sitting on shepherdesses, or birds and butterflies, from vulgar ornaments and other atrocities in taste, and for having made their homes homely and beautiful.*[43] Although initially Neo-Gothic, 'the Firm' differed from leading architectural practitioners like Pugin and Gilbert Scott, who were happy to apply a 'medieval' machine-made veneer. The Firm was ideologically committed to medieval craft techniques. Through its principles, it explained to rich customers that machine-made objects were vulgar and established itself as a fashionably radical purveyor of furniture, wood and stone carvings, metalwork and stained glass and murals. The Firm aspired to have handmade decoration accepted as a fine art and, to advance their ideal of a medieval guild controlling artisan output, recruited apprentices from the Industrial Home for Destitute Boys in Euston, London.

Not all partners had the same interests, so in 1875 Morris assumed control of the company. He drafted in effective financial management and Morris, Marshall, Faulkner and Co. became Morris and Co. The company flourished under the patronage of artistically inclined members of the upper and upper middle classes. It was not the clientele Morris the social reformer had hoped for but the business needed rich customers.

Morris became increasingly involved in various socialist experiments and funded many of them in pursuit of his vision of creating rural craft communities away from the destitution and pollution of cities. In the midst of his political manoeuvrings, he continued to design textiles and wallpapers, write poetry and translate Icelandic sagas. In 1891 he founded the Kelmscott Press to produce beautifully crafted books. When he died in 1898 it had published over 50, of which 23 were by Morris. His writings, particularly his novel *News From Nowhere*, are now seen as early examples of the fantasy genre. One might think that his vision of a social utopia in a world of flourishing capitalism was also a fantasy. He never managed to share profits with his workers.

The Arts and Crafts movement took time to formalise itself. In 1888 the newly formed Arts and Crafts Exhibition Society held its first exhibition – Burne-Jones concluded that it represented the first opportunity to make a retrospective assessment of what the movement had achieved in 20 years. In the same year C. R. Ashbee set up the Guild and School of Handicraft, a craft cooperative based on the model of a medieval guild, to train and elevate a few of the deprived inhabitants of London's East End. The Guild employed around 50 men and in 1902, in pursuit of the ideal of small rural communities of well-nourished and

Opposite
William Morris's 'Pomegranate' wallpaper in the home of the architect E. W. Edis, circa 1880.

Top left
C. F. A. Voysey, Holly Mount, Buckinghamshire, entrance hall, 1907. The chairs, the simple ceramic vases on the stretched fireplace surround, the door hinges and the clock on the mantelpiece in the room beyond are all typical of Arts and Crafts.

Below left
C. F. A. Voysey, 1880. Like a good Arts and Crafts architect, Voysey designed everything; the chair, the tabletop mirror, the wallpaper and the textiles.

Top right
C. F. A. Voysey, Holly Mount, Buckinghamshire, 1907. The furniture, including the piano, are all designed by Voysey, and all horizontal surfaces carry tasteful *objets d'art*.

Above left
C. F. A. Voysey, design for a fireplace, 1892.

Above right
C. F. A. Voysey, design for a clock for his own home, 1898.

well-behaved artisans, Ashbee relocated it to the Cotswolds. There, he designed jewellery and silverware which the craftsmen meticulously produced in silver that proudly bore the marks of their hammers. The objects were exquisite but necessarily expensive, not for general consumption. Nevertheless, the movement survived. Perhaps its most accomplished exponent was Charles Voysey who designed a number of irresistibly picture-book houses in irresistibly picturesque locations in the British Isles, their fixtures and fittings and every object within them.

A mildly subversive element had been insinuating itself into respectable middle class London. Areas of Kensington and Chelsea in particular were attracting businessmen's artistically inclined sons, and occasionally daughters, who were not seen as future assets to the businesses that were providing them with generous allowances. A few parents may even have enjoyed the risqué kudos in having an artistic offspring. Depending on parental generosity, these creatives could set themselves up in a bespoke studio house or in one of the romantic little studio blocks, built by developers every bit as sharp as the entrepreneurs who had constructed the terraces of Pimlico. There they could live *La Vie Bohème*, but free from concerns about hunger and cold. They became the dedicated foot soldiers of the Arts and Crafts movement.

Like most Victorian reformers with artistic aspirations, Morris inherited his wealth. Presumably he and the other reformers felt guilt about the sources of the financial independence that allowed them to indulge talents that were not necessarily of the highest order. Perhaps they had ambitions to be seen as all round good eggs. Osbert Lancaster, another scion comfortably cushioned by inherited wealth but one not inclined to egalitarian impulses, said that Morris's wallpapers 'were the only legacy of any artistic value bequeathed to us by the whole Arts and Crafts movement.'[44] That opinion is strictly a matter of taste.

A divine wind

In 1853 'barbarians' under Commodore Matthew Perry of the American Navy had sailed into culturally hermetic Japan and the discontinued trade links established 200 years earlier by Europeans were reopened. From around 1875 Japanese arts and crafts grabbed Western imaginations, matching the physical and spiritual presence of the Gothic-esque with added exoticism but also with restraint and no recognisable religious references that might disturb a pious Westerner. For those satiated with Gothic retro they offered an alluring alternative.

The tsunami of Japanese influence was not invariably for the good and the rather sparse aesthetic meant that faux pas of style and taste would not be lost in a fog of gewgaws. Mark Girouard condemns a 'wildly pseudo-Japanese boudoir in Bayswater', the owners of which had 'too obviously surrendered themselves to a smart decorator not quite out of the top drawer'.[45] Nevertheless striving for restraint, concentrated minds and more able designers began to get the hang of the basics of faux Japanese. It had nothing to do with British or European traditions, it was not Christian but its Japanese style seemed intrinsically and nobly spiritual.

Genuine Japanese artefacts, even those produced for the Western market, were not factory-produced but crafted by artisans with traditional tools and skills and that allowed the Japanese spirit to segue comfortably into the Arts and Crafts movement. Other radical British designers were seduced into changing course. The architect Edward Godwin had begun working in the mid-century polychromatic Neo-Gothic style, but Japanese influences crept into his Gothicism and became increasingly obvious as he opted for ebonised finishes and lighter elements. An affair with the actress Ellen Terry gave him the opportunity to expand these ideas into theatre design and to move in louche circles. His furniture, textiles, wallpaper and tiles were sold in Liberty and Co., the London department store that opened in 1875 to sell Japanese artefacts. Godwin designed a studio house for the painter James Abbott McNeill Whistler, and Oscar Wilde was an effusively appreciative client. Shared admiration for Japanese and Chinese art encouraged Godwin and Whistler to collaborate on furniture and interior design projects.

At the end of the 19th and beginning of the 20th centuries the influence of the cult of the artisan was clear across the decorative arts. Arts and Crafts and all things handmade was fashionable but, as the market grew and artisans proliferated, quality declined. The handmade began to look too shoddy against the machine made; machines could create a hammered finish as well as any doughty artisan.

Top right
William Godwin, dining room sideboard for Dromore Castle, Limerick, 1880.

Below right
William Godwin, wall frieze for Dromore Castle, Limerick, 1880.

In the 1890s British Arts and Crafts developed its effete side, the Aesthetic movement, led by Oscar Wilde. Its adherents indulged in pantomimes of confected taste, all the better to outrage the bourgeoisie. Wilde was reported to have expressed regret that he found it 'harder and harder every day to live up to my blue china' and was satirised when *Punch*, the ponderously humorous organ of the middle classes, published a cartoon in which a wife made exactly the same complaint to her plainly sceptical husband. Blue china, imported from China, was the height of chic but as an aesthete Wilde would have been distressed by the popularity of the – British designed and manufactured blue quasi-Chinese – Willow Pattern motif which became a *sine qua non* in humble homes and is now a junk shop stalwart. Tastemakers are generally unsettled when their discoveries are adopted by plebeians.

The Aesthetic interior was ascetic, denying itself the artistic gluttony that was devouring mainstream interiors. Osbert Lancaster dubbed the style 'Greenery Yallery' and wrote that: *a variety of strange breezes sprang from several directions at once which in combination succeeded in blowing the stuffy yet cosy atmosphere of the average Victorian interior to oblivion ... the cheerful magentas and sulphur yellows were banished ... in favour of sage green, peacock blue and every variety of ochre.*[46] The most significant of the 'strange breezes' wafted from Japan.

Lancaster, of course, did not approve of the Aesthetic movement's aesthetic: *a tangle of water lilies cast their tenuous roots from ceiling to floor; chairs, tables, mantle pieces ... shot skywards ... in letters of a tortuous and illegible craftiness suitable mottoes, punctuated with tiny hearts, were beaten on copper and incised with pokers on wood; and handmade pots ... entirely useless for any practical purposes supported with difficulty a spray of honesty or a single iris. Here and there on the walls were displayed a few of the rare pictures which could possibly compete with the decoration; Japanese prints the size of postage stamps in mounts like table clothes, a Beardsley drawing or two and possibly a Whistler nocturne.*[47] Arts and Crafts was a particularly British movement, the result as much of reaction against the Industrial Revolution as of artistic aspiration but some of its ideas spread to Europe and North America, both of which were coming to terms with their own industrialisation. Before settling down and committing to the self-denying cult of Modernism, mainland Europe had a fling with Art Nouveau in the last decade of the 19th century and the cult clung on for the first decade of the 20th. It drew heavily on convoluted and writhing natural forms and exploited the industrial processes of the end of the 19th century to achieve approximations to them. It had a lot in common with Britain's Aesthetic movement. It was fundamentally decadent and a retreat, conscious or not, from reality. It thrived in decadent European cities. Its only significant British appearance was in Glasgow where Charles Rennie Mackintosh and his wife Margaret Macdonald created a domestic world of their own which brought them a short period of acclaim in Vienna but little success in their home town.

It is perhaps appropriate that Britain, which gave the world industrialisation, should offer it the Arts and Crafts antidote. But the antidote was perhaps too idealistic, wrapped up in soul searching about the legitimacy of using machines or of having craftsmen make objects to the designs of non-makers who might not properly understand the integrities of materials and techniques. In Britain the argument led diehards to move in favour of hand-crafting and cherishing the marks of the making process. The awkwardly finished object was presumed to be authentic.

Peter York, the pathologist of contemporary culture, has pointed out in his *Authenticity is a Con* that to be truly authentic one must 'embrace the modern world',[48] which is what the Continental, and especially German, followers of Arts and Crafts did as they progressed towards Modernism. They accepted the potential of the machine and fed into it an understanding of how products might resolve the realities of function and production. They were distinctly less successful in finding a popular aesthetic.

We should wonder however if we can learn something about the fundamentals of taste from the persistent popularity of Arts and Crafts and Art Nouveau. Could it be that in ideas that draw from nature, which is where Ruskin advised his readers to look for inspiration, there is something to which those untutored in matters of taste instinctively relate?

CHAPTER 3

New Century, New Style

'The 1890s were the first decade in which a cadre of intellectuals began a kind of a countdown to a new century, and saw themselves as participants in the definitive end of something, the fin de siècle … The world was winding down; 1900 was to be the magical year in which it would be wound up again. The Twentieth Century! It was a good, round number.'

Bevis Hillier, *The Style Of The Century*, 1998[1]

Queen Victoria died in 1901 and was succeeded by her fun-loving 60-year-old son, Edward VII, by whom she had not been amused. Like his mother, Edward gave his name to an era, but a significantly shorter one; remembered not for rectitude but for his and his aristocratic cronies' moral laxity and conspicuous consumption. His lifestyle was prodigiously unhealthy and he died in 1910.

Edward the philanderer was succeeded by George the philatelist who preferred stamp collecting to debauchery and, with his wife, set his subjects an example of respectability. Britain however was running out of steam. She continued to enjoy the benefits of Empire and to think herself the pre-eminent world power but the 13 American colonies that had seceded from the Empire 125 years before had now created their own federal empire in the conquered territories of their mid and far west. Natural resources brought them extraordinary wealth and, apart from sending the daughters of its richest industrialists to marry and invigorate the finances of European aristocracy, the federation was not inclined to be proactive beyond its shores. When the west was won, pioneering spirits tackled new frontiers. In 1903 Henry Ford joined the ranks of car makers and perfected assembly line production. In the same year, with a hop of 37m, Wilbur Wright made the first flight in a heavier than air contraption.

Everyday 20th-century lives were being changed by Thomas Edison's 19th-century inventions which were spreading from the homes of the well-to-do to those of more modest means and from the USA to the UK. Osbert Lancaster took his customary jaundiced view of this filtering down of convenience and novelty when he wrote: 'there was one trait that found ample expression in the contemporary interior, that particularly distinguishes the Edwardians from their immediate forebears – their pathetic faith in the benefits of science'.[2] It may or may not have been pathetic but Edwardians would have been foolish to reject the benefits of electricity. Brighter, electrically illuminated rooms encouraged a retreat from Victorian gloom towards lighter colours and a thinning out of bric-a-brac. Art Nouveau had limped into the brave new century only to be redeployed in the service of household appliances. Lancaster recorded how, *from the heart of a tinted glass flower at the end of a terrifyingly sinuous brass stalk there now peeped the electric light bulb … [and] a complicated contraption of vulcanite, mahogany and polished brass carried the householder's voice, at the mere turning of a handle, to such of his neighbours as were similarly equipped.*[3] Lancaster, born in 1908, was too young to have experienced Edwardianism first hand but E. F. Benson, 33 at the turn of the century, was there. He wrote: 'these same years saw, glimmering from the darkness of the unknown, such manifestations of scientific marvels as no other short period can point to. Motorcars and moving pictures, telephones and electric lighting, X-rays and other ultra-spectrum potencies.'[4]

Motorcars and flying machines were the most spectacular examples of the new technologies that would shape the 20th century into something that had little to do with the patient and ponderous evolution that had gone before. Railways that had revolutionised the 19th suddenly seemed prosaically earthbound. The new technologies also changed the mechanics of warfare. The people and government of the United States had been keen to remain neutral in the Great War but in 1917, after Russia withdrew from the fight and weakened the position of Britain and France, they began to think otherwise. Germany's sinking of shipping in the Atlantic in 1917, with the loss of American lives, swung support behind intervention. American troops became heroes in Europe and, with their dashing uniforms and their intoxicating marching music by George M. Cohen and Irving Berlin, embodiments of cinematic glamour, exponents of the new music and dance crazes that had begun to excite progressive Europeans.

The devastation of the Great War seemed, to many, to demand and justify systemic change to the institutions and trappings of the pre-war world. Youngish artists and architects were particularly agitated. Even before the war Italian Futurists, excited by speed, machines and violence, had declaimed in their manifesto 'we will have none of it, we, the young, the strong, and the living FUTURISTS!'.[5] Russia's October Revolution of 1917 further fired up artistic radicals who prodigiously emitted hyperbolic tracts, proposing that after wartime violence only cultural anarchy could bring root and branch change. In 1918 the Dutch De Stijl group invited all who believed in the reform of art and culture to destroy those things that would prevent progress. An evolutionary rather than a revolutionary process might have engaged those of a more ameliorative mindset but avant-gardists, fired up by their own rhetoric, were disinclined to compromise and more interested in outraging all beyond their circle. The removal of incumbent dinosaurs left the way clear for totalitarians, both political and artistic.

Below
The Schröder House, designed in 1924 by Gerrit Rietveld, is the best known – and most extreme – example of De Stijl design. It sits like a jolly abstraction on the end of a conventional brick terrace and patently wants no part of the past.

Right
The interior of the Schröder House. The white chair in the foreground, also by Rietveld, confirms that theory took precedence over comfort.

Artistic revolution quickly acquired its own institution when, in 1919, Walter Gropius established the frantically progressive Bauhaus art school. It was committed to Gesamtkunstwerk, or the total work of art, in which, theoretically, all creative activities combined to make a coherent whole. It rejected conventional disciplinary boundaries. It taught what it held to be a pure design process that was common to all materials or techniques, which was a defining step away from the Arts and Crafts obsession with both. If it was not art for art's sake it was design for art's sake.

It was, like any good educational institution, totalitarian, imposing rules and practices but the rules and practices did not produce results of which the Nazi party approved and the school was shut in 1933. Idealistic staff went east to die in Stalin's purges. The less idealistic retreated to the USA and teaching jobs in liberal art schools. Former directors and architects, Gropius and Mies van der Rohe, went west and defined the steel and glass buildings that were to change the financial districts of cities across the world.

Nazi disapproval consolidated the Bauhaus's credibility, and its ideas infiltrated schools of architecture and design throughout Europe. For students it was heady to know that one could instigate enormous blights upon landscapes and justify them with theory understood only by one's peers.

Radical departures from architectural normality in the 1920s provoked a seismic schism between a self-regarding profession and a sometimes baffled public. The new style was different from any other architectural movement that had gone before it: here, the progressives decided that everything that had gone before them had been wrong – perhaps the idea of the 'war to end wars' encouraged architecture's iconoclasts to presume that they should wipe their own slate clean. Repudiation of ornament excited radical architects, outraged traditionalists and appalled and baffled the public whose appetite for decoration remained undiminished.

In any consideration of the modern domestic interior, and particularly its relationship to architecture, it is necessary to deal with Charles-Edouard Jeanneret, a.k.a. Le Corbusier. He began as a young provincial architect with ambition in a small city in the French-speaking part of Switzerland. He travelled to Italy, Budapest, Vienna and Paris where he worked for Auguste Perret, a pioneer of concrete construction, and to Berlin where, like so many nascent Modernists, he worked for Peter Behrens who had transitioned from Germanic Art Nouveau to Modernist austerity.

He spent the First World War in his neutral Switzerland, formulating the theories that he would set out, in 1923, in *Vers Une Architecture*. He could be as shrill as any Futurist; the book began: 'A great epoch has begun. There exists a new spirit.' He was excited by motorcars, aeroplanes and, more surprisingly, grain silos. He declared that the house should be a 'machine for living in'.[6]

His vision for housing was encapsulated in the diagrammatic drawing he made for his Dom-Ino House. Conceived during his Swiss retreat, its reinforced concrete floor slabs, supported on thin reinforced concrete columns, gave maximum freedom to subdivide floors with non-loadbearing walls and to design external walls. Theoretically, any inmate could determine the facade style they wanted but that freedom was never on Le Corbusier's agenda. People craved a symmetrical four-square house with solid walls regularly pierced by vertical windows, all beneath a pitched roof; Le Corbusier switched windows from the vertical to the horizontal and put them all under a flat roof.

In *Vers Une Architecture*, which was effectively his manifesto, he made a distinction between 'engineers' aesthetic' and 'architects' aesthetic' which produced 'harmony and beauty' and which, he proposed, might be arrived at by formulae derived from his studies and interpretations of Classical proportions. His rules were not dissimilar to those taught in the Neo-Classical Beaux Arts architecture schools and suggested, in effect, that, stripped of layers of ornament, buildings could be beautiful. The problem was that the hoi polloi liked the broken bones of the Parthenon, liked the surviving carvings and would have liked the building even more had its surfaces been painted in bright colours as they were when it was built.

The Roman architect Marcus Vitruvius suggested, that a good building needed '*firmitas, utilitas, venustas*', which is normally translated as 'firmness, commodity, delight'. The 15th-century Italian polymath Leon Battista Alberti divided 'venustas' into 'pulcritudo', achieved with harmonious proportions, and 'ornamentum', which he relegated to 'auxiliary brightness'. Le Corbusier may have had formulae for perfect proportions but none for 'auxiliary brightness'.

Below
Gesamtkunstwerk! The Bauhaus students' hostel designed by Walter Gropius, Dessau, Germany, 1926.

NEW CENTURY, NEW STYLE

Lost in translation

The useful, and unassuming, 16th-century English word 'modern', which might best be defined as 'contemporary', was appropriated as a label for the anarchic artistic movements of the 1920s. It has served that cause for a century and, by association, has become a term of abuse for anything disturbingly new.

Mistranslation, wilful or otherwise, has not helped English speakers cope with seminal architectural texts. *Vers Une Architecture* translates literally as *Towards An Architecture* and suggests a sober, perhaps cautious, search for a definitive answer, without ruling out the possibility of a return to something familiar, but its modification to *Towards A New Architecture* in the English edition might suggest novelty for novelty's sake.

We can see something similar in the translation of the title of Adolf Loos's German language essay of 1913, *Ornament und Verbrechen*. This precisely translates as *Ornament and Crime* and was published in France as *Ornement et Crime*, which, unfortunately, to anglophone ears, is indistinguishable from *Ornement est Crime*, which translates as *Ornament is Crime*: and that belief became a Modernist mantra.

Ornament und Verbrechen offered a curious thesis, arguing that contemporary society had no capacity to create, or need for, ornament. Loos explained, that prisoners guilty of violent crimes, such as murder and rape, are likely to be comprehensively tattooed, while non-violent criminals, such as bigamists and embezzlers, will be un-tattooed. Tattoos, he proposed, were the self-inflicted, self-abusing, self-loathing ornament of an underclass, for whom, he conceded, they might have a therapeutic benefit. With the right translator Loos's writings were by no means dull.

Those likely to join him in rejecting ornament were few and not necessarily clustered

Right
Loos's department store in Vienna – the building that alarmed the Emperor Franz Joseph, 1911.

TASTE

at the top of the social pyramid. The Emperor Franz Joseph of Austria changed his route to and from his palace to avoid an accidental sighting of a department store designed by Loos that was alarmingly free of mouldings.

Loos also proposed that architecture was only about the 'tomb and the monument'.[7] Everything else; – factories, railway stations, department stores or dwellings – was merely 'buildings' and, since they were not of a spiritual nature they could be garnished to satisfy untutored tastes. His distinction may be demonstrated by comparing the tomb he designed for Max Dvorak, in 1921, and his entry for the *Chicago Tribune* tower competition of 1922, condemned by its commercial function to be no more than a building. The tomb was a square stone structure under a ziggurat roof, with a narrow door and high square window, both free of mouldings. The proposal, presumably tongue in cheek, for the Tribune Tower building was a 'Doric' column 21-storeys high sitting on a 12-storey reworking of the Dvorak tomb. A tight regular grid of windows pierced both base and column. It purported to be a pun on the idea of a newspaper column and looked absurd, although not a great deal more absurd than the Gothic-esque competition winner. Loos's whimsy would have passed muster as Post-Modernist 60 years later.

Like so many before and after him Loos professed to hope that understanding of materials and their potential would evolve a new aesthetic. If he stripped his exteriors of ornament he did so hoping to find beauty 'in form instead of making it depend on [applied] ornament'.[8] In his interiors he used the grains and colours of woods and marbles and made abstract patterns. He defined beauty as the degree 'to which (a building) attains utility and harmony of all parts in relation to each other'.[9] To all this he added his *raumplan* strategy. Rather than subdividing interiors with walls he marked functions by changes in floor levels. When walls were unavoidable he gnawed them away to provide views from one area to another. Le Corbusier's Dom-Ino House, though unbuilt, had theoretically removed the need for structural walls and allowed casual connections between compatible areas. The *raumplan* offered the theatricality of changing levels.

Loos visited the United States in 1893 and was captivated by its exemplary plumbing. The following year the Chicagoan architect and mentor of Frank Lloyd Wright, Louis Sullivan, published *Ornament in Architecture*. Sullivan was admired for his ability to embellish huge commercial buildings with terracotta slabs of intricate ornament inspired by natural forms and so it was significant when he suggested that ornament should be temporarily set aside: 'ornament is an intellectual luxury, not a necessity … it would be greatly for our aesthetic good if we were to refrain entirely from the use of ornament'[10] to concentrate on making buildings that were 'well-formed and comely in the nude'.[11] It was an argument for de-cluttering which might have been applied to the Victorian drawing room.

Above
Loos's competition entry for the *Chicago Tribune* competition, a Doric column sitting on a tomb, 1923.

Top left
The Strasser House in Vienna, 1919: demonstrating Loos's reliance on the inherent patterns in natural materials to provide decoration. The change in level defines the music podium, the *raumplan* strategy.

Top right
Louis Sullivan's Bayard-Condict Building, illustrating his ability to decorate a monstrous hulk delicately and give it grace, Bleecker Street, New York, 1897.

In 1896 Sullivan declared that 'form ever follows function and this is the (natural) law', which gave Modernists the first draft of another article of faith; 'form follows function'. This was not a mistranslation but 'function' was presumed to refer only to the practical. The traditional function of a building, to give pleasure, was losing currency.

Mistranslation happened again, in 1932, with the MoMA exhibition, *International Style Modern Architecture Since 1922*. The United States' awareness of Modernism happened slowly and the elimination, in black and white photographs, of what little colour it sported suggested that white planes were a given. It was a misunderstanding shared by everyone who learnt about the style from books and magazines.

It is easy to appreciate why MoMA chose to replace 'Modernism' with 'International Style' in the exhibition's title. It was an international movement and their new label did not deny America's own modern architectural tradition, its skyscrapers and Frank Lloyd Wright's prairie houses.

Wright, exercising his great ego in the comparative isolation of the mid-West, had evolved a distinctive modern (not Modern) architecture. His 'Prairie' houses of the last decade of the 19th century and the first of the 20th were suburban villas, albeit large, but they were entirely radical, long and low with horizontal bands of brick and window. They inspired European pioneers of Modernism but their Arts and Crafts richness made them deliciously palatable. European Modernists generally rejected that richness.

With the help of European immigrants and refugees from Nazi Germany, and Mies van der Rohe in particular, the International Style became the default style of American, and international, business. The Getty Research Institute describes it as 'the style of architecture that emerged in Holland, France, and Germany after World War I and spread throughout the world, becoming the dominant architectural style until the 1970s'.[12] American modern architecture had, until the arrival of the Europeans, been dominated by the Chicagoans. Sullivan understood how to build tall but, more importantly, how to decorate the monsters. His small-scale terracotta ornament gave abstract texture to the naked shells when viewed from a distance and intricate, naturalistic natural forms when seen close up. The Europeans were not practised in making skyscrapers and applied smooth skins of factory produced materials. Their towers were best viewed at a distance. They did not reward close inspection. There was little that Wright's palette of organic materials and organic forms could contribute to refining the towers of corporate business. If Corbusian concrete and glass dominated Europe then Miesian steel and glass ruled North America and everywhere that the international business held sway.

The MoMA exhibition gave credit to the European pioneers but it would be wrong now to ignore how they had been influenced by the portfolio of 100 lithographs of Wright's Prairie Houses published in Germany in 1911 by Ernst Wasmuth. Images of the low horizontal planes of the prairie houses caused a stir in the Behrens office at a time when it was bursting with future Modernist talent, and the De Stijl group readily acknowledged its importance for them: an architecture created for the flat prairies resonated with inhabitants of Dutch polders.

Below
The Robie House: the finest of Frank Lloyd Wright's 'Prairie' houses, which inspired early European Modernists, Chicago, 1909.

NEW CENTURY, NEW STYLE

The baby and the bathwater

In *The Ascent of Man* Jacob Bronowski suggested that, in the first years of the 20th century, physics was a work of art because the 'notion that there is an underlying structure, a world within world of the atom, captured the imagination of artists ... and that modern art begins at the same time as modern physics because it begins in the same ideas'.[13] Perhaps that is the problem; people at large understand and care as little about modern art as they do about atomic physics.

Victorian thinking had been shaped primarily by Christianity but, as the 19th-century wore on, there was a dilution of the spiritual intensity that had driven men like Pugin and Ruskin. William Morris went from youthful aspirant clergyman to aged atheist. Whilst 19th century reformers had promoted social reform within established social mechanisms, Modernists were more interested in outraging the bourgeoisie, to confirm that they were indeed on a cutting edge. The conceit was captured in a *Punch* cartoon of 1936 in which a woman, chicly mannish in jodhpurs, stands in front of a Modernist house and urges a conventional couple: 'do tell me you hate it'.

Modernism's apologists like to explain that it is not anything as ephemeral as a style but a philosophy, a rational way of designing, immune to swings of taste. Modernist housing did deal efficiently with the mechanics of daily living but did not lift spirits. It offered new homes but in social ghettoes and in what looked suspiciously like a style, one designed to outrage the bourgeoisie, while those consigned to the ghettoes it created aspired to be bourgeois.

Auguste Perret, Le Corbusier's early mentor, questioned Modernist objectivity. In the magazine *L'Amour de l'Art* in 1924 he accused its designers of talking of nothing but straight lines and essentials but being still obsessed with composing elevations aesthetically. The whole building, he suggested, became a single ornamental abstraction but, because there was no recognisable traditional decoration, the whole was presumed to be rational.

The moment architects obeyed their instinct to arrange elements for an aesthetic end they were making ornament. In his 1954 book *The Natural House*, Frank Lloyd Wright came clean and explained how, by using natural materials, he could make ornament: 'A plain flat surface cut to shape for its own sake, however large or plain the shape is ... no less ornament than egg and dart.'[14]

Perret was supported by Amédée Ozenfant who said 'many, and not the least, invent feigned utilities for the pleasure of rationally solving the problems thus raised, as witness those balconies for urban haranguings'.[15] The flat planes of a Modernist facade are distinctly functional, but if one's instinct is to add an aesthetic dividend (according to taste) then balconies can prettify flat facades with light and shade. Modernists excused them as devices to enjoy sunshine and fresh air, an article of their faith – Le Corbusier's sketches do indeed show inhabitants of new blocks addressing their neighbours from little balconies, presumably with harangues about the virtues of utopian Modernism.

Le Corbusier was not entirely opposed to applied ornament. He liked to think of himself

Left
The Aghion House in which Auguste Perret cast bands of rudimentary mouldings in the exposed concrete structure, Alexandria, 1927.

as an artist and had a penchant for painting murals. With Amédée Ozenfant, a painter, he founded and edited *L'Esprit Nouveau*, a magazine for progressive art and architecture. For the *Exposition des Arts Decoratifs* in 1925 he designed the *Pavillion de L'Esprit Nouveau*, a realisation of his architectural ideas, that came complete with a mural and a double height living space, overlooked by a mezzanine. It was a romantic artist's studio coerced to perform as a family home. A lot of the building's charm depended on a tree that grew on its terrace and popped through a circle cut into its roof. Such idiosyncrasies prompting wit were rare in the tower blocks of social housing that have been Le Corbusier's legacy. His villa had critical attention but it was the decorative artefacts, exquisitely crafted and broadly influenced by rudimentary Modernist thinking, that found an appreciative Jazz Age market.

Osbert Lancaster offered his retrospective description of what he called a 'Functional' interior in *Homes Sweet Homes*. Acknowledging how, through the 19th and early 20th centuries' excesses of 'furniture, ornaments and knick-knacks of every variety' had crowded the domestic interior he conceded that it had perhaps been inevitable that there should be a reaction just as extreme in the opposite direction.[16] He conceded that, as 'the voice of the new Puritans', the Modernists had authority at the end of the 1920s and had continued to command ever-increasing respect but that 'the number of persons who felt compelled to act upon such advice as it so generously gave remained disappointingly small'.[17] He presumed that the lack of enthusiasm for Modernism in domestic architecture was the result of a failure by its exponents to understand, or respond to, the shortcomings of the human psyche. *The open plan, the mass-produced steel and plywood furniture, the uncompromising display of the structural elements, are all, in theory perfectly logical, but in the home logic has always been at a discount. The vast majority, even including many readers of the New Statesman, crave their knick-knacks, though not in Victorian abundance, and are perfectly willing to pay the price in prolonged activities with broom and duster*.[18] Modernists made a great thing about the hygienic advantages of their unornamented interiors.

Critiques of Modernism transcended the architectural press. The novelist Evelyn Waugh – an occasional contributor to the *Architectural Review* – devoted a significant passage in *Decline and Fall* (1928) to making Modernist architects look ludicrous. His character Margot Beste-Chetwynde, a rich, socially well-connected white slaver, wanted a Modernist country house, 'something clean and square',[19] and engaged the German architect Professor Otto Friedrich Silenus, having seen his 'rejected design for a chewing-gum factory which had been reproduced in a progressive Hungarian quarterly'.[20] The professor pronounced 'the problem of architecture as I see it is the problem of all art – the elimination of the human element from the consideration of form … I do not think it is possible for domestic architecture to be beautiful, but I am doing my best'.[21] He claimed to prefer designing factories and he had a dilemma: 'I suppose there ought to be a staircase. Why can't the creatures stay in one place? Up and down, in and out, round and round. Why can't they sit still and work?'[22] An enlightened admirer says of Silenus: 'I think that he's a man worth watching. He was in Moscow at one time and in the Bauhaus at Dessau … he's got right away from Le Corbusier, anyway'.[23] Another replied: 'If people only realized, Corbusier is a pure nineteenth century, Manchester school utilitarian.'[24]

That Waugh could presume that his readers would be familiar with his targets suggests that, even by the mid 1920s, the shock of the new architecture was enough to have brought it to the attention of his readers and to allow him to lampoon its excesses and perpetrators.

Laggards

Britain and the United States were slow to come to terms with the European phenomenon of Modernism. The American government had recognised this and opted out of Paris's seminal *Exposition des Arts Decoratifs* of 1925 because, they confessed, they had 'insufficient good modern design' to offer. Nevertheless, the event was a catalyst that stirred national pride and spurred official attempts to inform and inspire its citizens with exhibitions in museums and department stores.

European immigrants tended to produce the most radical work. Rudolph Schindler and Richard Neutra worked briefly with Frank Lloyd Wright before taking advantage of Californian climate, terrain, wealth and open-mindedness.

In the 1920s, American-born radicals saw Europe as the prime location for avant-garde activity, a more convivial and cheaper environment in which to spend their allowances and enjoy bohemian capers. Paris was their preferred destination. Gertrude Stein and her brother Leo had been snapping up Cézannes, Picassos, Matisses and other avant-gardists since settling in the city in 1903. The siblings' income came from investments made by their elder brother Michael who, with his wife Sarah, assembled another cache of Matisses and commissioned Le Corbusier to build them a suburban villa. When Gertrude and Leo quarrelled over Gertrude's live-in girlfriend, Alice B. Toklas, Leo decamped to Italy in 1914 and they divided their spoils. He is considered the more perceptive buyer of Modernist work; Gertrude has been accused of drifting towards more homely and decorative acquisitions. Is it dangerous, particularly where Gertrude is concerned, to suggest that her taste and her impulse to make a home rather than a gallery, was feminine?

Whatever Gertrude's true thoughts on décor, she established her celebrated salon for progressives of all nationalities living in and passing through Paris. American visitors included F. Scott Fitzgerald drinking copiously and Ernest Hemmingway crafting his fictional back-story. Other Americans settled elsewhere. T. S. Eliot was content to be a bank clerk in London but Ezra Pound found the city too capitalist and retreated to Italy where he became infatuated with Mussolini.

Britons, always intrigued by their own past, were incapable of taking anything too radical too seriously. Bright Young Things, the collective noun for the gang of socialites who set the pace and tone for London's nightlife in the 1920s, were louche, camp and inclined to be moderately modernistic. They were, themselves, excessively English but their instruments of self-destruction were American: cocktails, drugs, jazz and the Charleston. Three particularly self-indulgent Things, the siblings David, Richard and Olivia Plunket-Greene, commuted to New York to have their trousers cut *à la mode* and to visit jazz clubs. Less wealthy Things included the novelist Evelyn Waugh, the poet John Betjeman, the painter Rex Whistler, the stage designer Oliver Messell and the photographer Cecil Beaton for whom the others posed in narcissistic tableaux. The movement was languidly camp – and so were their interiors. Osbert Lancaster, one of their number, identified what he called Curzon Street Baroque, in Mayfair, as their milieu and described their abandoning French furniture and paintings for 'hand-painted furniture from Venice and a surprisingly abundant supply of suspicious Canalettos and ecclesiastical salvage'.[25] Or they might have favoured the First Russian Ballet period of 'modified Bohemianism' in artists' studios in Chelsea which were particularly good for parties, and 'electric light now took refuge in an old Chinese temple lantern and the telephone lurked coyly beneath the capacious skirts of a Russian peasant doll …'[26] Lancaster was habitually critical of the bowdlerising of practical gadgets. One suspects he considered prudery to be in bad taste.

In 1904 the German diplomat and architect, Hermann Muthesius, published *Das Englische Haus* and brought the comparatively simple lines and respect for materials that characterised Arts and Crafts houses and their contents to the admiring notice of many

Top
Rudolph Schindler's own house, Los Angeles, 1922.

Above
Richard Neutra, The Lovell Health House, Los Angeles, 1929.

Top right
Peter Behrens, the front elevation of New Ways, Northampton, UK, 1926.

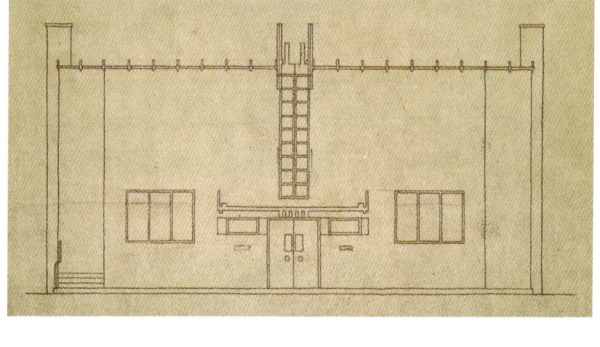

Middle right
Peter Behrens, a fireplace for New Ways with decidedly geometric tiling and a suggestion of Art Deco, 1926.

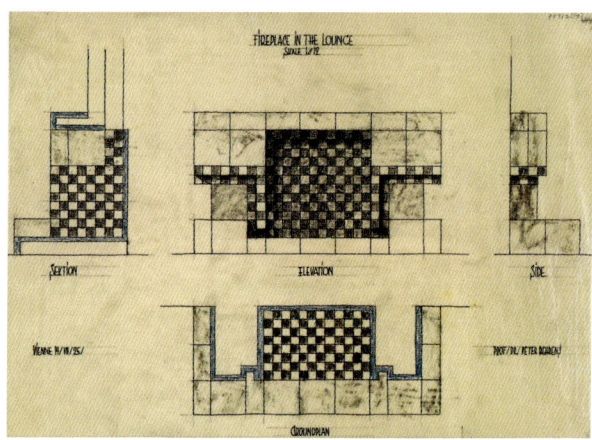

Below left
78 Derngate, Northampton, the entrance hall: when Charles Rennie Mackintosh moved on from the plant-based forms of his Art Nouveau phase to squares and triangles that appear to anticipate Art Deco, 1917.

Below right
78 Derngate, Northampton: stepped geometries that appear to anticipate Art Deco, 1917.

TASTE

Above
Amyas Connell, High and Over: the exterior demonstrates Modernist symptoms down to the little balcony that casts its decorative shadow, Amersham, 1930.

of Modernism's European pioneers. Peter Behrens had designed New Ways, Britain's first smooth cuboid box, in 1925. It was radical, with small steel-framed windows set in flat wall planes, under a flat roof and without the benefit of mouldings but its construction and composition were not truly Modern.

There were no native British pioneers of architectural Modernity and it was not until the 1930s as refugee architects and designers, fleeing from Nazi Germany, began to arrive in Britain that Modernism built up a modest momentum.

The client for New Ways was Wenham Joseph Bassett-Lowke, a manufacturer of model railways, who in 1917 had commissioned Charles Rennie Mackintosh to remodel his house, 78 Derngate, also in Northampton. There is a hint of a similarity between that house and New Ways, which may or may not be down to a client with a taste for obsessively geometric pattern. That may be why he chose Mackintosh in the first place and eight years later decided he would like a little square box. Mackintosh enthusiasts suggest that in Derngate he anticipated Art Deco.

High and Over is now generally recognised to be the first true Modernist house in Britain. Completed in 1931, it was designed by Amyas Connell, a New Zealander. It ticks the boxes with a roof terrace beneath a floating canopy, long horizontal strips of windows, is very white and has a little balcony should the owner wish to harangue the gardener. The interior, lined with rich red wooden panelling, looks more Deco than Modernist.

One might assume from the evidence of the Lowke-Bassett houses and High and Over that clients, however progressive and however willing to accept a Modernist exterior, preferred something distinctly more decorative for their interiors.

In 1934 another colonial, Wells Coates, a Canadian born in Tokyo, raised the bar. His Isokon Flats, a long low block in Lawn Road, Hampstead of 24 studio and eight one-bedroom units, were intended for creative individuals. These were to include Walter Gropius and Marcel Breuer en route to the United States and the novelist Agatha Christie, who compared its exterior to an ocean liner. Its external walkways, which gave access to each flat, contributed a pronounced horizontality in blatant contrast to the verticality of surrounding 19th-century brick terraces. The architectural critic J. M. Richards said it came closer to the ideal of a 'machine for living in' than anything Le Corbusier himself had designed. Coates was a First World War pilot, and understood Le Corbusier's enthusiasm for aircraft aesthetics. He was prodigally innovative and his product designs included Bakelite radio cabinets and the 'D' handle that has become ubiquitous in modern interiors. It is conjectured that his childhood in Japan, where his parents were missionaries, gave him a particular ability to elevate bare Modernist bones into something poetic. Also his mother, who had studied architecture under Louis Sullivan, perhaps passed on to him Sullivan's proposition that buildings should be 'comely in the nude'.[27] The interiors were undisputedly Modernist. That Agatha Christie the doyen of the country house murder mystery was happy to live there from 1941 to 1946 suggests she had an adventurous spirit and that Modernist buildings could be seductive. Perhaps Coates got it just right.

Opposite
High and Over, the dining room: the interior is decidedly Art Deco.

Left
Welles Coates's Lawn Road flats: the horizontal elements made Agatha Christie think of an ocean liner, Hampstead, UK, 1934.

NEW CENTURY, NEW STYLE

Top left
Lawn Road flats, 1934: a typical living room with no concessions to Art Deco frivolities.

Top right
Lawn Road flats, 1934: balconies on the southwest elevation for disagreeing with neighbours on philosophical matters.

Below left
Lawn Road flats, 1934: a 'sliding' table in a 'minimum' flat. A modest piece of machinery in a machine for living in.

Why so white?

The idea of the white interior did not entirely belong to Modernists, or indeed to men. At the turn of the 20th century, Charles Rennie Mackintosh and his wife Margaret Macdonald collaborated to decorate the drawing room of their Glasgow house entirely in white, apart from black lacquered wooden furniture and metal work details. Unfortunately, the Mackintoshes, who were better known in Vienna than in London, were drifting towards obscurity. Their palette was considered too idiosyncratic and they were too provincial to be taken seriously by the *haut monde*.

The shift from gloomy High Victorian to brighter, lighter interiors did become fashionable when promoted by two high society women. Elsie de Wolff was an actress who, after dabbling in set design, moved on to interior design. In 1913 she published *The House In Good Taste*, which moved *The New Yorker* magazine to suggest that she had invented the interior design profession. This was not quite true but she did radically affect its direction. She threw a schoolgirl tantrum when her parents redecorated their drawing room with William Morris wallpaper, an early demonstration of her talents for acting and decorating. She dominated the profession until the late 1930s, attracting glamorous clients, a Vanderbilt, a Frick and the Duke and Duchess of Windsor. She advocated to her clients brighter interiors, eliminated heavy drapes and clutter and substituted lighter colours, pale painted furniture and many mirrors to reflect natural light. She fused inside and out with *trompe l'oeil* wallpaper, and flowery chintzes.

Syrie Maugham was Britain's leading designer in the 1920s and 1930s. She learnt her trade in an established London decorating company. In 1922 she opened her shop and decorating business in London, later opening in Chicago and New York. After their divorce in 1928 the novelist Somerset Maughan gave her a house on London's chic King's Road and in it she created her (almost) 'all white' music room.

But a woman and a decorator could not live by white alone. Maughan never made another entirely white room but continued to work with a light palette. The salon of her seaside villa in Le Touquet was decorated in beige hues. By the mid-1930s she had progressed to greens, pinks and reds. She popularised mirrored screens and indirect lighting and preferred her furniture to be white and craquelured by a method of her own devising. In 1936 she and de Wolff holidayed in India where they threatened to paint the Black Hole of Calcutta white.

Early Modernists were not entirely against colour and had theories about its strategic use. (Early Modernists had theories about everything.) Alfred Roth, who had collaborated with Le Corbusier, talked about a change from painting walls to painting as a way of defining spaces within an open plan. Popular taste was disinclined to accept the elimination of walls between rooms and equally unsympathetic to the visual deconstruction of such enclosure as they offered. In the early 1920s Le Corbusier, always energetic and always keen to bring others to heel, collaborated with Ozenfant to produce a purist palette and together they concluded that it should comprise yellow ochre, red, brown, white, black, ultramarine and mixes of these. Alumni of the Bauhaus were less catholic and restricted their colour palette to the primaries and black, white and grey; it simplified decision-making and remains a default position for many architects who feel obliged to venture too close to colour. Keeping it simple was a manly thing to do.

Below
Syrie Maughan: her almost all-white room of 1927.

Modernism, misogyny, misanthropy and sound business practice

Below
Mies van der Rohe's Barcelona Pavilion with the chairs and stools he designed with Lilly Reich the only furniture. They became standard fitments in the entrance lobbies of International Style office blocks, Barcelona, 1929.

Frank Lloyd Wright travelled through Europe to promote his *Wasmuth Portfolio*, yet typically refused to acknowledge that anything he saw there influenced him. Also, half of the drawings in the portfolio were by Marion Mahony, but her contributions were not acknowledged. Now recognised as one of the great architectural delineators, she was one of a group of five men and two women – the other was Isabel Roberts – who worked on the prairie houses. It is wholly conjectural to assume that female sensibility helped shape the powerful sense of domesticity that characterises the houses, but Mahony does seem to have been particularly significant. When Wright felt obliged to retreat to Europe with his mistress in 1909, he offered her the studio's work. She turned it down but agreed to collaborate with the male who took up the offer.

TASTE

It would be wrong to presume that Wright had a particular prejudice against women. He shared credits with neither men nor women. He considered that his was the concept and his name was the brand. Architecture is a collaborative process so appropriation of credit requires forensic analysis but Wright's offer to Mahony suggests that she was not undervalued. He certainly had vituperative relationships with male employees and rivals. Whether Wright recognised that women were particularly adept at designing interiors it is impossible to say. But perhaps one dare conjecture that males presume themselves better suited to the grand gesture and grappling with the problems of construction and that females are more interested in the intimacies of the interior and the delicate refinements of its modest components.

Women's consolidating the reputation of male Modernists is a recurring phenomenon. Charlotte Perriand was a precocious Parisienne furniture designer who, having read Le Corbusier's writings, decided she would join his studio. In 1927, aged 24, she applied and was rejected with a manly: 'we don't embroider cushions here'. Shortly afterwards Le Corbusier saw an interior with tubular steel furniture she had designed and offered her a job. She became the crucial contributor to the tubular steel and leather furniture generally credited to him. She left his office in 1937 and built a distinguished international career for herself.

Lilly Reich, born in Berlin in 1885, played a crucial role in the development of Mies van der Rohe's 'modern classics'. She began as a textile designer and worked with Josef Hoffman in Vienna before returning to Berlin to design a prototype for the interior of a working-class flat. She organised and designed trade fairs in Frankfurt and there met Mies. They began collaboration, she moved to Berlin and they worked together until he moved to the United States in 1938. War curbed her professional opportunities but Albert Pfeiffer of Knoll, who manufactured the 'Mies' chairs under licence, noted 'that Mies did not fully develop any contemporary furniture successfully before or after his collaboration with Reich'.[28]

Le Corbusier was an admirer of the Irish designer Eileen Gray and particularly of a house she called E1027 on the Côte d'Azur. Completed in 1929 she designed it for herself and her lover, the critic Jean Badovici. When they split up, she built herself another house further along the coast, but Badovici invited Le Corbusier to stay and agreed that he could paint murals on eight white walls. These alluded to Gray's bisexuality and she denounced the daubs as acts of vandalism that destroyed her concept. She was primarily a furniture designer and the context for her pieces was crucial: they needed white walls. Le Corbusier, at Badovici's suggestion, left and built himself a small wooden cabin below E1027, the antithesis of Gray's, and his own, white purism.

Photographs show Le Corbusier painting the murals in the nude, prompted perhaps by Mediterranean heat, a desire not to soil his clothing or by sexual frustration. Gray had annoyed him by disagreeing with his declaration that a house was a 'machine for living in' and counter-declaring that it was a 'living organism', a reflection of the evolving lives of those who lived in it.

The house has been restored – or not quite restored since the murals have been retained. Anthony Flint, author of *Modern Man: The Life of Le Corbusier* summed up: 'brilliant but unassuming female designer from Paris builds an elegant minimalist villa on the shores of the Mediterranean, and boorish male architect takes it over. Le Corbusier towers in history,

Above
E1027, Eileen Gray's masterpiece on its rocky shelf above the Mediterranean, Côte d'Azur, France, 1929.

and Eileen Gray fades away'.²⁹ The male animal had marked his territory.

It would be disingenuous to think that the male protagonists were misogynistic rather than driven. The mores of the time made it difficult for women to establish themselves in conventionally male activities. Furniture and interiors were as far as they might venture. Perriand and Reich had self-confidence; Mahony, the daughter of an unsuccessful Irish poet, had not. Gray, the daughter of an Irish aristocrat, may simply have been uninterested in getting attention.

Female psyches may lack architectural grandees' commitment to self-promotion. The grandees are obliged, and driven, to find work where they can. A painter can paint and a composer compose without commissions but architects need to do more than work on paper and it is smug to condemn, with hindsight, those who sailed close to unappetising ideologies. Corbusian urban strategies, to flatten picturesque city centres and replace them with residential towers dotted across parkland, require totalitarian support. The problem with creative elites is that they feel obliged to impose their ideas.

TASTE

Top left
E1027: The living room.

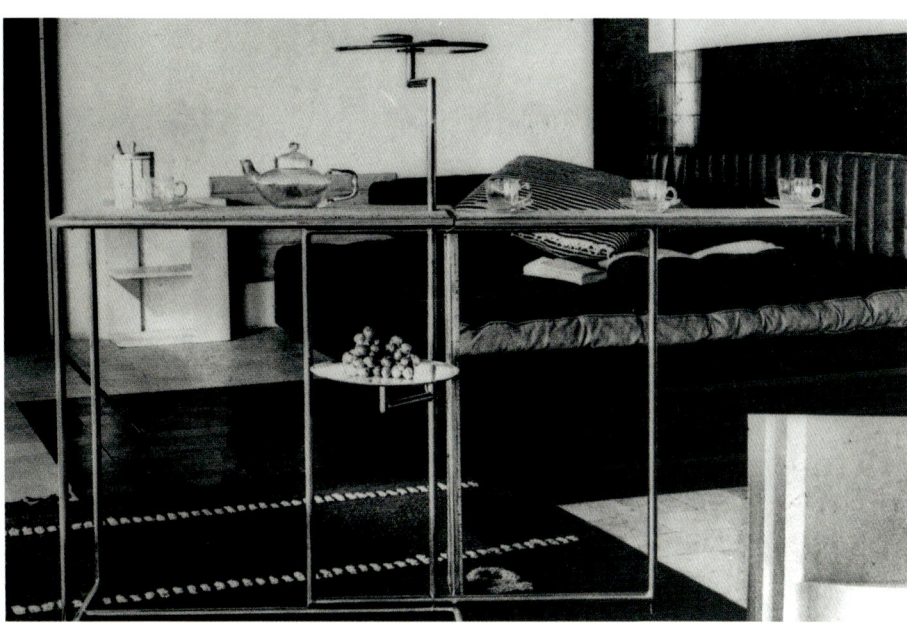

Middle left
E1027: An adjustable tea table in the living room.

Below left
A bedroom/boudoir for the XIV Salon des Artistes Decorateurs, 1923.

Lessons from history

In 1934, Mies was the sole member of the Bauhaus staff to sign a letter supporting the Nazis, but he left Germany in 1937 when it became clear that Hitler preferred Albert Speer's literal Classicism to his abstracted version. Le Corbusier spent a considerable part of the Second World War in Vichy, France trying to elicit work from Petain's puppet government. Having been feted in Russia where the edition of *Pravda* published on 13 October 1928 hailed him as 'the most brilliant representative of today's advanced architectural thought',[30] he was disillusioned when his proposal for the Palace of the Soviets was rejected in 1932. Embarrassingly, it was Hitler and Stalin who recognised the advantage of respecting popular taste for the familiar and the ornamented.

To fulfil his perverted desires for world domination, Hitler needed to increase the German population. He favoured earlier marriage to produce larger families and, in the cause of fecundity, also increased house building. The new housing of the Third Reich was diagrammatically traditional, with steeply pitched roofs and window shutters. Nostalgia nurtured national identity.

Below
Hotel Ukraina, one of Stalin's Seven Sisters, Moscow, 1956.

Below right
Mussolini's stripped-back Classicism: Palazzo della Civilta Italiana, Esposizione Universale di Roma, 1942.

Left
Louis Sullivan knew how to apply decoration – sparingly but significantly. Merchants' National Bank, Grinnell, Iowa, 1914.

Below
There is no particular precedent for Sullivan's decorative language, but the pure geometry of the major elements and the leaves and twigs and egg and dart of the secondary are instantly comprehensible.

Stalin rewarded Russians for their sacrifices in the Great Patriotic War with the Seven Sisters, seven tower blocks in the baroque-modernistic style that became synonymous with Soviet public architecture. They dominated the Moscow skyline, demonstrated that the country could surpass the architectural excesses of capitalism and were much loved.

In Italy, Benito Mussolini, a less prescriptive totalitarian, let architects get on with developing a stripped back Classicism that, though it lacked applied ornament, had a grandeur and enough hints of the familiar to please most of the people most of the time.

When Louis Sullivan suggested stripping buildings of their ornament he intended it to be a remedy rather than a terminal condition. He intended that, following a full recovery, 'comely' naked buildings should again be thoughtfully adorned – and viscerally adored. Loos had grandly conceded that, if his shoemaker took pleasure in crafting the patterns on his brogues, he would not deny the simple artisan simple gratification. As Modernist factions goaded each other with reductivist manifestos they herded themselves into progressively tighter corners and joined forces against the barbarians. The possibility of evolving a popular (appropriately) decorated modern style was lost.

CHAPTER 4

The People Decorate: the inter-war years 1918–39

'I consider modernity as a condition or experience while I consider Modernism – with a capital M – as an aesthetic practice'

Deborah Sugg Ryan, *Ideal Homes 1918–39*, 2018[1]

While Modernists fought their corner during the mid-20th century, householders knew what they wanted and kept their distance. Osbert Lancaster identified the self-effacingly modest home that most people wanted. It had been, he said, a constant from the Great Exhibition to the General Strike of 1926. In fact, it is a formula that has, with some editing of clutter and the intrusion of increasingly affordable generations of household gadgetry, persisted until the end of the 20th century and still survives, contentedly under the radical radar. He called the style *Ordinary Cottage* and the adjective explains exactly its appeal; it is a home for all who care about how and where they live, who want to be just like their neighbours, and have no interest in avant-garde fuss. It is the weekend haven of the city dweller and the final resting place of retirees. It is the shamelessly bucolic retreat of radical creatives. It is the universal safe place, the refuge from experimental fussing.

Ordinary cottagers persisted doggedly with Victorian decorative excesses and pointedly ignored Modernist oddities which, they assumed, were not to be taken seriously and would surely not last. Lancaster described an archetypical ordinary interior: 'Against a waxed wallpaper, dark in hue and boldly floral in design are ranged innumerable ornaments and pictures, for the true cottager still retains that passion for objects, which the cultured have so signally abandoned.'[2] He listed in detail the subject matter of the oleographs (sovereigns and military men), the photographic memories of 'long forgotten beanfeasts' and the unforgotten 'dear deceased', the embroidered scriptural texts, the sentimental and occasionally comic objects and trophies that hung from the walls and sat on the mantelpiece, and the 'striking collection of potted ferns' that sat on 'the round central table and the window cill'.[3] Cosiness, prettiness and simplicity prevailed: like innocent children 'they abide and they endure'.[4]

The best of all possible worlds

In 1919, the United States felt confident after its intervention in the Great War. The two decades that followed saw unfamiliar prosperity for some, devastating poverty for others and, for many, a taste of both. The change from wartime to peacetime industrial production stalled the economy but a quick recovery saw the USA become the richest country in the world and set the pace for the rest of the world in the pursuit of happiness.

Despite its hold on overseas imaginations, some historians see the period as one when Americans, having completed the colonisation of their vast land mass and becoming self-sufficient in natural resources, became inward-looking and a little paranoid. Uncontrolled immigration was ended, fear of communism spread, the Ku Klux Klan reappeared. But it was also the Jazz Age, with speakeasy bars and nightclubs in which otherwise law-abiding citizens could flout prohibition on the sale of alcohol and dance the Charleston long into the morning.

Henry Ford had sold 16 million Model T cars by 1927. Mass-produced gadgets, like refrigerators and radios, reached large markets and suggested that modernisation had begun in earnest. For example, by 1959 only 13% of UK homes owned a fridge; in the US that was 96%. As demand for factory workers grew people began to desert the uncertainties of country life for steady wages in cities. The influx meant housing shortages and, with financial security, many wanted to buy a home, away from apartments piled high above noisy treeless streets.

Inner city living could be circumvented. Electric streetcars increasingly reached out to suburbs and improved roads, blossoming private car ownership made longer commutes feasible. Detached houses, with front and back yards, were desirable even when minor commutes were needed to reach shops. For those who could afford membership country clubs bound communities and fostered consensus on matters of taste. Period styles ruled, but the details were tuned to reflect regional precedents.

Away from the east coast, with land to spare, plots were bigger and the Californian 'ranch house', a modest combination of Wright's Prairie style and Arts and Crafts details, provided a model for single-storey living. The climate was benign and every room could have direct access to the outdoors. The 'bungalow', easy to build with American timber frame construction, became the most popular house type. 'Bungalow mania' created real estate booms.

The bungalow with its veranda had been exported from India to Britain and re-exported to the USA, along with Arts and Crafts principles. At a time when American humanitarians were expressing concerns about the well-being of factory workers, a Pugin-esque return to a pre-mechanised society built on craft skills was seen, by eccentrics, as a social palliative. It was a pretty theory but unlikely to be welcomed by the majority of citizens who were without the inclination, or the ability, to survive in a pre-industrialised economy. The newly affluent wanted 'things' – and they preferred to buy rather than whittle them.

Gustav Stickley introduced Arts and Crafts principles and self-sufficiency in the *Craftsman* magazine and other publishers followed suit. Stickley saw the bungalow, with well-wrought Arts and Crafts detailing, as ideal accommodation for the enlightened and the artistic. 'The bungalow's unassuming demeanour and informal character was particularly conducive to enrichment by the use of simple, natural materials and restful colour palettes in harmony with its natural setting.'[5] For the enlightened 'practicality, simplicity and individuality in an affordable and fashionable package was irresistible'.[6]

The bungalow satisfied the modest working- and middle-class dream of owning a house and garden, and not only for Americans. The model was promoted wherever there were cinemas, as modest examples provided backdrops for the misadventures of Charlie Chaplin and the Keystone Cops. Arts and Crafts ideals and practices faded away.

Homes on the range

American suburban expansion was not subjected to the anxieties that would bedevil its equivalent in Britain; there was less need to worry about unspoilt country being desecrated. Unspoilt American country was not in short supply. And because there was a surfeit of space, houses could be bigger, rooms could be bigger and furniture could be bigger than in suburban Britain.

American citizens had very little awareness of, or anxiety about, Modernist styling even after the Museum of Modern Art staged its 'International Style' exhibition in 1932. Few of them visited MoMA and they lived in a new world, one that was about fresh starts. Although they might prefer things to look old-fashioned, Americans had a penchant for modern conveniences. In the booming house market, style was important. Choice lay with buyers: they called the shots and tended to choose revivals of familiar styles. There was a bias towards rough and reductive variations on local traditions, since immigrants from particular countries (often European) tended to settle in particular areas. Dutch Colonial and Carpenter Gothic flourished in the northeast and Spanish Colonial and Mission revivals in the southwest. Typical Spanish Colonial materials were wood, stucco and tiles, terracotta floor tiles, wrought ironwork on balustrades and window grilles. Mission used similar elements but was less refined. Mayan and Egyptian elements, popular on film sets, trickled into domestic interiors.

Public buildings tended to favour Colonial Revival, a reworking of the Neo-Classical and Georgian architecture that had prevailed at the time of the Revolutionary War. It was resolutely conservative. Modernism which lent itself to corporate attention-seeking fared better in commercial buildings; in 1930 the Chrysler Building succeeded 1913's Woolworth Building as the world's tallest, for a year, until the Empire State was completed in 1931, which with no particular corporation to promote was distinctly less flamboyant and relied on its height for its singularity. All three were successful attention seekers but no one wanted to live in them.

A decade of heady prosperity ended in October 1929 with the Wall Street Crash. Savings were lost, debts were unpaid, loans were foreclosed and ruined financiers jumped from high windows. The repercussions dug deep into the economy: unemployment peaked at 25% in 1933 and persisted throughout the decade, with 15% still unemployed in 1940. It was a time of soup kitchens and shanty towns. Nature added to the devastation. Pioneering farmers in the mid-West had not understood the implications of intensive farming methods and had replaced deep-rooted native grasses, which anchored the soil, with shallow-rooted commercial crops. A succession of droughts turned soil to dust and winds blew the dust as far as New York. Two and a half million people lost their homes and went west. Their hardships were recorded in Dorothea Lange's photographs, John Steinbeck's novels and Woody Guthrie's songs. Housebuilding was curtailed; those ready to move to suburbia were those most likely to be affected by the slump.

Although anxieties about communism and state control were endemic in American politics the government found ways to create employment, by financing state construction projects like the Grand Coulee Dam. In 1941 Woody Guthrie, always pragmatic in tuning his political stance, accepted a government commission to praise the dam in song, dismissing the ancient wonders of the world he declared '… now the greatest wonder is in Uncle Sam's fair land': it was the world as seen from an American perspective.

Despite depression and deprivation, the United States continued to shape the aspirations of the rest of the world through films; even the poverty portrayed in Hollywood features would not have seemed unduly harsh and was likely to offer a more promising future than the prospect of eternal poverty in Italy's Mezzogiorno or Ireland's Gaeltacht.

Where next?

After the First World War British citizens were generally enjoying modest prosperity. Nevertheless, unrest bubbled. The General Strike of 1926, called to support coal miners, lasted nine days and was the biggest industrial dispute in the country's history. It fizzled out as middle-class volunteers, including a few Bright Young Things who thought it such fun, helped run essential services. It was a skirmish between classes but workers were not, on the whole, inclined towards revolution. Some did think they deserved more and the state had accepted that returning soldiers deserved 'homes fit for heroes'. It did not, in the deteriorating global economy, deliver on the promise. But a skilled working class, with more and better paid jobs, were becoming the 'new rich'. The incomes of the upper echelons of blue collar workers matched those of the lower echelons of white collars whose earning power decreased in adverse proportion to levels of literacy and numeracy in the wider population.

Britons understood the template of class and were resigned to the limits it might impose on their personal social mobility, but relative prosperity allowed them to think that they might climb a few rungs of the social ladder and they understood the importance of demonstrating, when they got there, that they were taste compliant.

The *Daily Mail* newspaper had organised its first *Ideal Home Show* in 1908 when it promised 'streets of a town lined with hundreds of bright little buildings of varying shape and design – red roofed cottages, brown bungalows, and gaily coloured pavilions – and moving between them endless lines of interested visitors'. It became an annual event and there were indeed long lines of interested visitors, all imagining how they might enjoy the futures on display. Apart from full-sized show houses manufacturers demonstrated how domestic appliances could ease the tasks of keeping one's home in a constant state of readiness for those visitors who might penetrate beyond the front door to scrutinise one's housekeeping skills. Scaled-down regional versions of the show took the excitement and aspirations beyond the capital.

Women over 30 were enfranchised in 1918 and all over 21 got the vote in 1928. Politicians were obliged to listen to the new voters who wanted better houses, with kitchens and bathrooms, more bedrooms and a parlour. They were presented with a provocative option in the *Ideal Home Show* of 1928; a Modernist *House of the Future* was dropped amongst the Georgian and Tudor replications. The paper summed up the diverse collection as a comprehensive compilation of modern housing and made no judgement on the relative merits of periods or styles. The Modernist model fussed about how its horizontal strips of window bathed its interiors in natural light but visitors noticed that the flexible planning of the 'Tudor' models allowed rooms and windows to be orientated to catch the sun as efficiently. Tacked-on timber 'frames' satisfied consumers' taste for the fanciful. One exhibit in which the timbers decorating the gable were arranged as a 'sunrise' motif melded Tudor and embryonic Art Deco. Houses that made allusions to historical styles demonstrated that they could be modernistic, satisfying demand for light, bathrooms, kitchens and labour-saving devices without being offensively Modern.

When consumers shied away from Modernism, they found themselves in the amenable arms of the speculative housebuilder. In post-war Britain, home ownership filtered down through the classes. The middle class, the 'old rich', were finding that they could no longer afford three servants and were making do with one. Those who did inherit large houses had difficulty maintaining them and those obliged to buy got significantly less than they might have been accustomed to. The 'new rich', the tradesmen and the skilled manual workers, expected less and were pleased to receive warm, dry and well-serviced, retrospectively styled dwellings.

Getting cosy

Suburbs were the habitat of first-time buyers and increasingly so as house prices, which peaked in 1931, fell for the rest of the decade. Building societies offered cheap loans to both blue and white collar workers. Speculative builders understood the importance of making their products distinct from social housing. Buyers wanted to make it clear they were doing well and builders introduced small variations in decorative detail to suggest individuality. They favoured historical allusions, principally the 'Tudorbethan' pastiche of white walls subdivided by decorative black timber strips whose function was not structural but the declaration of ownership.

Rents, frozen during the war, stayed low. Landlords found property unprofitable and a million modest houses were sold to owner-occupiers. They were often in poor condition but gave the 'new rich' the possibility of security and the chance to improve their circumstances

Right
An ideal and generously sized 'cottage', designed by Castle and Warren in 1910, sponsored by the *Daily Mirror* newspaper. A romantic vision of bucolic bliss but for a small prosperous sector of the middle class.

gradually. The 'old rich' dreamt of retreat to country cottages in which they could regret post-war realities. The grander of these bijoux became the staple of lifestyle magazines but bucolic bliss was primarily a middle-class aspiration. Former inhabitants of town and city slums had fewer illusions about a romantic past, or future, and were pleased with their own modest versions of a respectable heritage.

An amateur decorating aesthetic evolved – again, primarily the work of the women who were usually responsible for the day-to-day running of households. Suburban houses required significant effort if appearances were to be maintained. As time passed, their chatelaines could afford more artefacts and ornaments, the selection and presentation of which loomed larger in the daily round. Men, when they came home from work, had dinners to eat, pipes to smoke and, at the weekends, lawns to mow and, increasingly, cars to wash. They tended to concede the interior to their wives who, since they spent most of their time within its walls, had opportunities to ponder the finer details of taste. Maintaining standards was time-consuming: household gadgets were increasingly available but they were rudimentary, refrigerators were significantly rarer than in the United States and those without them had to make daily journeys on foot to shops that, in suburbia, were unlikely to be convenient. Few had a car and fewer could drive.

Arguments may be made for a female modernity, distinct from male modernity. Sugg Ryan writes that: 'suburbia was associated with a particular kind of feminised modernity that embraced the trappings of mass culture, such as magazines, cosmetics and cinema'.[7] Alison Light, a feminist analyst of working-class cultures, declared 'the suburban semi and bungalow [to be] the only truly modern form of life in the 1930s' and considered hard-line Modernism a peripheral phenomenon.[8] Sugg Ryan suggests that 'a specifically

Left
A living room in a cottage in Surrey by Elie Mayorcas completed in 1939: the various elements are mildly modern but the exposed rafters and beam, although modern and cut cleanly and smoothly, are reassuringly cottagey.

Right
Two proposals for semi-detached houses for Romford District Council by Leonard Culliford in 1930. These are obviously of a high standard, and are good examples of public housing rivalling and bettering private developments.

suburban Modernism emerged in the interwar years, embodied most fully in the suburban semi-detached house' and that it was a place where seeming incompatibles, 'modernity and nostalgia, urban and rural, masculine and feminine could be reconciled'.[9]

In more salubrious suburbs, Tudorbethan became 'Stockbroker Tudor'. Detached replaced semi-detached, usually the work of traditionally trained architects who knew how to add elaborate folderols to demonstrate that these 'villas' were a level up from speculators' more expedient offerings.

In contrast to housebuilders' decorative ploys, those architects who were senior enough to make strategic decisions about social housing were old enough to have been seduced by Arts and Crafts houses. Council properties were likely to have brick facades and steep tiled roofs and, free of an obligation to turn a profit but required to be economical, forewent fanciful devices. Councils took responsibility for the maintenance of their developments and imposed uniformity as front doors shared a single colour, standard handles and letterboxes. Behind front doors the compulsion to demonstrate individual taste ran free.

Council properties were respectably tasteful, but their architecture signalled their council pedigree and could not match Tudorbethan's gimcrack glamour. One wonders what effect such heritage-signalling might have had on tenants' satisfaction if it had been applied to public housing.

In 1919 the Tudor Walters Report – named after its principal author rather than a prophetic affinity for Tudorbethan – had set out minimum standards for room sizes and amenities in council housing, which profit-sensitive speculative builders frequently failed to match because experience told them that customers preferred appearances to practicalities. Decorative nostalgia was more seductive than practicality. Buyers wanted an exterior that spoke, not necessarily honestly, about their status.

Critics lined up to scorn suburbia and its inhabitants. In 1928 the Classical scholar turned social commentator Harry Joseph Birnstingl, had had enough of popular taste and, in his book *Lares et Penates, The Household Gods*, was contemptuous and superior: *the vast and variegated range of lower-middle-class houses [have] for the most part, one characteristic in common. It is their vulgarity; utterly devoid of taste in their outward appearance and their inward furnishings, and in the very names that are inscribed in distorted letters upon their gate rails, they reflect from ridge to foundation this besetting characteristic of the present age.*[10] Sugg Ryan suggests that what Birnstingl called 'meretricious' was a 'modern aesthetic … that has little to do with either utilitarian functionalism or Arts and Crafts "good" design' and writes of fusions of traditional and modernistic decorative elements, about 'the third type of furniture', condemned by critics but which represented a respectful response to suburban tastes and 'simultaneously looked backwards to the past while looking forward to the future'.[11]

There were precedents for identifying and defending the suburban hybrid. F. R. Yerbury, secretary of the Architectural Association (AA) from 1912 until 1937, contributed regularly to the Ideal Home exhibition and championed what he called 'old English' architecture. From 1913 he lived in Hampstead Garden Suburb, the grand inspiration for all the less grand suburbs that were to follow it in the UK. In collaboration with the principal of the AA, Howard Robertson, he wrote about traditional and modern architectures and managed to cause offence to protagonists in both camps. Championing 'old English' architecture inevitably offended Modernists, and supporters of Arts and Crafts objected to suburbia's careless borrowing of style and the industrialised construction techniques. Factories were churning out 'old' English artefacts, Toby jugs, horse brasses, brass repoussé coal scuttles and companion sets. Householders who had seen some service in the Empire, however brief and distant, were prone to display their trophies. Ebony elephants and brass dinner gongs implied exotic connections, and status, in a colonial outpost.

In 1929 Yerbury and Robertson visited Stuttgart's Weissenhof exhibition of Modernist working-class housing in which 60 dwellings, in 21 buildings by 17 architects, all shared open plan interiors behind horizontal window bands and under flat roofs that doubled as sun terraces. The exteriors were uniformly white. Yerbury and Robertson concluded that: 'A little more plumbing, heating and light and air, a little reconsideration in replanning for the furtherance of the labour-saving ideal, are all that is required to make the English cottage type serve admirably for the working or middle classes'.[12] Unseduced by symptoms of Modernism they judged that 'so far it has not been found that any of the more radical departures in design and construction (pre-fabrication had been used to speed up construction) have justified the disadvantages attendant upon their introduction'.[13] And for them the disadvantages were matters of taste and a strong suspicion that there were virtues in the materials and details of traditional form that evolved from their context, which they judged to be missing in Modernism. They considered the obsessive concern for hygiene and labour-saving gadgets to be fetishistic and a by-product of quasi-rational rationale for the removal of ornament.

J. M. Richards, editor of the *Architectural Review*, the profession's high-minded glossy monthly, also recognised the importance of *terroir* and the significance of the suburban appetite for tradition. He suggested that 'tradition-rooted architecture' offered comforting echoes of 'good old times when the immediate world was a self-sufficient place' and a stock market crash in New York did not affect prosperity in quiet British backwaters.[14]

He also wrote: *It takes all sorts to make the suburban world, and its essential quality lies in a mixture of familiarity and novelty, glamour and homeliness. The suburb is neither the refuge of dowdiness, tolerated for the sake of old associations, nor the playground of slick modernity, but is something of both and everything in between … Familiarity breeds no contempt, liberty does not lead to license and the new wine improves in the old bottles into which it is consistently decanted.*[15] The *Architectural Review*, and Richards himself, had been early enthusiasts for Modernism and its social ideals. Increasingly, however, they were expressing doubts about the capacity of its visual language to create a viable alternative to traditions. Richards's contributors included a number of former Bright Young Things: John Betjeman, Evelyn Waugh and Osbert Lancaster, all of them untainted by formal architectural training, all of them instinctively reactionary and happy to denounce Modernism and its modernistic offshoots.

Money talked

Art Deco was the foremost of the frivolous modernistic offshoots. It took its name from the *Esposition Internationale des Arts Decoratifs Et Industriels Moderne* held in Paris in 1925. It was organised by the French government to highlight the new *style moderne* in architecture, interior decoration, furniture, glass, jewellery and other decorative arts. Modern ideas were debuted, including Le Corbusier and Ozenfant's *Pavillion d'Esprit Nouveau*, but it was the exquisite materials and craft techniques in the decorative arts that caught popular attention. They were distinctly of their time but made very few concessions

Below
Mulberry House, Smith Square: The dining room by Bradley and Deane demonstrates how Art Deco retuned Classical decorative strategies, London, 1930.

Below right
Denys Lasdun's upgrading of this flat illustrates that, while the dining furniture may work with the lack of mouldings, the period pieces are left stranded, London, 1938.

to Modernist reductivism. For that they were criticised, by, amongst others, Le Corbusier for pandering to the taste of the wealthy. An interior designer, Paul Follot, offered a defence: 'We know that man is never content with the indispensable and that the superfluous is always needed ... If not, we would have to get rid of music, flowers, and perfumes.'[16] The artefacts displayed were for the rich – indeed the very rich – but they offered ideas to mass manufacturers who, in the 1930s, would supply affordable variations to the un-rich. Follot was pointing out an obvious truth: one would not get poor by satisfying the popular taste for decoration. As the style's exclusivity slipped *Arts Decoratifs* evolved into the jauntier *Art Deco*.

Deco had the virtue of being comprehensible. Its language was primarily abstract, but the underpinning geometries were comprehensible and it easily engaged non-doctrinaire imaginations. The sunrise motif that appeared ubiquitously in stained glass panels and garden gates suggested suburban summer idylls. The long and languid girls, in bronze or painted plaster, who danced with elegantly contorted abandon, who walked their borzoi dogs and served as table ornaments, were distinctly of the time, products of machine production but damned for their sentimentality. Had they not been such hits in suburbia and had not so many been churned out, these little figurines might have been better regarded: one might just have seen something of Brancusi or Modigliani in them.

Osbert Lancaster described the glut of modernistic style cultivars and Art Deco in particular as: *the fruit of a fearful union between the flashier side of Ballets Russes and a hopelessly vulgarised version of Cubism ... elements ... popularised by the Paris Exhibition of 1927 [sic], such as the all too generous use of the obscure and more hideous woods ... unvarnished wood and chromium plate, relentlessly applied.*[17] He identified and labelled a tranche of substyles, amongst them *Aldwych Farcical*, for those who could not resist Tudorbethan rusticity and *Vogue Regency*, of which he tended to approve since the modest restraint of Regency artefacts sat reasonably comfortably in modernity's stripped back rooms.

Below left
A flat by Clive Entwhistle: The elements within the room, the bentwood furniture, the figured veneer of the sideboard and the adjustable table lamp, are elegantly modernistic but the blank walls make the whole sterile; the electrical fire at the level where a cornice would have been draws attention to the bleakness. Mayfair, London, 1937.

Below
The living room of the Maharajah of Indore in the Temple of Rubies suggests that Art Deco had universal appeal, Madhya Pradesh, India, 1933.

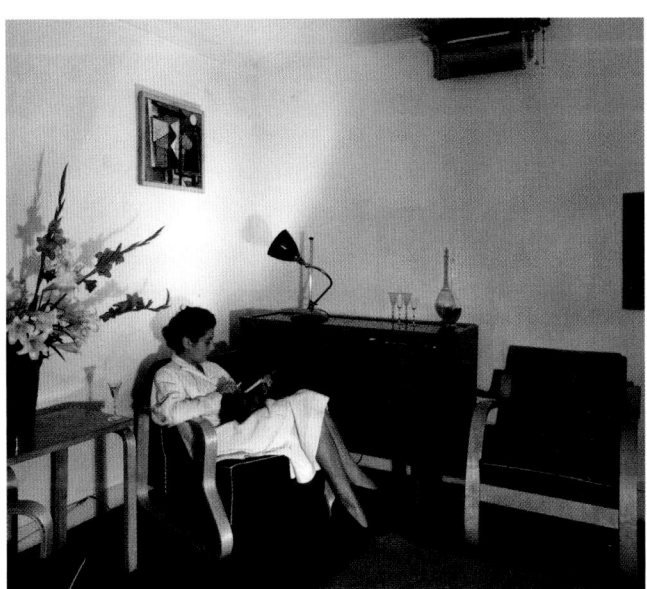

Above
A Streamline corner on flats on the Oaklands Estate in Clapham Park, southwest London, 1936.

Top right
Streamline flats by Ernst Ludwig Freud in Hampstead, London, 1939.

Below right
The dining room in the Hampstead block with curved window and built-in shelving and a stone fireplace. The furniture is modestly Art Deco. London, 1939.

He complained that: *the old English fondness for disguising everything as something else now attained the dimensions of a pathological affliction ... Gramophones masquerade as cocktail cabinets; cocktail cabinets as bookcases; radios lurk in tea caddies and bronze nudes burst asunder at the waist-line to reveal cigarette lighters, and nothing is what it seems*.[18] He was writing in 1939 as Britain was embarking on the Second World War after a period of wistful thinking that Germany would not precipitate a war and optimistic but wholly futile peace negotiations. As a result, he drew a broader conclusion, suggesting that 'it is perhaps not surprising that disaster should have overtaken a generation which refused so consistently to look even the most ordinary facts (about household objects) in the face'.[19]

Modernists tended to ignore any trifling with their curious priorities but market forces invariably prevail. Designers of interiors and furniture are always less doctrinaire than architects because, professionally, they sit below the salt, more directly influenced by popular taste as expressed in the marketplace. With their noses held close to the economic grindstone they were obliged to bowdlerise Modernism's uncompromising principles. *Art Moderne* evolved in France, a form of *Deco* with the whimsy and wit removed, and the very similar *Streamline* appeared in the USA. Both were retorts to the craft-based and the handmade and picked up on the Modernists' infatuation with the machine. Both were antidotes to what their originators, who were primarily product designers and shared some

Left
Model AD-65 ECKO radio by Welles Coates: The plastic-bodied darkly serious and successful model of 1934.

of architects' machismo, saw as Deco's unmanly frivolity. They stripped away its cornier decorative details and substituted curved corners. They switched from exotic and expensive hand-crafted woods and metals to plastics, principally Bakelite, the first wholly synthetic plastic developed, curiously, in unassuming Yonkers by a Belgian, Leo Baekeland. The marriage of cheap materials and cheap production sat well with the economic problems of the 1930s.

The curve, although inherently frivolous, was not wholly anathemic to Modernists who used the curved ramp and the spiral stair to counterbalance straight lines and right-angled corners. But *Moderne* and *Streamline* were primarily the work of those who styled cars, toasters and kettles, clocks and radios and every other domestic gadget and it was successful in the market place: few consumers could resist curved plastic. Sales suggested that popular taste would accept modernistic design, as long as it ventured beyond the wholly rational, and plastic was a perfectly acceptable alternative to woods and metals when tweaked into rounded corners and rolling curves. It could also deliver bright colours, but colour tolerance appeared to depend on context. The Wells Coates circular radio set sold well in shades of brown but significantly less well when brightly coloured. If the radio was becoming the new focus of the living room then it seemed to require the gravitas of dark brown quasi-wood.

In deepest suburbia

In Britain, a proselytising quango, the Design and Industries Association, with the maxim 'nothing need be ugly', had been founded in 1915 by designers, businessmen and industrialists who presumed to take responsibility 'for the advancement of knowledge to promote, organise and encourage education of the public in the appreciation of good design, more particularly in connection with things in everyday use'.[20] Householders ignored these missionaries and carried out their improper activities behind their closed doors. Those with budgets stretched thin by monthly mortgage payments put their initial spending into the hall, to make a tasteful first impression and to confirm that they rightly belonged to the community of owner/occupants. The second priority was the parlour, the 'best' room, where visitors were entertained and family events celebrated. Technology changed the artefacts and, to a certain extent, behaviour as the piano gave way to the radiogram and the cocktail cabinet.

Below
A suburb of good-quality houses in south London designed by the London County Council Architects' Department, 1920.

Above left
'Design for Dingley Dell' for a private client by Marshall Harvey: a trace of Pugin and Tudor half-timbering, Kent, UK, 1926.

Above
A suburban dining room in Enfield, with traces of Arts and Crafts, 1928.

Left
Hampstead Garden Suburb, a few Arts and Crafts influences, 1920.

Snobs and more snobs

The sacrosanct status of the parlour brought down the wrath of those who judged themselves to be by intellect and inclination un-suburban. Social snobs and design snobs abused the most sacred suburban place on the grounds that it was the bastion of snobbery.

A general contempt for suburbia was shared by the intelligentsia of both right and left: the former because suburbanites failed to understand or wantonly disregarded nuances of behaviour and taste and did so in accents that confirmed their un-genteel origins, the latter because suburbanites were uninterested in the niceties of class warfare and had vested interests in preserving the status quo on which they hoped to have gained a foothold. Suburbanites found it hard to believe that Modern art and architecture were to be taken seriously. That offended both right and left.

There was a pecking order within British suburbia, and the bungalow was at the bottom. It may have been that the word 'bungalow' is phonetically amusing but more probably prevailing taste in the UK considered that a dwelling should have two floors and that sleeping should be undertaken on the upper. The intricately carved verandas and eaves of the original wooden bungalows had a modest scale that charmed but, when the form was reinterpreted in brick or render, the devices that worked for two-storey semis seemed overwrought. The spread of bungalows ('bungalow blight'), their failure to be 'villas' or country cottages and their capacity to cover huge tracts of land, along coastal fringes in particular, added to resentment. Perhaps in cost-conscious suburbia they did not represent a sufficient investment or maybe it was that those who bought them were retirees without families *in situ* and suburbs were family enclaves; bungalow dwellers were memento mori.

Rooms could be squeezed into the roof voids of bungalows but that, it was generally held, did not make them houses. It made them 'chalet bungalows', and 'chalet' with its connotations of quaint wooden houses on Swiss mountains did not make them any more glamorous. They were uppity bungalows with aspirations to be houses with aspiring owners who could not afford the real thing.

Even more than dwellers in semi-detached houses, those in single storeys, whose age makes them less likely to be well-informed about progressive decoration, seem particularly susceptible to the garish or sentimental decorative objects that arbiters of higher taste resolutely designate to be 'kitsch'. (Those with tutored tastes will sometimes profess an amused regard for such things, an affected affection that pre-empts scrutiny of their own core taste: those who sneer first cannot easily be sneered at.)

Below
A 'keyhole' door to a suburban house in Devon with the geometry and easy allusion that makes Art Deco popular, 1930.

Opposite
An inglenook doorway with 'sunrise' framing to the glazed front door. The name of the house, Insanity, is another example of suburban wit.

TASTE

Right
Glass lampshades became more translucent as memories of Victorian gloom faded and higher light levels and less serious decoration became the norm.

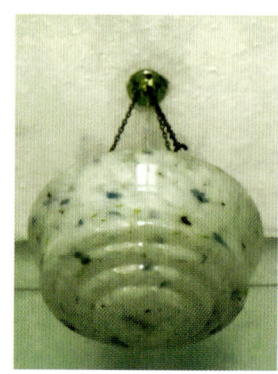

The nature of kitsch is complex but has much to do with class: the ornamental contents of a country cottage, particularly if lived in by a *bona fide* country person, will be viewed tolerantly while an identical object in a suburban bungalow will be viewed suspiciously. Both may come from the same factory but the second bears the stigma of suburbia. Suburbanites are perhaps considered to have had opportunities to absorb the criteria of appropriate taste and are not to be forgiven their transgressions.

The majority of interiors, whether for the new rich or the new poor, whether in isolated cottage or suburban avenue, demonstrated enthusiasm for traditional decoration. The new poor embraced the antique, real and reproduction. The idealised country cottage provided their prototype. The marks of age were prized and 'period' pieces, real or reproduced, were indisputable signs of good breeding and, therefore inevitably, of acceptable taste. The new poor in their cottages were likely to have inherited furniture and artefacts but suburban new rich were the sort of people who had to buy their own furniture. Critics like the superior Birnstingl approved of genuine antiques but were upset by the hold of old ideas on new designs which led to 'furniture which is at once pretentious and vulgar in design, shoddy in manufacture; in two words – utterly meretricious'.[21]

The new rich had their own pastoral visions, but had to start from scratch and were prepared to settle, when they had to, for second-hand furniture. If they had not inherited pieces with provenance – however modest – they were content with reproduction, without the kindly light of candles and gas mantles and in an electrical glare, genuine age could look shabby, unhygienic and cheap. The preferred reproductions looked staunchly old English; legs of chairs and tables were embellished with twists and bulges. Suburban room dimensions were modest but tables with gate legs and pull-out leaves accommodated extended family gatherings. Bulky sideboards ate up space but were symbols of plenty and their flat tops could support many ornaments and family photographs. The Victorians' magpie instincts survived. Upstairs things could be lighter and less status conscious. Bedrooms could dabble with Deco. The rare households inclined to be modernistic found it difficult; local retailers catered for the majority taste.

Cast iron fireplaces disappeared; grates for coal fires were set in stepped tiled surrounds that flirted with Deco. Whatever its detail, the fireplace remained the focal point of the room, and the major source of un-Modernist dirt. Central heating lay 40 years into the future. The new poor were liable to have doubts about anything modern that reminded them that the world was no longer entirely theirs but the new rich relished gas fires and electrical gadgetry and were particularly appreciative of manufacturers' efforts to gloss over raw practicality. Floor and table lamps were prettified with barley twist supports. Rooms had a single central pendant fitting, but the bulb was concealed behind a glass bowl hung on delicate chains, which efficiently collected the dead flies that had flown too close to the hot bulb. Bowls were abstractly patterned, and, while early examples had Edwardian traits, later models became more modernistic. The glass became more translucent to deliver lumens more efficiently. Visible bulb holders were likely to mimic candles, fairly unconvincingly.

Wallpaper was more popular than paint, and the antithesis of the white wall. Patterns, traditionally figurative or abstractly modernistic, were enhanced by 'borders'; narrow, more intricately patterned paper strips pasted on at what would have been picture rail height. Corners were often embellished by ornate paper pieces that elaborated the border motifs. These were generally triangular and folded along their centre line to turn the corner. Classical symmetry was not dead.

Painters could upgrade cheap timbers. 'Graining', the simulation of the patterns and colours of expensive woods, had been popular in the 18th and 19th centuries. 20th-century house painters knew enough of the techniques to enhance doors and wall panels. In halls and reception rooms, plywood or wallpaper performed the same illusion. Painted anaglypta wallpaper, with its raised pattern, could suggest intricate plaster decoration.

Carpets were not fitted. Naturalistic floral motifs were popular. Uncarpeted floorboards around the edges of rooms were stained dark or painted black. Parquet was popular but expensive and usually appeared in facsimile on linoleum, particularly in kitchens, bathrooms and halls. Neither the new rich or new poor, had problems with illusion or allusion. The message was more important than the medium.

For those not seduced by images of semi-detached suburban villas and hymns to the efficiency of the public transport systems that could whisk them from home to city centre workplace there were flats. Lancaster, in a category he labelled *Modernistic*, listed a number of prevalent genres and speaks, approvingly, of a 'complete misunderstanding of the ideals of the Corbusier-Gropius school of architects'. He suggested that, although 'neo-Tudor enthusiasts waged their olde-worlde campaign they were never able completely to stifle the opinions of those who held that the brave new world of the 'twenties and 'thirties demanded a brave new style'.[22] But the developers of blocks of flats recognised the need to tempt buyers' aesthetic palettes, however unreformed

Below
Old Barn: A Tudorbethan-style lodge with drive-through carriageway. The house was a 17th-century tithe barn from Worcestershire, moved and converted into a house. The search for authenticity could result in confusion. Stanmore, London, 1915.

they might be. Flats, or the structures that contained them, could not easily, or convincingly, be dressed up with Tudor motifs so their creators turned to *Arts Deco* and *Moderne.* Mildly modernistic gestures, leavened with lingering traces of Arts and Crafts and Art Nouveau, became the acceptable face of modernity. Those keen for change, but without an appetite for austerity, found in the potpourri a decorative style that represented progress with a mild and satisfying suggestion of decadence.

There was less scope for Deco cultivars in architecture, other than in the curved corners of the long horizontal elevations of factories and offices and a few speculatively built villas with quadrant corner windows that had their curves emphasised by horizontal metal framing. But it took a pioneering suburbanite to commit to that degree of modernity; the market preferred Tudorbethan slatherings.

The pain of plain

With the ever-looming threat of a Modernist-induced famine of ornament, those without benefit of a sub-Bauhausian education gorged on ornamental sweetmeats. In 1935, in *New Architecture and the Bauhaus*, Gropius wrote that the first rationalising stage of modern architecture was only 'a purifying process' and that the ultimate goal was a 'composite but inseparable work of art, the great building in which the old dividing line between the monumental and decorative elements will have disappeared for ever'.[23] Was he expecting a new palette of ornaments to evolve that might satisfy popular hunger, or would the new architecture persist with abstractions, which required a taught understanding of theory if they were to delight?

Modernism had been given a fair crack of the whip. In 1934, Kenneth Clark, then Director of the National Gallery, described it as 'the architectural revolution which is familiar to everyone – at least it ought to be because no aesthetic movement has been more relentlessly publicised' and he offered an explanation for its unpopularity: 'We have abandoned the conventions of architecture before abandoning the conventions of life.'[24] Traditional building had evolved in harmony with human instincts, communicated pleasure and was understood. Modernist building talked about anything but itself.

Clark went on to make what may seem a contradictory argument, one that was then made by everyone sympathetic to the idea of a new architectural style. There could be no return, he said, to the ornamental conventions of the past because the 19th century's 'battle of the styles' had demonstrated that a return to historical form could not answer the needs of a society transformed by technologies. When Modernist revolutionaries abruptly rejected the idea of applied ornament they precluded the possibility of an evolutionary transition, which might have found the decorative veneer that would make their architecture digestible for those with no alternative but to live with it, and in it. He understood the difficulty when he said 'Ornament should be a common language. It should grow up slowly.'[25] He might also have said that without ornament there could be no acceptable common language of architecture. It would have been unreasonable, in the long gestation of architecture, to expect to find evidence of a coherent new language after 15 years but time was not on evolution's side. Modernists were committed to revolution and throwing pretty babies out with bathwater.

Clark questioned the rigour of the revolutionary process: 'Modern simplicity does not always arise from a fastidious self-criticism but from a poverty of invention.'[26] He might have recognised, as did Perret and Ozenfant, that the instinct to beautify was irresistible, even for architects but the definitive premise of Modernism, the banishment of ornament, tied architects' hands and forced them to conjure up the 'feigned utilities' in a search to bring light and shade to their elevations, without benefit of the intimate scale and intricate variations of traditional ornament.

In 1940, J. M. Richards, in *An Introduction to Modern Architecture*, wrote that Modernism was becoming 'merely decorative, an imitation of itself', suggesting that for architects the absence of ornament gave the same visceral pleasure that the unenlightened found in its presence. In the 19th century traditional ornamental devices had drawn veils over the bare bones of the new engineered structures, the railway stations, the bridges, the Crystal Palace. It had not been enough to calm traditionalists, but it sugared the pill, and suggested that links to the familiar past had not been wholly severed. For the uninitiated there was nothing reassuring about the flat roof, the moulding-free doors and windows, the horizontality of it all.

Throughout the 1930s the United States continued to shape popular culture across the world, with its cinema, its music, its idyll of car ownership. The vast sets for Fred Astaire and Ginger Roger's films and the lavish apartments and restaurants for the protagonists of romantic comedies promoted the modernistic cause. In black and white, rather like the photographs in Johnson and Hitchcock's International Style exhibition, they offered an ideal of bright white interiors.

But even cinematic visions could not sell whiteness and emptiness: these were not enough to satisfy appetites for intricacies, patterns and colours, wholesale. It would be 50 years and a systemic cultural shift before white and empty became desirable. The impulse to decorate appears pervasive and it transcends class. Whenever they could householders made the effort and sometimes the sacrifice to decorate, as is evident in Ryan's description of a photograph of a working-class family's kitchen/living room: *on the wall there is a startlingly Modernistic wallpaper … a riot of 'Jazz Modern' patterns which could be purchased cheaply … a vase depicting a camel, no doubt influenced by the Egyptomania craze that followed the discovery of the tomb of Tutankhamen. These elements sit alongside traditional Windsor chairs and a piece of lace covering the mantelshelf over the range. A photograph like this suggests the evolution of an interior and a sense of 'making do'. It points to a very real human need for colour, pattern and modernity. It also goes some way to explaining why such wallpaper might have been seen in its time by designers and cultural critics as cheap, nasty and vulgar – in 'bad taste' and as an example of 'bad design'.*[27] Making do requires prioritising and wallpaper was a cheap way to apply a wrap-around transformation to which could be added piecemeal the artefacts that money permitted, the 'traditional Windsor chairs' may have been second-hand or hand-me-downs but they had enough distinction to elevate the room. The photograph, taken in 1939, is a reminder that while not everyone could climb the social ladder the impulse to enhance one's environment was universally human.

CHAPTER 5

Post-War Populism 1945–50

'The mid century period was an age of dreams and optimism. In the post-war years, after all the chaos and crisis of a global conflict, the world began to rebuild and rethink itself.'

Dominic Bradbury, *Mid-century Modern Complete*, 2014[1]

In 1939 Osbert Lancaster's last entry in *Homes Sweet Homes* was headed '*Even More Functional*'. He drew a room prepared for war, fortified with sandbags, its walls covered in official diktats about precautions to be taken and restrictions to be observed. He doubted that: 'when Monsieur le Corbusier first propounded his theory of the house as *une machine à habiter* ... he foresaw the exact form in which it would be translated into fact'. He allowed 'that other well-known architectural authority, Herr Hitler' credit for introducing 'the insular British' to 'the extreme dictates of the continental functionalists ... all attempt at applied decoration ... has been abandoned'.[2] It was, at the beginning of the Second World War, a patriotic quip, suggesting that the island race had no truck with bizarre Continental ideas and, since his sympathies were not with Modernism or the modernistic, it was a chance to tar them, in passing, with a particularly undesirable brush. Meanwhile in Berlin, Hitler looked forward to the time when he had conquered the world and could roll out the works of Albert Speer, his preferred Neo-Classicist.

Lancaster wondered if 'enforced familiarity with this rugged décor over a prolonged period will in fact have any marked effect on the average person's taste in interior decoration'.[3] Forty years after the war's end corrugated iron and other brutish materials were, briefly, staples for a small group of professional interior designers who specialised in designing shops and restaurants and liked to think of themselves as rather artistic. Lancaster assumed that 'after the first air-raid much of that enthusiasm for vast areas of plate-glass, which has been so marked a feature of the modern movement, will vanish for good'.[4] Eighty years after his observation the appetite for floor-to-ceiling glass has increased and shows no sign of abating.

Throughout the war Britain was on the front line. In 1940 the German air force bombed London for 57 successive days, and their planes could reach the most far flung cities. Most damage was done in poorer areas, around docks and industrial hubs. The government encouraged and assisted the construction of private air raid shelters but, in London, 150,000 slept in Underground stations every night. A quarter of a million houses were destroyed and two million seriously damaged. The homeless were frequently obliged to billet themselves with relatives.

Raw materials: food, clothing and other essentials were rationed and the country had accumulated debts to the USA and Canada so huge that they were not paid off until 2006.

Misery was intensified by the severity of the winter of 1946–7. The root vegetables that were staples of winter menus were frozen into the ground and railways could not carry coal to power stations, or domestic grates. Domestic electricity supply was restricted to 19 hours a day. Radio broadcasting and the nascent television service was put on hold, newspapers were reduced in size. And, with the March thaw, came flooding.

In contrast, the USA actively entered the war in November 1942, three years after it began, and for the two and a half years of their involvement American civilians' experience was quite different from that of the British. Their mainland was never attacked and war production ended the 25% unemployment rate of the previous decade. There was a return to prosperity and jobs for all, as men joined the forces and women took their places in factories. Rosie became a riveter and a feminist pin-up.

American prosperity continued to grow after the war but, in Britain, shortages and rationing lasted another ten years. Citizens had reasonably assumed that things would get better after victory, that shops would be full of necessities and affordable luxuries, that they would have decent houses in a more egalitarian society. Optimism provoked something of a revolution but it was a British revolution, fought out in an election campaign between the end of the war in Europe in May 1945 and victory, three months later, in the Far East. The Labour party had contributed to the coalition wartime government and a few of its leading lights had earned credibility. Winston Churchill was adulated as a war leader but not seen as the working-class champion who would deliver a caring new world. Labour won the election decisively. Churchill had underestimated the appetite for a return to dull normality and the modest appeal of Labour's mildly socialist leader, Clement Attlee, of whom Churchill said 'An empty taxi drew up and Mr Attlee got out'. Churchill may have been a warrior, but Attlee looked like a bureaucrat who would be capable of delivering utopia. Social reform was in the air: the Conservatives had introduced free education in 1944 for children up until the age of 16; Labour trumped that with the National Health Service.

In February 1947, Christian Dior launched his 'New Look' which required prodigious amounts of fabric. For some in Britain its long and voluminous silhouette was an irresistible alternative to the government sanctioned economies of Utility clothing, others saw it as an unpatriotic waste of fabrics and others were insulted that such self-indulgence originated in France which had been spared German bombs by speedy defeat and occupation. Continuing clothes rationing incited fashionable women, who might have once cared for their interiors, to take down curtains and remodel them into facsimiles of the New Look.

If capitalism gave American householders the means to determine their own lifestyles, Britain's benign post-war state presented its citizens with radical but limited housing templates, and they were obliged to take what they were given. The aesthetics of Modernism suggested that its buildings would be cheap and quick to build, which appealed to national and local governments but produced social housing that failed to recognise that it had any aesthetic obligations. Modernists have excused themselves by explaining that, if properly executed, their buildings are not cheap: cost cutting, by philistine bureaucrats, was responsible for their shortcomings. Whether the philistines would have been justified in sanctioning expensive Modernism and whether this, shorn of recognisable ornamentation, would have been appreciated by those obliged to live with it is another question.

In post-war Britain, building materials were rationed and private house building curtailed: there were new schools to build for the expanded pupil population and new hospitals for the NHS. The new government was assuming control of vital services, like the railways, and industries like coal mining, and, in this spirit, government departments and local councils set up their own architectural departments and those who worked in them, excited to be building a new world in a new way, were free to ply Modernist principles. In hospitals and community health centres large windows and plain, palpably hygienic, surfaces made Modernist sense but it was not long before the institutions began to appreciate the therapeutic importance of decoration. The remedies that were applied – whimsical murals in reception areas and modernistic prints hung in long corridors – were inadequate dressings applied retrospectively to aesthetic wounds. They were gestures that were lost amongst the grubby sheets of instructions and exhortations that spilled over the edges of noticeboards to gather unhygienic dust.

The programme of new school building allowed Modernists to download their principles and a formula quickly evolved. As Hopkins stated: *The new primary schools were the first to appear – and nowhere was the revolution in attitude more strikingly declared. Their architects – or the best of them – had studied the ways and needs of children to some purpose. There was a feeling of space, of expanding horizons, even of adventure. Gay, often strongly contrasting colours were now becoming almost as standard as the old dark green partitions and 'institutional' brown glazed tiles had been formerly.*[5] It would be disingenuous to suggest that dour Victorian school buildings, in which window cills began above the eye level and heating was rudimentary, were joyful places in which to learn but they had a presence and made education look like a serious matter. The new prototypes, single storey where site size permitted, with low-cilled windows that stretched the length of at least one wall of every centrally heated classroom, introduced their innocent young inmates to the basics of Modernism and, perhaps, helped cushion the blow for those who would later find themselves living high in tower blocks, gazing at the discouraging empty space that separated their block from the next one along.

The new schools also gave tasters of modern furniture. Esavian, a company that adapted its wartime techniques for the use of plywood and aluminium in warplane construction, evolved a range of lightweight stacking chairs and desks that became standard issue in new schools. They were smaller and much lighter than the traditional heavy wooden and cast iron couplings of seat and desk, traditionally incised with initials carved by the pen knives of long gone pupils. The ingenuity and elegance of their curved and angled aluminium legs, with their hints of Streamline and Moderne, and their light coloured plywood veneers was recognised by the Italian magazine *Domus*, then the essential monthly record of progressive design.

Left
An infant's stacking school chair in curved plywood and aluminium by Esavian and now a collectable object for enthusiasts of vintage furniture.

Right
An Esavian prototype for a storage unit with curved plywood legs and a plastic laminate top. The angled drawer fronts make elegant finger holds.

TASTE

Above
A row of temporary prefabricated houses designed by the Ministry of Works in Croydon, UK, 1942.

Furniture for the home, new or old, was less radical. Rationing of materials meant manufacturers were not inclined to take risks with their allocation and retailers were unprepared to ignore conventional taste. 'Utility' furniture, designed during the war to be 'simple, functional, unadorned and therefore patriotic'[6] had been conceived by a government committee manned by representatives of the Council of Industrial Design, who felt obliged to nudge public taste towards something modernistic but the products were stolid and dull with dark brown wooden frames and veneers. As time passes, nostalgia prevails and, like Esavian's school furniture, Utility pieces have admirers and have become desirable amongst collectors of mid-20th-century design.

Having assumed that they had won the war, Britons were disillusioned when rationing continued and those bombed out of their homes had to resort to squatting, sometimes in the bomb-damaged shells of grand town houses, sometimes in the corrugated tin huts that had housed wartime service personnel. Local authorities could only turn blind eyes to this trespassing. Before his defenestration Churchill had promised a short-term solution to the wartime housing shortage and proposed half a million compact factory-produced prefabricated dwellings. Those who had lived in pre-war slums were delighted to find 'prefabs' were warm and dry with well-appointed kitchens, running hot water, refrigerators, inside

Right
A view from the dining room to the living room. Sliding doors increased the perceived sizes of rooms and introduced the idea of open plan living, UK, 1945.

Below left
A fold down 'breakfast table' incorporated in a fitted 'prefab' kitchen cupboard, UK, 1945.

Below right
The prefab kitchen featured modern appliances which many tenants would not have seen before, UK, 1945.

lavatories and plumbed baths, mod cons that most privately owned houses did not have, all squeezed into a 59 m² rectangle which was, nevertheless, excitingly spacious for families who had previously crowded into single rooms and shared kitchens and lavatories. These single-storeyed little boxes, although their external asbestos cement cladding panels were not admired, allowed tenants to experiment with making an agreeable home. Interiors came ready-painted, walls were cream and woodwork green but tenants had to decide about furniture and decorative details. The little boxes were designed to last ten years but many exceeded that and many former residents were nostalgic for the simple comforts, their own front doors and tiny gardens.

Above
Fitted wardrobes in one of the two bedrooms, UK, 1945.

Left
The prefab bathroom introduced many tenants to running hot water and privacy, UK, 1945.

The American way

In the United States in 1933, 49% of mortgage repayments were in arrears and each week in the region of 1,000 houses would be repossessed. It was not a time for average householders to concern themselves with the niceties of interior decoration. In 1934 the National Housing Act had reduced down payments from 40% and 50% to 20% and, to support other arms of the housing industry, loans for upgrading existing premises and buying appliances were also available. To organise this, the Act also set up the Federal Housing Administration, which issued *Technical Bulletins* in which it promoted 'modern' principles but these were purely practical, about efficient use of space, materials and technology, not about styling. In fact, it explained that well-considered practical solutions would be viewed favourably by officials while 'modernistic' aesthetics would not. In 1940 it offered innovative and acceptable planning variations and material palettes for a single-storey house: the elevations were traditional, with pitched roofs and small windows. It became known as the 'minimum' house' and seemed to recognise that, while decoration might be an imperative for the newly installed householder, it could be a short-term matter – a house could change hands and be redecorated without compromising its soundness or efficiency.

The Second World War, like the First, was a social and aesthetic watershed in the USA but this time principles of taste were not determined by radicals and foisted on a respectful public. The new suburbanites had stretched and tested themselves in a foreign war and were not inclined to be told how, and in what, to live and they were served by retailers who felt no obligation to offer unpopular products in the service of promoting an elitist taste.

Families, free of the stresses of living cheek by jowl in apartment buildings, were more relaxed and had more space in which to entertain themselves . A bright world of gaudy colours and loud patterns evolved, made possible by the advent of new materials, oil-based plastics, foams and fibreglass. They shaped the new interiors which became the defining image of post-war America. Art Deco seemed very pre-war; too white and comparatively staid.

Prefabrication techniques which had evolved to speed wartime arms production were adapted to a different end than they were in Britain with its social welfare and social housing programmes. The USA remained committed to the market economy and, on the east coast, a real estate company, Levitt & Sons, developed enormous tracts on the peripheries of major towns and cities. Their first 'Levittown', on Long Island, began in 1947 and was completed in 1951. Six others were developed simultaneously. They were aimed at returning servicemen who, subsidised by government grants, could buy without deposits and with monthly repayments that were no more than the rent for a city apartment. Levitt & Sons borrowed techniques from manufacturing production lines and wartime military construction. Their workforce was divided into autonomous teams and each team member performed only one of the 26 separate assembly tasks which resulted in a completed house, on average one every 16 minutes. William Levitt described the company as manufacturers rather than builders.

The new suburbs attracted those who wanted away from crowded, rented city centre tenements. Levittown men commuted to jobs in city centres but they and their wives wanted children and these pristine communities provided wholesome environments for post-war baby boomers. Each house had grassed 'yards', front and back, a place to park a car and included, as standard, built-in television and hi-fi sets.

No matter how excited the inhabitants might be about owning real estate and how pleased they might be to see their children play on grass, Levittown houses were never going to meet with critical approval. They were, after all, suburbs and inevitably criticised for conformity: there was one basic house type and it was stolidly traditional with a pitched roof, and familiar cladding materials. Malvine Reynolds wrote *Little Boxes*, a smug quasi-folk song that complained that suburban homes were 'all made out of ticky-tacky and they all look just the same'.

The suburban uniformity of Levittown was an easy target for novelists, particularly those who had grown up in such developments. Most were predictably critical of conformist communities that supposedly stifled individuality but the hero of *The Man Who Loved Levittown*, a short story by W. D. Wetherell, gave a full-blooded rebuttal: *Sure they were little boxes when we first started ... (but) ... the minute we got our mitts on them we started remodelling them ... thanks to Big Bill Levitt we all had a chance. You talk about dreams. Hell, we had ours ... We had ours like nobody before or since ... We were cowboys out there. We were the pioneers.*[7] It may be that places like Levittown present canvases so blank that those who lived in them felt a need to brand their property (as any good cowboy would), and the customising of individual houses contributed to the collective customising of neighbourhoods. Exteriors remained men's work, interiors, women's. Office-working husbands demonstrated manly handling of tools and their wives ruled on matters of taste. It was they who defined the new interiors and it was their image that defined the Norman Rockwellian American lifestyle, in which a contented mother, in a frilly apron, served a smiling father and happy children at a table surrounded by built-in kitchen units and a towering fridge, with glimpses of a sprawling open plan living room beyond. The rest of the world gazed in envy.

The inspiration for the suburban tract house was primarily the early long low 'ranch' houses of California, but suburban reworkings of the 'ranch' were smaller and their plans, confined by regular site boundaries, sprawled less. They retained the open plan, the fusing of living, dining and kitchen, the essential strategy that characterised the interiors of everyone else who dabbled in Modernism. 'Ranch' planning was the indigenous American way and those who bought into it were not interested in white walls. They had flowing space and could see no reason not to fill it and fill it plenteously.

Traditional formalities were challenged and Mid-Century Modern, typified by bright colours and bold patterns, evolved. Natural and manufactured materials were mixed, splayed legs on tables and chairs supported bright upholstery and colourful plastic laminates. Compared to traditional forms the component parts were frivolous but they offered a diversity that could match traditional styles for excesses of detail.

A view from the centre

In 1940, Daniel S. Defenbacher of the Walker Arts Center, in Minneapolis, which was involved in the Federal Arts Project, initiated a project to present the Minnesotan public with the positive and pleasurable realities of a modern house and to invite their comments. Defenbacher, who had trained as an architect, saw in the Federal Arts Project's mission to foster creative employment and interest in the arts amongst the general population an opportunity to promote contemporary design.

Presuming that models and drawings would neither be an attraction nor an effective conduit for showcasing principles, he established the Idea House project, a prototypical suburban home, designed by local architects, Malcolm and Miriam Lein. It was built within the Walker Arts Center's grounds, and was fully furnished and open for six months, closing in November with the arrival of the Minnesotan winter. Thereafter it would operate as a place for teaching design and home decoration.

Promising publicity, Defenbacher persuaded local suppliers and retailers to donate materials and artefacts, although he was careful to insist that, in the grander scheme of things, the centre's educational project would be unpolluted by commercial pressures.

The Minnesotan initiative was not entirely unique. Manufacturers and builders were in the habit of proffering model homes at the 'world fairs' and exhibitions that had become established phenomena in the American calendar. In 1939 the New York World's Fair featured a *Town of Tomorrow*, with 15 houses, aimed at different price brackets and sponsored by producers of building products. Participating architects were warned that the town should be 'neither traditional nor modernistic in design, it should be modern', it should assist consumers to get 'value for money' and the houses would offer inspiration without prioritising Modernist tropes over uninhabitability.

Idea House I followed the same principles and those of the Federal Housing Administration's 'minimum house', accepting that 'modern' referred to technology and not style. Its intention was to demonstrate sound planning principles and a practical palette of materials to allow prospective homeowners to assess the merits of the houses they would buy or build. Weekly progress reports in the local newspaper recorded the evolution of the project. Building began in January 1941 and continued through the Minnesotan winter.

It described the open plan organisation of the 'minimum house', with sliding partitions providing options for privacy and a leather-veneered screen between living and sleeping areas. The house provided a living room, a kitchen/dining area, a bedroom, a guestroom/study and a bathroom. Large windows in the living area maximised winter sunlight and overhanging eaves kept the interior cool in high summer. With its emphasis on modern efficiency the kitchen had an electric cooker, a refrigerator and a dishwasher; its walls and ceiling were lined with stainless steel sheet. Bathroom finishes were easy to clean, and a utility room housed a washing machine. The open plan was radical, a demonstration of how a limited floor area could be made more flexible, and useful, with movable partitions. The modest decorating scheme provided no distractions; visitors could concentrate on the practical.

Defenbacher argued that 'as a consumer, every man uses art … his medium he obtains from stores, manufacturers, and builders. His composition is his environment'.[8] He was suggesting that composing the interior, and perhaps the exterior, offered everyone the opportunity to be creative, to develop personal skills and ideas over a period of time. He had identified a folk art.

The project received very little government funding and Defenbacher was obliged to work with whatever materials were donated by local suppliers. All the furniture came from a single supplier, which did not demonstrate product diversity but gave the interior the coherence that the personal taste of any householder might impose. The Center resisted attempts by donators of materials and services to have sales representatives on site and instead added details of suppliers to printed information about the concept. It encouraged enquiries about the principles that underpinned the design. 'Rather than selling goods the Walker claimed it was selling "ideas" and the implications of these ideas were highly appealing to businesses with real goods to sell.'[9]

Towards the end of the war, in late 1945, Defenbacher began working on *Idea House II*, which was usefully timed to examine the priorities and problems of the post-war housing. In September 1947, the month *Idea House II* opened, *McCall's* magazine had sympathised with housewives overwhelmed by the responsibility of operating new appliances and *Idea House II* was intended to prepare its visitors to face those distinctly American challenges. It foresaw that a modern way of living that would be shaped by new domestic gadgetry as much as it was by aesthetics, which, Defenbacher proposed, should be left to householders emancipated from strictures *de haut en bas* about good and bad taste.

The Walker's press release worried that a market, supported by cheap government finance, would lead to expedient building and expedient buying. *Idea House II* was a place where visitors to the gallery could 'absorb new concepts in design, building materials, furnishings and technology, and apply them where and how they wished in their own homes …' The absence of proselytising on behalf of one style suggested that decoration, and matters of taste, were better left in the hands of the homeowner. This time the project was primarily funded by the Home Institute Unit of the Northwestern National Bank, which assisted with financial planning and supplied an extensive collection of wallpaper, fabric and paint samples. Interior designers advised on strategies for their application but offered only a support service: decision making lay, ultimately, with householders, which had an unexpected hint of Ruskin's proposal that Victorian customers should be provided with impartial advisers to protect them from sales persons.

Like its predecessor *Idea House II* was a modest proposition, a home for a family of four with a flexible use of communal areas and privacy for individuals. It used readily available materials, gypsum board, concrete blockwork and plywood, and well-tried North American construction methods.

The principal room was flexible and designated for relaxation, eating, working or entertaining and was visually connected to the outside by large window 'walls'. Storage units also acted as 'walls' and defined activity areas. The chimney breast, of fair-faced concrete block and brick, was large, as if trying, not wholly successfully, to retain its status as the focal element in the open planned area. Furnishings were more radical than in *Idea House I*, supplied by the Knoll company and included pieces by Charles and Ray Eames and Eero Saarinen. Lighting was designed by Walter von Nessen and built-in furniture by George Nelson. To drum up visitors, the Walker and the *Minneapolis Morning Tribune* initiated a competition to select readers who most convincingly explained their interest in experiencing this modern way of living. Representatives of four typical family units were selected: a young married couple with no children, a couple with two small children, a working couple with teenage children and a couple with one child at home and one away at college. A fifth kind of 'family' was added when three women reminded the paper of the 'large army that falls under [the heading of] the three girls who share an apartment.' They were particularly keen to experience the pleasures of hot water on tap, the comprehensive battery of domestic appliances and to test the capacity of the clothes storage provision to cope with the demands of three women. *They explained that they had no in-laws or teenage children, in fact we don't even have husbands ... Don't you think you're overlooking a major factor in your household selection? We buy food and subscribe to the papers and pay our phone bills just like any family ... and we know what we want in the way of comfortable living.*[10] Their confident, good-natured description of their circumstances and obvious relishing of their independence was a convincing demonstration that, the young professional woman had arrived and felt no need to deny the validity of her particular circumstances while reminding the organisers that when she married as she would expect, and be expected, to do she would play the major part in determining the nature of domesticity and domestic taste. A photograph from the Walker Arts Center archives shows the three women confidently sprawled in the living room of *House II*, relishing their coup.

The house attracted interest across the US and inspired some to ask challenging technical questions and others to ask for copies of the plans. The Walker reminded the second group that it was a house of ideas and they should employ an architect to find their own bespoke solution.

Defenbacher had maintained that because 'a man's house is his art', each house should be unique, defined by its owners' taste. Housing had become a 'national preoccupation'. His public-spirited and public-funded initiatives informed buyers about options and quality, a bedrock on which individuals could create their own homes. They charted the change in lifestyles for the average Americans, from the cash-strapped uncertainties of the 1930s to, no more than six or seven years later, the prosperity and confidence that followed the war; a booming economy reinforced by the realisation that their popular culture, their household goods and their baroque 'limousines' had seduced the world. It was an attempt to retain something of Vitruvius's firmness and commodity at the time when popular taste was let off the leash.

If Minnesotans were being invited to make up their own minds about how they might dress their own homes, architects and fellow travellers continued to be appalled by suburban aesthetics and thoughts of lost commissions. With the moralising certainties of any group of missionaries, *Art and Architecture* magazine commissioned architects, approved by *bien pensants*, to design model suburban houses in Los Angeles, a long way from the offensive Levittowns in the east. However, even if elevations could be prescribed by architects, not even *Art and Architecture* could police what went on behind them.

Other museums followed the Walker's example. Philip L. Goodwin, co-designer of the MoMA building revealed, a touch pompously, in a letter to Defenbacher, that he and Philip Johnson, on behalf of the museum, had discussed with 'a well-known architect' building a house in the garden of MoMA and that he understood Defenbacher 'had done something of this kind recently'. He then cadged information. The MoMA project went ahead with a 'family house' and Marcel Breuer was the 'well-known architect'. Plans could be bought and, given MoMA and Breuer's predilections, the end result was distinctly Modernist. The museum's imprimatur and architect's reputation ensured that the design was reiterated precisely in several east coast locations – for clients who wanted a trophy rather than the house they needed.

Charles and Ray Eames were invited by *Art and Architecture* magazine to contribute to the Case Study programme. Their proposal, completed in 1949, and number eight in the series, became their home and studio. Their general output was a complex mix, from an utterly practical wartime plywood splint moulded to cushion wounded legs to didactic films bordering on abstractions. Neither Eames was formally trained nor qualified as an architect, and they brought an unorthodox vision to house design and demonstrated a pragmatic solution to producing fast and flexible houses that coped with the demands of chronic suburban expansion. Whether it would have been to the taste of suburbanites is another question. It was constructed, by hand, with a speed that rivalled that of Levitt's production teams, using prefabricated steel products intended for the construction of industrial units and its empty shell looked like a lofty, comprehensively glazed warehouse. There were few subdivisions of the plan: it made an undeniably elegant empty shed, but when the Eameses moved in they filled its lofty spaces with plants, scatter cushions and a collection of stylish objects that, if assembled by less illustrious figures, would have been considered knick-knacks. Their inhabited home demonstrated ways in which something aggressively modern could be tuned by a talent for accumulating and orchestrating decorative clutter. The collection was the product of well-tuned eyes and confirmed that inessentials add humanity.

Judith Gura suggests that the USA was 'the last of the major Western powers to embrace Modernism'.[11] Its designers were aware, however, of what was happening through magazines and immigrant European designers and architects were teaching in the more progressive art schools. Scandinavian ideas did much to shape the Eameses. They met when studying under the Finn Eliel Saarinen at the Cranbrook Academy of Art and acquired a Scandinavian taste and talent for exploring and respecting the structural and shape-making potential of bent plywood. Their 'lounger', with fat 'chocolate' leather cushions held within the curved edges of red-grained walnut-faced plywood supporting planes has, with its matching ottoman, become the accepted comfy chair of choice for hard-line architects and designers. The softer lines and timber of both components are significantly more accommodating of the possible configurations of the human body at rest than Corbusier and Perriand's tubular steel framed, leather upholstered chaise longue, which remains first pick for those in need of a 'sculptural' piece: *In the Nordic countries, good design was considered a democratic right rather than an elitist privilege … They pursued the goal of socially responsible design, focusing on human needs as much as, and occasionally more than,*

Above
The Eameses' prefab, built from standard materials for the construction of industrial sheds, introduced the high-tech house, and elegantly integrated the interior with the garden, Los Angeles, 1950.

Opposite
The construction methods of the Eames house gave complex internal spaces and abundant natural light; a catholic collection of artefacts humanised and personalised it, Los Angeles, 1950.

aesthetics. The resulting objects, and the interiors that surrounded them, offered a less radical and more accessible option for those who were put off by severe European-born Modernism[12]. Minnesota was home to many immigrants from Scandinavia. They knew how to deal with hard winters. And perhaps their instinct for non-elitist, socially responsible design accounts for the Walker Arts Center's democratic intentions.

Apart from a brief period in the 17th century when the militarily accomplished King Gustavus Adolphus made Sweden a leading European power, Sweden, Norway, Denmark, Finland and outlying Iceland have been physically and culturally on the fringe of Europe. However, they blossomed in the 20th century, each country with its own version of the 'Nordic model' of democratic government, an envied meld of a comprehensive welfare state and free market capitalism.

Sweden had remained precariously neutral during the war, counterbalancing supplying iron ore to Germany with passing strategic information to Britain, and its non-combativity made it well placed after the war to demonstrate its vision of modern domesticity. The other Nordic states had been subjugated by the Nazis but spared the intense warfare that destroyed mainland Europe. They, and especially Denmark, were quickly able to add to Sweden's example of amiable modernity.

Both modernists and traditionalists, in Europe and North America were, and continue to be, seduced by the Nordic vision of the home, internally and externally. Modernists can see abstinence from blatant ornamentalising. Traditionalists see respect for an indigenous past. In the 19th century Scandinavian architecture was unassuming, even when it dabbled

with Neo-Classicism, perhaps unsure that Mediterranean traditions were entirely appropriate for its rhetorical needs. Its own traditions of timber and brick buildings did not translate comfortably into the grandiose, and its understanding of working with natural materials sat more easily with Arts and Crafts and Art Nouveau, but all influences from abroad were tempered with nostalgia and respect for its own traditions.

The climate means that it was not a region given to working in concrete, nor to expanses of glass, nor inclined to mimic French and German models of Modernism. It had to worry about making warm houses. It found its own humane modernity, which was radical but realised in bricks and timber. Even its eclectic exteriors, sometimes clad in painted timber boarding and sometimes in painted corrugated metal, all under steeply pitched roofs have a diagrammatic simplicity that can cruelly tug at a Modernist's heartstrings. Modernists can explain their acceptance of deviation from their own clear rules as appreciation of inherent 'honesty'. Traditionalists are simply delighted by houses that look like proper houses.

Scandinavians are not inclined to create furniture with tubular metal frames. They enjoy curves as much as the next designer but prefer to mould plywood, like the Finn Alvar Aalto, or to bend solid timbers, like the Dane Hans Wegner. Modern, non-Nordic, designers turn to their pieces when they want natural materials and curves in their interiors. As well as furniture the stubbornly persistent Scandinavian craft tradition produced textiles and ceramics and glass that were demonstrably of their time but had a humane modesty that insinuated itself into popular imaginations far beyond its shores.

Scandinavian design comes from the dour North but something subliminally good-humoured lurks in its tactile, colourful detail. It is accessible without pandering to a presumed low common denominator of taste. It has never been accused, even by the loftiest critics, of vulgarity and has defined ways of living that come closer to satisfying the aesthetic needs of the deserving hoi polloi than anything that Modernism's social agenda has achieved. It comes from simple roots and nourishes needs that have been neglected by Modernity.

Opposite
Finnish Design Limited,
Finland House, Haymarket,
London, 1958.

Below
Finmar showrooms, Soho,
London, 1953.

CHAPTER 6

1951 and All That

'I can't imagine there has ever been a more gratifying time or place to be alive than America in the 1950s. No country had ever known such prosperity.'

Bill Bryson, *The Life and Times of the Thunderbolt Kid: A Memoir*, 2006[1]

After the Second World War and into the 1950s the United States demonstrated to the rest of the world all that was desirable for a mid-20th-century lifestyle. Its happy families lived in suburban idylls and owned three-quarters of the cars in the world. The myth was consolidated and exported in films and television sitcoms.

But even the happiest families have concerns. The United States had been a reluctant combatant but having done so and given the post-war confrontation of capitalist and communist ideologies, it found itself leading the non-communist bloc. It found itself, with some support from Britain, fighting with capitalist South Korea against the communist North. Fear of communism, which had first emerged as an immediate response to the Russian Revolution, increased when the Soviet Union tested their first nuclear device in 1949 and intensified when a number of spies, working on the American nuclear programme, were discovered to have given information to the Russians. Defence spending was high and in the Cold War, as in a hot war, the economy benefitted.

Anxiety about a Russian nuclear attack and a campaign by Senator Joseph McCarthy to eliminate communist sympathisers from public life nurtured national paranoia. The novelist Richard Yates, who grew up in a Levittown, suggested that the 'general lust for conformity'[2] bred support for McCarthy while McCarthyites suspected that Levittowns' homogeneity encouraged socialist communities. William Levitt responded: 'no one who owns his own house and lot can be a Communist. He has too much to do'.[3]

And the style guru Anne Fogarty helped focus minds on more pressing matters. In *Wife Dressing: The Fine Art of Being a Well-dressed Wife* (1960), apart from tacitly confirming wives as strategic weapons in their husband's career, she advised 'if you give small, informal dinner parties, have a few long or short colorful skirts and dresses in jersey or flannel with gay party aprons to make your role of hostess festive yet comfortable'.[4] British wives had not the resources to cope with such detail.

Britain had hung on through the 1940s, cold, hungry and drab. There had been little evidence of post-war economic recovery and low national morale prompted the government to adopt a proposal made in 1943 by the Royal Society of Arts, with defiant wartime optimism, for an event to mark the centenary of the Great Exhibition of 1851. It was agreed that an international exhibition would be too expensive and there may have been a suspicion that immediately after the war the country would not be ready to give a good account of itself on an international stage. The expedient alternative was probably more productive: it gave the British the chance to get a glimpse of their possible future and it looked like it might be fun.

A 'Festival of Britain' was proposed, to feature home-grown arts and sciences. It was to be, its director Gerald Barry explained, a 'tonic for the nation' and despite scepticism about its succeeding in a time of austerity, it was characterised by a lightness of touch that enraptured the nation. Events were organised in towns and cities across the British Isles and an exhibition ship and a travelling show brought a taster of the main event to distant outposts. The proposed number and scale of events was enough to convince citizens that the country had ambitions and the festival's style, whether in its graphic imagery or its major structures, caught the national imagination. Hugh Casson, a 38-year-old architect, was appointed the festival's Director of Architecture. He was by nature good humoured and ensured that the

Opposite
The Festival of Britain logo designed by Abram Games, 1951.

structures were jaunty. The extravaganza he orchestrated prompted a shift in taste that became evident in domestic interiors for the next decade.

The main festival site was in London, on the south bank of the Thames. A faction of architects, presumably including some disappointed when not invited to contribute, objected to the buildings as insufficiently innovative but an open-minded public was entranced. Suddenly they were reconciled to modernistic design. That the buildings, apart from the Royal Festival Hall, were temporary allowed visitors to set aside the anxieties that permanent modernistic structures might have induced. They could treat them as festive novelties – and they did not have to live in them. It may also have encouraged the designers to set aside their more philosophical concerns. The Festival Hall was permanent and heroic but memories of the industrial squalor that had previously occupied its site cast it in a positive light. Its internal detailing, its stairways, light fittings and furniture were restrained but not out of tune with the bravado of the temporary structures.

Ten million visitors saw for themselves, in one venue or another, modernistic ideas presented with light-hearted whimsy. Eight and a half million people visited the main site on London's South Bank, got a taste of what the future might hold and liked it. Everything from the logo, to the street furniture, to the banks of loudspeakers and floodlights, to the elevated walkways that connected extraordinary building to extraordinary building suggested a future to be relished. Decorative devices without precedent were subliminally familiar; modernistic reinterpretations of traditional devices. They were a considerate and considerable step forward. A popular style had been delivered.

Photographs of the festival are enlightening. At a time when clothing was still rationed, visitors dressed soberly and similarly: they had little choice. But at the Festival site they could sit on cheeky little chairs under striped umbrellas and looped lengths of fairy lights in open-air cafes, all within plain sight of the Houses of Parliament and St

Below
The festival was enjoyably frivolous, with fairy lights and the sprightly little Antelope chairs by Ernest Race.

Below right
Visitors wandered about a futuristic world; the antithesis of the bomb-damaged city that surrounded them.

Pauls, the two symbols of wartime survival and victory. They were introduced to a modernistic world and they enjoyed it. They could take away souvenirs in the festival style, which was: *clean, bright and new. It looked neither to classical Athens, nor Imperial New Delhi, nor to chromium-plated skyscraping New York, but to the modest, model social democracies of Scandinavia. It caught hold quickly and spread first across London and then across England. And the name it acquired in doing so was significant, too: 'Contemporary'.*[5] Hopkins described how the municipal 'gravy browns and drab greens' were displaced by the bright colour palette and cited 'a woman reporter' who wrote 'After the long grey winter this galaxy of colour was like a glass of champagne. Everywhere I looked brought fresh impact – vivid reds, blues, greens, lemon yellows – bubbles pricking my nose'.[6]

The festival demonstrated that the future could be made with a light touch and, with their appetites whetted and the ways and means to achieve it, householders took matters into their own hands. They called their new style Contemporary. The critic William Feaver listed its fundamentals: 'braced legs, indoor plants, lily-of-the-valley sprays of light bulbs, Cotswold type walling with picture windows, flying staircases, blond wood, the thorn, the spike, the molecule'.[7] There was much more. Light hued woods of splayed-legged Ercol and G-plan furniture began to usurp Utility's glum browns. A 'feature wall' usually containing a fireplace, whether of heavily patterned, brightly coloured wallpaper or garish and rather unconvincingly

Above left
Converted double decker buses took first-hand encounters with modernity far beyond the capital, European Publicity bus tour, 1950.

Above
Local architects and designers mounted regional exhibitions. This, in Belfast, featured a full scale mock-up of a modern house, Belfast Modern Architecture Exhibition, Ulster, 1951.

Below
Plastics, bright colours, shiny finishes became common and popular in the aftermath of the festival.

Above
Chairs by Robin Day and table by Ercol.

Below
Trio textile design by Lucienne Day.

Below right
Flotilla by Lucienne Day.

reconstructed 'Cotswold' stone cut in random sizes and of random tints became focal points in open plan ground floors. Glass and plastics, for tableware and table lamps, brought sleek shapes and brighter colour. Fittingly, for what was essentially a domestic movement, much of the most radical work was done by the husband and wife team of Lucienne and Robin Day. Husband and wife teams were commonplace at the time, particularly in architecture. Couples met in architecture schools and drifted into joint practice but each had specialist responsibilities. Husbands played golf and sought clients while wives dealt with child rearing and domestic chores but the female 'eye' was considered an asset when it came to dealing with interiors. Males were generally responsible for less frivolous exteriors and dealing with the practicalities of weatherproofing and plumbing.

Lucienne and Robin Day, Britain's equivalents of the Eameses, had contributed to the festival. Lucienne was the leading textile designer of her day and her work brought brightly coloured abstract imagery, derived from natural forms and scientific symbols, into progressive homes. Robin was a furniture designer and, apart from his stacking plastic and metal chairs which became ubiquitous in public places, he combined chrome frames and plywood carcasses to make domestic pieces that showed a distinct Scandinavian influence. The Days became the poster couple for a modern lifestyle and spent 60 productive years at opposite ends of a shared worktable.

The festival helped make real the images of colourful and irreverent domestic interiors that were coming over from the United States; the market-driven aesthetics of American product designers and the popular taste of Levittown, with a leavening of Scandinavian values.

Top left
Lucienne Day's *Spectators* curtain fabric on a stand for Heal and Son at the Ideal Home Exhibition, Olympia, London, 1953.

Top right
The fireplace remains the focal point of the room but becomes frivolous and is complemented by furniture from Heal's, the reworkings of the winged armchair and the standard lamp and the skeletal magazine rack. London, 1953.

Above left
Fireplaces that were readily available in shops across the country were less eccentrically 1950s and retained Deco'd geometrical clarity. With an enormous stretch of the imaginations this could be seen to have affinities with Loos's tomb.

Above right
No style is an island: This 1950s chair could have belonged as easily to the 1940s and 1930s.

The New Elizabethan age

By the mid 1950s, when rationing ended, Britain had begun its peacetime recovery. The coronation of Elizabeth II had encouraged growth in ownership of television sets, from the 350,000 in 1950 to 3.2 million in 1953. By 1960 three-quarters of homes would have sets. The family living room was becoming a primary place of entertainment and the increased prosperity that bought televisions encouraged decorative upgrades, even if the little grey images were best viewed in darkened rooms.

Improvements to education and the instigation of the National Health Service had satisfied post-war enthusiasm for change but they were proving difficult to finance and housing remained a problem. The threat of increased taxes to meet escalating social provisions suggested that a period of prudent bedding down was necessary. After six years of Labour's social engineering a Conservative government, still led by the stubborn Churchill, was re-elected, in 1951, on promises of consolidation.

The immediate post-war ambition to create Utopia had proved ruinously extravagant. Hopkins described a new school in the new town of Stevenage: *set in twenty acres of countryside, with a fully equipped stage as big as the Haymarket Theatre's, with murals by leading artists, statuary by Henry Moore, as well as such now standard features as gymnasia and domestic science rooms, laboratories, craft shops and architect-designed animal hutches and potting sheds.*[8] The new government steadied the economy. Streets of slums, usually privately owned, were condemned and demolished and a quarter of a million council houses were being built in a year.

Planners and architects, intoxicated by Corbusian visions of residential tower blocks scattered across parkland, persuaded councils in the larger conurbations, keen to appear forward-thinking and anxious for a quick fix, to opt for high-rise blocks of flats. Generously sized self-contained flats, with bedroom numbers appropriate to family numbers, central heating and bathrooms and kitchens were distinctly more comfortable than overcrowded, rot and rat infested two-up two-downs. These practical improvements helped dampen tenants' initial reservations about being stacked high but those decanted into the monsters were quickly and predictably disgruntled. Whatever freedom tenants might have to indulge their individual decorating tastes could not reconcile them to the high life.

High-level living was an acquired taste and there was an additional stigma attached to living in a tower block: one had drawn a short straw in the competition for council accommodation. Terraced houses looked like real houses. Even when former neighbours were reassigned to the same tower block, the communal lift lobby did not offer the same opportunities for casual interaction as the street in which people had previously congregated to escape their overcrowded homes. (Or perhaps it is human nature to close the regulation front door to relish self-containment in a hot bath and forget one's neighbours.)

The first tower was completed in 1951 in Harlow New Town and, with the ameliorating passage of time, is now listed, presumably because of it social significance but, isolated amongst mature trees in its parkland setting and with its articulated facades, it is elegant. All but a few of the tower blocks that followed lacked its refinement.

Since Modernism's avowed intent was to improve social well-being its adherents might have resisted the temptation to impose an alien style, and lifestyle, on those obliged to use its buildings but in rented council houses and flats, free of market forces, its tropes have been freely applied. Architects, keener for peer rather than popular acclaim and doused in Modernist dogma, were reluctant to find nuances more agreeable to public taste. Making towers was more stimulating than making terraces. Those who commissioned them perhaps assumed that something unpalatable could only be good for their tenants. Or it may have been that negative responses in newspapers made architects stubbornly defensive, unable to retreat with honour intact. Or perhaps they presumed that they knew best. Le Corbusier advocated residential towers and in the 1950s architects wanted to be Corbusian.

Hugh Casson explained the problem: 'scratch an architect and you'll find a boy scout with a power complex'.[9] They were the sort of well-meaning boy scouts who would help old ladies across roads, whether they wanted to cross or not.

The interiors of tower block flats did offer bland, blank canvasses to be enhanced as their occupants might fancy. Similar problems and pleasures affected those decanted to new towns. In 1946 the Labour government had designated seven locations for these, two in Scotland, one in the far northeast of England and four close to London, just beyond its encircling green belt. Decantees were allocated semi-detached and terraced two-storey houses with gardens, good infrastructures and job opportunities. Some found the alien environments exhilarating; some missed pubs, corner shops and robust interactions on the old hugger-mugger streets. In 1951, only 15% of British families owned a car: the bicycle and the bus remained the means of getting to work.

Left
The Lawn: The first residential tower, built in Harlow, UK, 1951.

Right
The town centre in Stevenage with maisonettes above shops. The pedestrianised street was convenient but lacked the memories and rawness of those the new inhabitants had left behind. UK, 1958.

Below left
The ubiquitous public sculpture by, or in the style of, Henry Moore: a signal of municipal good intent. Harlow Civic Centre, 'The Family' by Henry Moore, 1954.

Below right
A new terrace in Essex: Not quite traditional, not quite popular. The form is familiar but the materials are not. Basildon, Essex, 1960.

Housewives walked to small 'parades' of shops: there were no malls. It was all a bit pedestrian. *… as the Fifties ended, the New Towns were already beginning to look like lonely monuments to Good Intentions. The generous social impulse of the war years had worked itself out. … the nation had willed the end but had neglected to will the means.*[10] New towns were British equivalents of American suburbs; not inhabited by owners but tenants who moved to them with a sense, not of achievement but of relief that their patience had brought them to the top of a long waiting list. There was not the sense of personal validation that came with ownership in Levittown nor the freedom to set about customising the standard model. Notoriously, council tenants were denied the right to choose the colour of their own front doors. Prole taste was not trusted: it was better that it was perpetrated behind closed doors.

Doing it oneself

For those Britons who could afford to buy modest houses, the end of rationing offered opportunities for home improvements. Homeowners were willing to take a hands-on approach. Doing it yourself was already an established option. It had begun in the house-buying boom that followed the Great War when instruction manuals were published to guide the New Rich who might be stretched to pay their mortgages and the Old Rich who might be unable to afford tradesmen. In the 1930s, enthusiasm for DIY generated a radio audience of a million for *Your House In Order*, a programme in which W. P. Matthews tackled the considerable task of explaining, in words only, home improvement techniques. After the war he reappeared on both radio and, more effectively, on television.

Matthews was succeeded by Barry Bucknell, who began by offering home improvement advice on an afternoon radio programme to housewives whose wartime experience in factories and on farms was presumed to have equipped them to tackle the lighter aspects of home improvement. They could paint, hang wallpaper, change plugs. Husbands were pleased to accept lines of domestic demarcation and the feminisation of the domestic interior was assured.

Towards the end of the 1950s and now with a regular evening television programme and an audience of seven million (there were only two channels), Bucknell became a celebrated advocate of DIY and DIY became a virtuous pastime. Bucknell's demonstrations were primarily about refurbishing old houses and his preferred strategy was to remove mouldings, in the name of hygiene and easy maintenance. Crumbling cornices and old fireplaces, which collected dirt and were difficult to repair, were removed. Door mouldings were hidden behind sheets of hardboard, the rudimentary, easy to paint sheet material, the forerunner of MDF which would take the same role 50 years later. The Contemporary style's energetic fabric patterns offered a substitute for decorative mouldings.

Television technology of the time meant that Bucknell had to demonstrate his techniques and proposals in real time. There were rehearsals but no second takes and inevitably things went wrong 'live'. He was unsympathetically nicknamed 'Bodger' Bucknell, primarily by men who wished to imply that they knew better and were too shrewd to attempt home improvements themselves.

The Second World War and its aftermath were being forgotten; prosperity was allowing households to find their identity. Bill Taylor had completed the first three years of an architecture course before joining the Royal Air Force as a navigator in 1942 and met Daphne Atkins, who worked at Bletchley Park. On being demobbed and reluctant to return to being a student he joined Esavian as publicity officer. He and Daphne married in 1947 and, after working their way up the property ladder, were able to afford a four bedroom house in Potters Bar. Their daughter Lindsay, remembered how it looked to her seven-year-old self and her ten-year-old sister and how modernity caused them more pain than pleasure: *The hall and dining room had Heuga dark brown felt tiles, which had been salvaged from an Esavian exhibition stand – very scratchy. Father thought they were a marvellous invention as they could be so easily laid, mother was not so keen as they were very difficult to 'hoover'. Esavian had offices off Tottenham*

Court Road, near to Heals, where father would have spotted Lucienne Day's 'Calyx' fabric, in the mustard yellow colour-way for the hall curtains and Barbara Brown's 'Sweet Briar', the brown and purple colour-way, for the dining room. The dining room furniture was oak and had been a wedding present from the boss at Esavian and also came from Heals. There were two Russell Flint prints which were thought rather racy.

The living room had an Eames revolving chair, with footstool, which had been a prototype made by Esavian but never taken up under license so my father had acquired it for himself. My sister and I considered it extremely ugly and christened it 'the horrendous chair'. There was a coffee table with a map under glass, which my father may have added and which was considered rather clever and a talking point for visitors. Above the fireplace was a framed tableau containing father's old violin and some spray-painted plastic flowers (can't remember what else – a book perhaps) which he had made and my sister and I thought downright embarrassing. There was also a large mahogany sideboard, which was a cast off from a wealthy friend and a Dansette record player, red and grey. The main bedroom had a navy blue ceiling and long navy blue velvet curtains. There was a 'feature' wall of wallpaper with a pattern of large scale meandering sweet peas, very beautifully painted on a white ground (Heals too perhaps) which made a strong contrast to the otherwise dark room and was thought very daring. The provenance of the house is interesting. Bill Taylor had found himself an interesting job, closely involved with Jim Leonard Esavian's principal designer, but abandoning his architectural ambitions left him frustrated and prompted his hands-on contributions, however witheringly reviewed by his daughters, to the house's decoration. The fortuitous proximity of his office to Heals, then the most progressive furniture shop, made the sourcing and choosing of fashionable fabrics easier. Daphne journeyed in from Potters Bar when necessary to adjudicate selection. Childish disapproval of the Eames chair was predictable. No child likes to think that their parents' taste, however progressive, is out of step with that of the friends' parents. Both girls inherited their parents' progressive instincts

Right
The Taylors's oak sideboard from Heals. It retains some of the robust simplicity that characterised wartime Utility furniture.

TASTE

and went on to disconcert their own children. Environment matters: the younger daughter became a textile designer.

Enthusiasm for Contemporary styling was a grassroots movement. Its elements were radical but undeniably entertaining and unacceptable to faithful Modernists who took a further step towards alienating their captive public by discovering an insatiable appetite for lumpish concrete. The style was dubbed New Brutalism, which unintentionally explained the nature of its imposition on a baffled public on whose behalf planners swept aside Victorian brick buildings to make way for multi-storey car parks which seemed to be New Brutalism's most frequent vehicles of expression. The style had its own motifs: the marks of the rough timber moulds into which the concrete had been poured, the mechanically battered surfaces designed to give texture and precipitate decrepitude. None of this decoration, which architects could claim to be 'honest', was pretty to untutored eyes. It wallowed in its lack of delicacy, macho posturing by men wearing bow ties.

It did not have to be concrete. The Barbican residential towers in London, a late example of the style, were elegantly designed, beautifully built and connected with brick paved walkways through landscaped gardens. The battered concrete was sparingly used and complemented by deep red bricks. When the original tenants were able to sell their leases the flats were snapped up as pieds-à-terre by bankers from the neighbouring financial district.

Alison and Peter Smithson were early Brutalists, admired by their peers for a school they completed in 1954 on the Norfolk coast and which, with its metal cladding panels and picturesque plumbing, was ill-equipped to deal with the winds blowing in from the Russian steppes. The designers explained that their intention was to find a relationship between 'culture, industry and society'. Architects were thrilled; society was not.

Their later housing scheme, Robin Hood Gardens in East London, for which they coined the poetic image of 'streets in the sky' to describe its deck access, had no brickwork to relieve its concrete. Its landscaping was rudimentary and it became a model for tenant dissatisfaction and criminal activity. It attracted no bankers and was demolished in 2017 despite emotional protests from architects who remembered it in its uncompromising

Top left
A living room in an outer London suburb. Patterns are strong and colourful. The coffee table shows tapering splayed legs typical of the period, and the seating units are an early sighting of the genre. Hendon, London, 1950.

Top right
An inner city two-storey 'maisonette' within a purpose-built block. The timber-framed screen to the kitchen, the wood block floor and the metal balustrade to the cantilevered stair are typical of the more ambitious public sector housing. The rug and the rubber plant are typical of the more ambitious tenants. Finsbury, London, 1957.

pomp. Comparison between it and the Barbican would explain perhaps how social housing might be made to work best. For all its size, the Barbican has intimacy.

The serious Smithsons, perhaps surprisingly, agreed to design a *House of the Future* for the 1956 *Daily Mail* Ideal Home Exhibition, and a full scale mock-up was shown in London and Edinburgh. It was intended for a childless couple 25 years into the future. Its prefabricated plastic partitions were extravagantly curved and there were no windows in exterior walls; rooms looked into an inner courtyard. Entry was by a blob-shaped, electronically controlled entry door, a table and a bed rose from the floor when electronically summoned. It was already a cliché and could have been

Top
Barbican Brutalism is softened by brick paving and human-scaled spaces between monumental machine-textured columns. There is a recognisable structural logic. London, 1982.

Left
Robin Hood Gardens could seem forbidding. The texturing of the surfaces seems arbitrary here. Tower Hamlets, London, 1972.

TASTE

Top
The Smithsons's House of the Future: The hexagon in the middle of the living area floor is the table top, which rises when summoned by pressing a button. London, 1956.

Above left
The Smithsons's House of the Future: Looking towards the internal garden. London, 1956.

Above right
A room setting for *Woman's Own* magazine gives an art-directed synopsis of late Contemporary style: the feature fireplace, the coffee table, the fabrics for curtains and upholstery, the increasingly ubiquitous television set. London, 1959.

scribbled by a schoolboy in the margin of his jotter, more inspired by images in science fiction comic books than by a credible attempt to speculate about the world in 1981. Such speculation always will be futile and embarrassing. Predictably, predictions 50 years into the future are always wide of the mark.

Morphosis

Britain continued to be a well-defined society, a place for everyone, everyone in their place and enough satisfied citizens to prevent any dangerous groundswell of popular dissent. Until the 1950s, the young were happy to transmogrify into their parents but sustained absorption of American images and sounds brought about the sudden and unexpected arrival of the teenager with its disconcerting codes of dress and behaviour. It was primarily a working-class phenomenon: middle-class children expected a comfortable future like their parents and tended to dress in anticipation of it. The emergence of feral teenagers had something to do with their having more money and not having to work as hard for it as earlier generations. They could no longer leave school at 14 as many of those destined to be manual workers had done. They were isolated from the adult world a little longer, and could concentrate on evolving rituals of their own for a crucial two more years.

Imaginary America, or imaginary white America, had little to be unhappy about. Popular culture was dispensed by corporations and customer-driven. There was no reason, other than youth's capacity for complaining about its lot, for the young to be dissatisfied. It was quite the opposite in Britain. If American teenagers could while away their time in drugstores and soda fountains, drive-in cinemas and drive-thru fast food franchises their British equivalents made do with greasy spoon cafes and fleapit cinemas. They did not have convertibles. The mechanically minded bought motorbikes which they rode too fast on arterial roads. Their death rates were romantically exaggerated. Others expressed their otherness by dressing outlandishly and a willingness to indulge in violence, dubbed Teddy Boys and Teddy Girls. The name came from the males' supposed resemblance to Edwardian dandies, but the look was more probably inspired by the long jackets of 'zoot' suits of black American musicians in the 1940s, to which they added narrow trousers and thick crepe soled shoes. Girls borrowed toreador pants, voluminous, many-petticoated skirts and wore their hair in ponytails. Male fashion was particularly bizarre when judged against the prevailing adult male's grey suit, white shirt and tie. Robert Elms, the authoritative voice on teenage fashion, holds that for any youth cult clothes come before the music and when rock and roll arrived from America in 1956 Teds found their background music and a pretext for destroying auditoria and dance halls. They were studiedly discontented, too sullen to explain themselves, rebels without a cause.[11]

They wanted something that post-war Britain did not offer and as the British economy steadied itself in the 1950s they had, for the first time, a degree of financial independence. They lived, like their American role models, with their parents but their homes lacked the extravagances displayed in films and on television. Interior decoration was left to their 'square' mums but they were the first young plebeians able to afford to express sartorial independence and concern for personal appearance that would, for some, transmute into concern for their interiors once they left the family home. The Contemporary's similarity to American Mid-Century Modern aligned very well with their tastes in clothes and music.

Middle-class youth tended to abide by the social and dress codes of its parents. The few grammar school boys and girls who aped Teddy dress were destined to end up in art schools rather than universities. A few others dressed with studied scruffiness and preferred jazz to rock and roll and chose to congregate in the coffee bars that first appeared in 1953 in London's shady Soho and then in cities and sizeable towns across the country. Coffee bars distinguished themselves with interior design of varying degrees of sophistication. The novelist and early television personality, Marghanita Laski, said of them that it was 'nice to have somewhere nice … somewhere outside the home that isn't hell to look at'.[12] The coffee was rudimentary but the idea of a non-brutish, non-British lifestyle that flirted with Continental sophistication, made tangible by hissing Gaggia espresso machines, was seductive. Coffee bars were modernistic but not Modern. Their full-blooded interiors suggested to their customers that there was no reason why they should live like their parents. Laski described typical coffee bar elements that could have easily been found in a Contemporary home: 'Vertical wooden slats … fleshy green plants, taper-leg wicker-seated backless stools, strings of garlic, periodicals on bamboo racks, thick glass coffee cups on the bare inorganic table tops …'.[13]

In 1954 Alan Ross, professor of linguistics at the University of Birmingham, published a paper on the difference between British upper class vocabulary, which he called 'U', and middle, which he called 'non-U'. Matters of class always command attention in Britain and a former Bright Young Thing, Nancy Mitford, promptly incorporated the professor's conclusions into a magazine article on the British aristocracy.[14] Tearoom habitués were disconcerted and Mitford received letters seeking advice from those terrified that they might be 'common'. So hot was the topic that in 1956, her essay, augmented by contributions from fellow former Bright Young Things Evelyn Waugh and John Betjeman – together with a more accessible version of Ross's paper – was published as *Noblesse Oblige*. It was, supposedly, all a bit of a joke but the middle classes knew the joke was at their expense. They had presumed to think that, apart from aristocrats' enormous landholdings and unearned income, they as decent middles were more or less indistinguishable from gentry and were disconcerted to find that, even if they mastered the look and the accent, their vocabulary would betray them. Mitford offered a glossary of 'U' words and their 'non-U' equivalents. Non-U words for furniture created doubts about interior decoration. Drawing room was U,

Below
Piazza conformed to the image of the progressive coffee bar with its plastic counter front and patterned floor, the undulating ceiling and the coffee making machine: very Italian. Marylebone, London, 1955.

lounge was decidedly not, sofa was U, settee was not, looking-glass was U, mirror was not, chimneypiece was U, mantelpiece was not. Those who got the words wrong feared that they might also be wrong on matters of visual taste. Did a settee look different from a sofa? Unfortunately it did, for settee owners were the sort of people who bought their own furniture. It was galling when Ross also pointed out that, while the middle class tended to adopt neologisms and euphemisms to sound refined, aristocrats favoured good old-fashioned words which they shared with the working class. This depressed the middle class even further.

Mitford and her fellow contributors (perhaps apart from Waugh) inevitably claimed not to be snobs, but they were unavoidably patrician. Betjeman's contribution to the book, *How To Get On In Society*, was a poem satirically packed with non-U-isms. The genteel butts of his doggerel where those who enjoyed his work but had failed to recognise that they were his targets. In matters of taste, when the middle class take on the upper class, they can only lose.

Taste trends tended to begin in London but the provinces liked to think that they had their own quirkily independent take on national values so that, in 1957 when the sociologist Richard Hoggart published *The Uses of Literacy*,[15] an accessible academic text widely read beyond academia, provincials were emboldened. Hoggart regretted the retreat of British popular/working-class culture in the face of its imported American equivalent. He eulogised the unadulterated native strain that survived beyond the metropolis. There followed a vogue for working-class novelists and gritty films of working-class life with working-class actors with working-class accents. Hoggart and the other proletarian heroes of the sort, including the Smithsons, were almost exclusively from the industrial 'North'. Suddenly, their backgrounds brought them kudos and they decided to be unashamed of their working-class idiosyncrasies and relished airing their unfamiliar vowel sounds. But with material success came ambitions to settle in more auspicious environments, inevitably somewhere in London and particularly in the comfortable bohemian enclave of NW1. There they could hope to rub shoulders with established northern overachievers whose cosmopolitan success encouraged the pluckier younger provincials, talented or not, to join the southern drift. Those who stayed behind resented the émigrés.

In 1959 the satirical review *Beyond the Fringe* lampooned politicians, clergymen and all the pillars and presumptions of the establishment. The theatre critic Michael Billington said the review had a greater and longer lasting impact than the 'kitchen-sink' dramas by the 'angry young men' who were, grumpily, attacking poor old middle-class values. It set the tone, he said, for 'an era of snook-cocking disrespect'.[16] The educational reforms of 1944 were bearing fruit. Two of the four creators of *Beyond the Fringe* were working-class boys who found their way, via grammar schools, to Oxford University. Alan Bennett, came south from Leeds, and Dudley Moore came north from the uncouth London suburb of Croydon. The other two were considerably posher.

As the supposedly dully conformist 1950s approached their end rumblings of dissent and social change were clearly audible. The ground had been prepared for the startling changes that would blossom in the following decade.

Opposite
Mocamba was differently exotic: its wicker stools referred to coffee growing rather than coffee drinking, but the Gaggia machine still had pride of place. Knightsbridge, London, 1955.

CHAPTER 7

The Empire Strikes Back

'England swings like
a pendulum do ...'

Roger Miller[1]

Convention requires that the 1960s be described as 'swinging'. Oscillation began in Britain and with it leadership in popular culture was wrenched back for a time from the United States.

The shifts in social mores that have come to epitomise the 1960s were, in the first instance, a British phenomenon, an effete blossoming of the heavy lifting that had been done in the 1950s when times were tougher and barriers higher. Mary Quant, who opened her first shop, *Bazaar*, in 1955 confirmed that: 'the whole 1960s thing was a ten-year running party, which was lovely. It started at the end of the 1950s …'[2]

The poet Philip Larkin was equally accurate when, in 1967 he reminisced in *Annus Mirabilis*:

So life was never better than
In nineteen sixty three
(Though just too late for me)
Between the end of the Chatterley ban
And the Beatles' first LP.[3]

The 1960s did see the erosion of accepted social parameters and a flowering of debauchery. The lifting of a ban in 1960 on D. H. Lawrence's sexually explicit novel *Lady Chatterley's Lover* confirmed that state control over private lives and public morality was slackening. The ending, in 1963, of National Service, an extension of wartime conscription that required all males aged between 17 and 21 to spend 18 months in the armed forces, confirmed a softening of the state's inclination to interfere with the affairs of its citizens. Young men were suddenly free to grow their hair as long as they wanted.

Society at large was strangely supine in accommodating the upheaval and content to be labelled 'permissive'. There was a frisson of moral laxity in the air and an implication that everyone really ought to be more promiscuous, if they could possibly manage it.

The Beatles were a strange phenomenon. Their music, and prankish humour, appealed to teenagers but also, unaccountably, to adults. They were cheeky chappies but serious musicians and critics seriously performed and analysed their music. It could be seen as a low point for high culture. The Beatles are acclaimed but the conceptualist Jeffrey Deller argues that it is their manager, Brian Epstein, who deserves credit for changing the known world. Epstein plotted the strategies, from wardrobe to wit, that shaped their success and that of the other performers, many of whom he managed, who followed in their wake. He seemed to understand how to embellish a promising core product and make it irresistible. For a few years Britain became the dominant force in popular culture but the USA continued to be content with its lot, unconcerned about who or what was entertaining it as long as it was entertained.

The country that had, ten years before, been stolidly staid was suddenly desperate for frivolity. Pop music was ubiquitous. The BBC lost its broadcasting monopoly as 'pirate' radio ships broadcasting from just outside territorial waters in the North and Irish seas spewed out pop 24 hours a day. The localised values of working-class culture eulogised by Richard

Hoggart were swept away. Successful pop groups deserted their places of origin for the more substantial pleasures of London.

Provincials who stayed put had comprehensive weekly briefings about metropolitan trends when, in 1962, the *Sunday Times* launched its colour supplement magazine. Other weekend papers, broadsheet and tabloid followed and increasingly they featured home decoration. These magazines were crucial sources of advertising income for the papers and of mail order offers for aspirational readers. The science of mail order was rudimentary but progressives living in remote wastelands could ease the pain of wanting with small items; a bright orange plastic storage unit or a small matt black and chrome desk lamp and such details could, by their sheer incongruous modernity, connect a provincial bedsitter to swinging London.

Clothes were as important as music, and little shops, nominally upgraded to 'boutiques', opened in even the shabbiest cities. The clothes were often shoddily made but since fashions changed precipitously that did not matter. Boutiques' interiors made token gestures to being trendy but, because they were small and packed with clothes, the decor was seldom visible let alone inspirational. It was a token gesture but shoppers had begun to suspect that trendy lifestyles deserved to be conducted in trendy interiors.

Good and getting better

In 1957 the prime minister Harold Macmillan had told the country that 'most of our people have never had it so good', which for the population at large was mainly true. He also promised that 'you will see a state of prosperity such as we have never had in my lifetime – nor indeed in the history of this country' and that was also true. It became a rite of passage for young married couples to buy houses in poor repair and to dedicate years to titivating them, with occasional help from tradesmen, before selling and moving on to bigger, better located properties and to begin reclamation and refurbishment again. House prices were kept low because, to claim a mortgage, couples had to be married and because borrowing was restricted to two and a half times their combined salaries with only half the lower salary included in the calculation. Mortgages were awarded by building societies who operated as a cautious cartel.

Many potential householders wanted to avoid the suburbs where they had grown up; urban Victorian brick terraces, however small, became more glamorous. Enthusiasm for eliminating period detail was waning and the rich mix of the Contemporary style was beginning to cloy and was too reminiscent of suburbia. Fledgling homeowners were beginning to think that modernity a was no substitute for traditional decoration and began to look for houses that had their mouldings intact and to hunt in scrapyards for discarded cast iron fireplaces, panelled wooden doors and Victorian sanitary wares. Period detail suggested period furniture and for the pioneers of eclecticism pieces were cheap; until dealers realised they had a finite supply and an increasingly less finite customer base. Enough time had passed for Victorian and Edwardian furniture and fittings to look stylish

Above
A flat retains some elements of the previous decade: Tapering wooden legs on the table in the dining recess and the three armchairs. Blackheath, London, 1962.

Opposite
A living room three years later: The furniture becomes bulkier and more generously padded, the paper lampshade, perhaps from Habitat, appears. Weybridge, Surrey, 1965.

again and what had been bought to consolidate a respectable place in society now had the weight, the crafting and the materiality to take the place of polychromatic plastics and to signal radical rather than respectable. It was the new modern.

So heavy, dark, distinctly wooden period furniture began to replace bent plywood and laminates. The furniture, the enormous sideboards, the over-stuffed Chesterfields and wooden-legged, leather-upholstered, sternly upright armchairs became focal points in rooms that did not attempt to match the clutter favoured by Victorians. The *zeitgeist* demanded that occupants no longer sat upright but sprawled, and to stretch out one needed legroom.

In the reaction against Contemporary, colours and patterns were played *sotto voce* and walls and ceilings were painted bright white. Cornices and skirtings that had survived the Bucknellian onslaught were treasured and correct taste required that they too be painted white. Those who failed to resist the temptation to pick out their details in colours failed to understand properly the rules. Carpets were abandoned in favour of bare wooden floor-boards, which, although occasionally painted, were normally sanded smooth and varnished to accentuate their grain. Threadbare rugs were permitted.

Since the advent of Modernism, householders with pretentions to being progressive would embrace, as best they could, modernistic offerings. Yet suddenly it seemed that the most progressive people in the most progressive city had decided to become regressive. They appeared to have found the confidence to ignore the cajoling from advocates of modernity.

Swinging London was quite sure that it was utterly modern, but it had eclectic taste across all fronts. Young men of fashion snapped up scarlet, intricately buttoned and braided military tunics, which were also just long enough to serve as mini frocks for the more adventurous 'dolly birds'. Sales of vintage dress uniforms began on a street stall and grew into the boutique chain *I Was Lord Kitchener's Valet* and the more flamboyant the uniform the better it was deemed. Taste, like a First World War infantryman, went over the top.

British youth, amusingly outfitted and guilelessly contrary, indulged itself. Its elders were not sure that they liked developments but contented themselves with making jokes about the length of boys' hair and the brevity of girls' skirts. A few curmudgeons were less sanguine. In his book, *The Neophiliacs*, the comparatively aged 32-year-old Christopher Brooker diagnosed a national psychosis.[4] Paul Johnson complained in the *New Statesman* about the 'bovine' conformity of Beatles fans while hitherto serious music critics analysed Beatles tunes with the solemnity they brought to the classical repertoire.[5]

Some thought it a sardonic comment on Britain's militaristic past, perhaps an acknowledgement that those days were over and the country's present and future were Ruritanian. The Union flag become a primary source of graphic iconography and while its use may have been ironic and a little churlish it was a potent rallying device for fashionable lemmings. The annexation of national heritage upset the crustiest amongst the old but was generally presumed to be evidence that healthy British iconoclasm was alive. The middle-aged were determined not to miss out on the new spirit and be thought square. They may have been making up for their own youth circumscribed by the war and the years of rationing. Men's hair crept over collars and women's skirts rose ill-advisedly high, conductors of symphony orchestras sported colourful cummerbunds and swapped polo-necked jumpers for bow ties.

While most people were preoccupied by the hit parade, in 1968 Ronan Point, a 22-storey block partly collapsed only two months after its completion, killing four people. The structural failure was the result of an innovative concrete prefabrication system, used to speed the supply of public housing. Its disintegration did not stop the building of residential towers and they continued to fall short of popular aesthetic aspirations nor could they any longer claim to be as safe as houses.

While Britain obsessed about its past the United States was committing to the future. Russian men, a woman and a dog were orbiting the Earth and in 1961 the President was forced to announce an American intention to put a man on the Moon by the end of the decade, which they just managed to achieve in 1969.

While Britons obsessed about pop singers Americans had astronauts for heroes. They were short-haired, married men in their thirties who drove enormous finned American cars to work through the suburbs of Houston. Their glamour helped keep alive the American ideal of the ranch style tract home, single storeyed and open planned. The bohemians and the beatniks, in New York's Greenwich Village, may have preserved fantasies of an alternative lifestyle but they had been replaced in the public awareness by the astronauts who demonstrated that the suburb was the home of the brave in the land of the free.

In 1964 the Beatles flew to the USA and seduced its teenagers (and a sizeable proportion of their parents). They established Britain's pop hegemony in the USA and after 1964, in a late flowering of colonisation, groups of raw white British youths from the industrial cities of the north appropriated the unexploited reserves of black American musicians, processed it, and shipped it back to the USA. Black performers were grateful for royalties but resentful that the accolades were not theirs. London-based record companies rushed north to sign up performers.

Every provincial town and city seemed capable of producing at least one 'beat group', capable of making approximate replications of black American music and consequently their home towns seemed less drab. American performers began to disappear from the hit parade. If British teenagers were less interested in American music the country itself continued to give every appearance of being a utopia for teenagers driving to school in baroque convertibles and hanging out in drugstores. Even the British pop singers who found themselves hysterically adulated in the United States expressed their excitement at experiencing its realities at first hand. Mythic America remained desirable. Chuck Berry might have been black, but wrote and performed songs that celebrated the American Way. Two lines he wrote in 1964: *'Cruisin' and playin' the radio/ With no particular place to go'* summed up the enviably languorous lifestyles of white American teenagers. Nuclear war with the USSR loomed as a possibility, but even the nuclear cloud had a silver lining: defence spending was high and in the Cold War, as much as in the hot war, the economy boomed.

For the slim majority of socially progressive American citizens, the election in 1961 of the photogenic President Kennedy suggested the dawn of a more progressive and elegant society. He and his wife Jacqueline were considered to be preternaturally glamorous and their entourage of show business cronies so dazzling that it was compared, favourably, with the court of Camelot which was being celebrated in the eponymous Broadway musical at the time.

Richard Nixon had opposed Kennedy in the 1960 presidential elections but failed to meet the standard of pulchritude set by the photogenic Kennedy. In policy debates between the two candidates broadcast simultaneously on television and radio, Kennedy won the viewers' approval and Nixon won that of the radio audience. Kennedy won the election by 0.2%. However peripheral, matters of visual taste can have serious consequences.

The young and the optimistic, across the world, were infatuated with 44-year-old Kennedy and, in 1962, he consolidated that admiration by negotiating the removal of Russian nuclear missiles from Cuba, 300 miles from the coast of Florida. A possible nuclear fracas had offered a plausible existential threat to the world and terrified the young. The crisis lasted 13 days and the relief that followed its peaceful resolution may have contributed to the hedonistic impulses that blossomed in 1963. No one wanted to waste their time being serious.

Mrs Kennedy, possibly as a distraction from her husband's quotidian adulteries, undertook to redecorate the White House. Her intention was to rescue it from the running repairs carried out by the wives of recent presidents, who lacked her much-publicised social credentials and the taste that was presumed to go with them. She undertook to restore it to an appropriate level of grandeur, perhaps finding inspiration in a couplet from the musical: '*In short, there's simply not a more congenial spot. For happily ever after in than here in Camelot.*'

She recruited the doyen of American decorators, Dorothy Mae 'Sister' Parrish, to help with some of the bedrooms, Henry Dupont, a collector of Americana, to source appropriate artefacts and the Parisian designer Stephane Boudin to 'add more vigour and sophistication'. The end result has been described as French Provincial, a style inspired, it is said, by the romantic, slightly shabby 17th- and 18th-century châteaux of Provence, which had in their turn been inspired by Louis XIV's Versailles. The improvements tended, appropriately, towards the court rather than the country. Colours were lightly earthy, creams and off-whites, greys and muted blues and greens. Early in 1962, in a very deferential television programme, supposedly aimed at female viewers, Mrs Kennedy, to critical acclaim, conducted a tour of refurbished parts of the building and explained her vision. The refurbishments were appropriate and improvement was clear, but there were no frissons of modernity.

They'd never have it so good

Opposite
The first Habitat shop, on the Fulham Road: A mix of modern with the coffee table and the spotlights; the exotic, the bamboo and woven furniture; and the nostalgic, the chesterfield sofa. London, 1964.

Born in 1931, Terence Conran had been a precocious contributor to the Festival of Britain. His modest little stand for a pot plant had been included amongst the images on Enid Sheehy's *Homemaker* plate, which had been decorated by a smattering of the festival's chicest artefacts. He had studied design at the Central School of Art in London and was an instinctive entrepreneur. He began by designing and manufacturing Summa, a range of flat-pack furniture. Only a couple of upmarket shops, cautiously committed to modernistic design, were interested and unfortunately their customers were not the type to assemble their own furniture. He also opened *Soup Kitchen*, a sort of restaurant where he sold soup by the mug, bread by the hunk and exotic (for London at that time) French cheeses in a white-tiled room dominated by the hissing of the second Gaggia coffee machine ever to arrive in Britain. It anticipated the virtuously simple peasant aesthetic that was to shape his next more ambitious venture.

In 1964 he opened his first Habitat shop in Chelsea, London's wealthy and most artistically inclined quarter. It was a short walk from Zeev Aram's shop, which also opened in 1964 on the increasingly fashionable King's Road, just opposite Mary Quant's first boutique. Aram, a Romanian who had come to London via Palestine and studied furniture and interior design at the Central School had begun to promote the idea of 'Modern Classics', principally tubular framed furniture, nominally by Le Corbusier, Mies van der Rohe and Marcel Breuer. If Aram's stock excited and informed enthusiasts for modernity his prices put it beyond the reach of most of them. Thanks to Conran's initiative frustrated salary men and women who might scrimp to afford a Mies chair or a Corbusian chaise longue could turn to Habitat and there they could afford to furnish a whole house. They found the modern furniture and artefacts to which they aspired and they saw other exotica, like the terracotta 'chicken bricks' in which to roast fowls, that they had not known existed or

realised that they needed them so very badly. They craved the lifestyle implied by the merchandise but were not exactly sure what it was they craved. Many were troubled by a false memory of a foreign idyll. Currency restrictions made travel abroad difficult but books by Elizabeth David and other bohemian wanderers increased longings for the Mediterranean littoral. Britons longed for France, Italy and Greece. Spain was politically too far to the right for the caring liberals who shopped at Habitat. Greece would become problematic when it succumbed to a military junta in 1967.

Conran was susceptible to the lifestyle and accoutrements of wise old peasants and correctly presumed that his fellow citizens would share the weakness. The Contemporary style had provided an antidote to rationing but that rich dish, delicious at first, had cloyed. Habitat seemed to demonstrate and provide the ingredients for a healthier aesthetic lifestyle. Nothing in the shop was too Modernist because everything chimed with a vision of a bucolic Mediterranean.

The Habitat shop floor was laid out to suggest how pieces might work together. Potential customers who lived too far away for a first-hand experience could pore over the annual mail order catalogue, a primer for the lifestyle. It was glossy and thick, with full-page photographs of room settings with models demographically appropriate to the furniture and actively engaged with it, exuding excitement and satisfaction. There were a few representatives of ethnic minorities but the old, the fat and the ugly were excluded. They belonged in bungalows.

Habitat customers wanted, above all, to live in a Victorian terraced house. They might declare an enthusiasm for things that were disconcertingly modern, but they wanted high ceilings, plaster mouldings and marble fireplaces in every public room and cast iron ones in every bedroom. They 'knocked through', demolishing most of the wall that divided the former ground floor sitting room at the front from the former dining room at the rear, to accommodate a modern family life in which formalities and generational demarcations were ignored. The perfect house had a semi-basement to house a fitted kitchen that segued into a dining area which doubled as a play room until children grew and retreated to sulk in their bedrooms. The terraces built by 19th-century speculators adapted well. If a Victorian terraced house was unaffordable a suburban detached would do and more modest Habitat pieces could sit comfortably in it.

The fruits of foraging in Habitat were best displayed within white-painted walls, one of which, with plaster chipped off to reveal brickwork, often painted white, might perform as a 'feature' wall, although such blatant texture might have better belonged in the 1950s. Stripped wooden floors were desirable on upper levels with red quarry tiles in the basement. Extant cornices and ceiling roses mouldings were prized. Ceiling mounted spotlights washed walls and highlighted the artisanal artefacts essential to consolidate the vision. Not everything had to be Habitat. The introduction of alien objects was condoned. Such trophies, obsolete and quaint, were used to dress sets for catalogue photographs and were particularly prized if they had formerly belonged to a French peasant. They could be artfully arranged on the shelving that was a Habitat staple. Shelving was always adjustable. Habitat customers were continually fine-tuning. Bulky Victorian heavy wooden furniture, preferably black but dark brown was acceptable, could be included and it could be big.

Above
Habitat's large warehouse and showroom at the centre of an area of prosperous towns and villages, none big enough to justify their own shop. The curved corners and corrugated cladding were very fashionable. Wallingford, Oxfordshire, 1974.

Left
The out-of-town showroom with room sets and exposed roof structure and ductwork: Fashionably high-tech.

It demonstrated that one could think outside the Habitat box and had been clever in a second-hand shop. A salvaged chesterfield sofa with buttoned upholstery was particularly desirable, so much so that Habitat produced its own version, excusing its retrograde styling with flamboyant textile patterns.

In pursuit of its vision of a fusion of the modernistic and the rustic Habitat sold Vico Magistretti's Carimate chair, with its woven straw seat and heavy, bright red wooden frame and Thonet bentwood chairs with woven seats, which Le Corbusier had declared to be an *objet-type*, an archetypical product, so rationally evolved that it perfectly, and elegantly, fulfilled its function. It sold heavy iron kitchen equipment, batteries of kitchen knives and tall, thin, clear glass cylinders for conspicuous storage of spaghetti, one of the few pasta varieties then known to Britons. It sold heavy cotton, blue and white striped butchers' aprons that men could wear with manly confidence. Cooking no longer respected gender. There were things that were comparatively expensive and things that were surprisingly cheap, like the flat-packed, wire-framed paper lampshades that opened up into huge spheres and declared to all that a room had been Habitat-ed. People were proud to have taken their first steps into the modern world and enjoyed having passers-by look into their lit un-curtained living rooms. Hunter Davies, a journalist, the authorised biographer of the Beatles and a quintessential 1960s man, wrote 'We keep our curtains and shutters open in our street, all the better for others to enjoy our tasteful middle-class décor'.[6]

Throughout the 1960s, 1970s and 1980s Habitats opened across Britain, one in every city and sizeable town that had a decent sized middle-class population. In 1978 it opened in New York, where it was renamed Conran but was never so successful, perhaps not American enough or, perhaps not British enough. After 50 years the chain lost its hold on the middle class. It could not compete with increasing competition, from online retailers and, most destructively, from Ikea. When all but three London stores had closed in 2011 journalist Yvonne Roberts expressed regret and described how 'in the 1960s, the shop had offered to those who had grown up amongst their parents dark brown furniture in gloomy interiors, the model for, and the means to create, a bright and light future'.[7]

Stephen Bayley – director of the Design Museum Conran founded and financed in the 1980s – said in 1977 before becoming a disenchanted former employee, that Conran had done more for 'what used to be called "good design" than any of the educators who have laboured in the public interest in acts of persuasion on behalf of manufactured reality'.[8] 'Good design', rather like 'good taste', is a contentious idea and best kept in inverted commas.

An outlier

If Conran catered for something approaching a mass market there was another 1960s designer who experimented outrageously, using a succession of his own homes as his laboratory. Max Clendinning grew up in rural Northern Ireland, keen on drawing and with a particular eye for colour and materials. He remembered how, when a child, he found that he felt fonder of an aunt when she wore a dress whose colour particularly pleased him.

In rural Ireland the role of interior designer was generally unknown and he trained as an architect, informally in Belfast where he worked on the local Festival of Britain exhibition and more formally in London. When as an adventurous apprentice in the late 1940s he visited Paris, he was surprised when owners of houses designed by Le Corbusier invited him in to look around. He had not yet appreciated the pleasures an owner might take in flaunting their perch on the cutting edge. He was to attract the same kind of clients, eager to own something extraordinary, when he became recognised as the generator of radical interior design.

While he was a salaried architect, without the autonomy of his own practice he exorcised his frustrations in the flats and houses in which he lived. His first small flat was in Belgravia, a rather expensive and exclusive area but, in the 1950s, good addresses in war-damaged London were accessible to a plucky provincial. Eaton Terrace was a short stroll from Chelsea and a promenade along the King's Road ensured regular bumpings into other progressive spirits. He claimed the flat, completed in 1954, to be 'no different' in spirit from his later work but in the 1960s there was something in the air that encouraged radical thinking.

Clendinning's family owned a furniture factory in Northern Ireland and it was his habit to bring back to London flat-pack pieces of his own design. The mechanics of flat-pack prompted him to develop interlocking plywood framing side and back components to contain and support cushions. The quadrant plywood corners, inspired by early computer fonts and the geometry of stacking coffee cups, were practical, capable of dealing with rough handling in transit. Diagrammatically simple forms and curved corners were very 1960s.

Below
Where it all began: Max Clendinning's flat in Eaton Terrace, London, 1954.

In the early 1960s Clendinning was project architect for Crawley Town Hall and, as public bodies were then less circumspect about spending money on their buildings, he also designed the furniture. The connections he made strolling on the King's Road paid off. He showed the furniture to a friend who had a friend who was a buyer for Liberty, early champions of Arts and Crafts furniture. Clendinning's plywood pieces were clearly not products of artisans' toil but they were distinctly progressive and attracted Saturday crowds and the attention of Race Furniture, a UK-based maker of handcrafted furniture. The company and Clendinning agreed that the plywood should be painted and the cushions upholstered in a bespoke tweed. The range was sold in the United States, revived the fortunes of Race and made Clendinning's

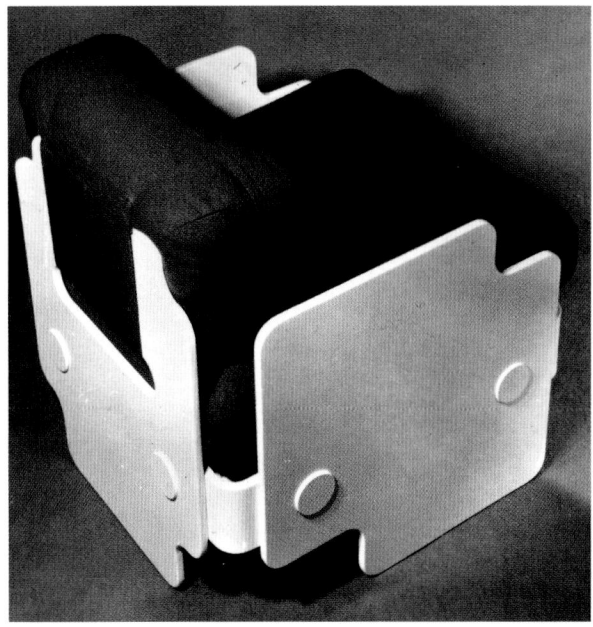

Top
A typical example of Clendinning's flat-pack, 1966. The cushions had a foam core, the sides and back were painted plywood and the discs cover fixings.

Bottom
The 'Maxima' range: Experience showed that plywood panels could be dramatically cut away. Curved corner and feet remained constant. Alwyne Road, Islington, London, 1965.

reputation. From this he was commissioned to design seven shops in Covent Garden's fashionable Neal Street. Their fat plywood window frames had quadrant corners borrowed from his furniture. He then designed a number of domestic interiors for one of the founders of the G-plan furniture company which had produced the splayed legged tables and chairs that had been all the rage in the 1950s and still have admirers.

Clendinning steadily attracted commissions for domestic interiors but his most interesting work was, inevitably, in the carte blanche of his own homes. He left the Belgravia flat for a terraced house in newly chic Islington. He began with a white room. Like Wharton's and Maughan's it was not entirely white, but his variations were more tonal than pigmental. White painted plywood with almost white upholstery sat on off-white painted floors between off-white painted walls and ceiling. But the emphatic divergence from others' earlier white rooms was the emptiness, the elimination of any furniture other than chairs and essential tables and since these were his creation, they did nothing to pull the room back towards convention. It was as close to Modernism as one could get in an early 19th-century terraced house but the sobriety of the living room, the emptiest room, was lightened by long fat and flat cushion/seating that lay on the floor like beached whales. In the 1960s sprawling was considerably more fashionable than sitting upright on a boring old chair. Any remaining suspicion of austerity was eliminated by a 3m high 'tulip' light by Ralph Adron. One could not take oneself too seriously in the 1960s.

In the dining room Clendinning began his serious move away from whiteness. Existing mouldings remained white but the walls are grey/green with sinuous painted strips, by Adron, that bend through quadrant corners and seem to disappear behind the original (now white) cornice before reappearing on the ceiling. He wanted to 'destroy the corner', a conceptual rather than literal, Modernist, assault on the compartmentalised plan. It was also a glimpse of the much more colourful decorative painting with which he transformed the same space in 1973.

The idea of the white room was pervasive. *The Knack ... and How To Get It* was a film in the swinging-London genre designed by Asheton Gorton and directed by Dick Lester in

Top left
Almost monochrome and almost white, plywood framed chairs have been replaced by saggy floor cushions. The irregularity of floorboards is eliminated by a grid of square off-white tiles. The tulip lamp lightens the mood. Alwyne Road, Islington, London, 1969.

Top right
Clendinning in his whitest creation. Foam plastic core replaces the plywood structure. Alwyne Road, Islington, London, 1967.

Above
Coloured variations and the beginning of the increasing use of colour. Alwyne Road, Islington, London, 1968.

1965, between his two Beatles films. It was a surreally whimsical look at the life of young men of diverse characters, each desperate to seduce a rather innocent and wholly indifferent girl. All shared a desirable brick terraced house, with walls, floors and ceilings painted blaring white throughout, and there was no furniture; it was a *tabula rasa* that dispensed with the colours of the 1950s and the physical clutter of every period that had gone before. It was indisputably modern but not strictly Modern since it relished the whitened period mouldings.

Opposite
Colour arrives in the dining room: The rounded corners of the coloured stripes match the quadrant corners of his plywood furniture frames, and were a persistent motif in 1960s graphic design. Alwyne Road, Islington, London, 1969.

Sour notes

It is here worth noting Sir Edward Elgar's criticism of English music in 1905: *An Englishman will take you into a large room, beautifully proportioned and will point out to you that it is white – all over white – and somebody will say 'What exquisite taste'. You will know in your own mind, in your own soul, that it is not taste at all, that it is want of taste, that it is mere evasion, English music is white and evades everything.*[9] This would seem to be an argument for detail in music but should perhaps be paired with the Emperor Franz Joseph's rebuke 'Too many notes Mozart'. Elgar's metaphor suggests that a white room offers a bland experience and no food for thought other than that it is very pleasant. Franz Joseph on the other hand might be presumed to say that a room overburdened with detail will be incoherent and likely to annoy, as did the first performance of Figaro, leading to angry frustration because one suspects there is merit in the design but no organising structure to make sense of it. Creatively discarding passages of which one is proud is painful.

If *The Knack* swept the interior clean, three years later, *2001: A Space Odyssey*, directed by Stanley Kubrick and designed by Oliver Morgue, visualised a future in which interiors were white tending towards grey, antiseptic, inhabited by serious people who had neither seduction or repelling seduction on their mind. It offered a familiar version of the future, which equated white with a placidity and aridity that seemed, at the time, to be an inevitable technological future. In the same year the much less portentous *Barbarella*, directed by Roger Vadim, proposed a libidinous future and portrayed a languid, pleasure-focused and untidy world and it proved to be closer to the truth, at least of the world of the hippies who appeared to believe that the secret of making the world a better place was to be self-indulgent.

Hippies were a countercultural movement that first flourished in San Francisco at the end of the 1960s and recaptured for America some territory in mainstream pop. It caught the imagination of the privileged young who, with youthful perversity, decided to complain about not having enough freedom to indulge late adolescent proclivities by purporting to reject established economic mechanisms. If British youth had been excited by Americans' conspicuous consumption they were equally ensnared by the hippies' rejection of conventional social mechanisms and money in particular since evidence appeared to suggest that hippies had found a way to circumvent boring old ways and means. And the hippie lifestyle retained the most appealing aspects of American teenage life: cars remained, but chrome and fins were out, and Volkswagen Beetles and old American pick-up trucks were in, particularly if they were painted in swirling Day-Glo pastels. The thought of riding in an overcrowded pick-up with one's legs dangling over the lowered tailboard became every bit as exciting as driving a finned convertible with an elbow resting on the window cill. Hippies talked, in a passive aggressive way, about peace and love. They were self-righteously self-congratulatory, purporting to have absorbed wisdom from Indian and Red Indian religions. They meditated, transcendentally. Some were sincere, some enjoyed abandoning dreary wage earning on principle and some lived by preying on the others. They abandoned Coca-Cola in favour of drugs, soft and hard. Those not supported by their parents declared property to be theft and 'liberated', or stole, what they needed. Women wore long dresses which allowed them to make extravagant shapes when dancing. Men wore headbands, tie-dyed T-shirts and bell-bottomed trousers. In large gatherings both genders seemed eager to take off their clothes.

They enjoyed mass gatherings, sometimes to listen to the music that grew up around the cult and sometimes to 'protest' against inconvenient social or legal restraints. Mass protests became fashionable. In 1968 French students rioted in Paris and brought something chic to the process. Their black and white posters were very elegant. When the USSR suppressed an uprising against Soviet rule by military means there were rallies in support of the Czechs across Western Europe but no intervention. Students across Britain felt they needed to participate and 'occupied', or entered and refused to leave, university administrative buildings until their hastily concocted demands were met. The most protracted occupation was in London's Hornsey School of Art, demanding greater say in the content of their curriculum. This spread particularly to the bland campuses of the newer 'plate glass' universities. Students in Belfast were a little late to join in but were unique within Britain in that they had a credible political cause supporting the disenfranchised local Catholic community. They precipitated sectarian violence and 3,500 people died.

Hippies were not homemakers. Property was theft and they preferred to squat in empty city buildings or, more primitively and more spiritually, in tepees. They specialised in passivity but when they did set about decorating they painted walls with swirling shapes and bright colours. They found furniture in skips and tips. They prized battered old sofas which were good for sprawling and covered torn upholstery with brightly coloured shawls and rugs. They seldom had access to electricity but candles were conducive to meditation. Where they had electricity the slowly distorting blobs of lava lamps were mesmeric and deserving of meditation. Patterned diaphanous scarfs draped over table lamps would cast coloured abstract shapes. Plants demonstrated respect for nature. Burning joss sticks scented the air and represented the most significant hippie contribution to interior decoration, surpassing potpourri's modest contribution.

Hippies had transmogrified into the politically minded Yippies. Their name was derived from Youth International Party but they were essentially an American phenomenon, radical, countercultural and proceeding on the assumption that with youth came wisdom. They swapped protestations of peace and love for increasingly acrimonious political protest rallies. Rancour and violence replaced confected expressions of all-enveloping love for humankind. They mustered huge support amongst students and in 1967, in the 'Summer of Love', proposed levitating the Pentagon with mystical chants on the presumption that these would cleanse the building of evil intent and end war in general and the Vietnam War in particular. They applied for a government permit to raise it 300 ft in the air. This was refused but a permit was granted to raise it 3 ft, which would suggest that the authorities had their own sense of humour. Despite the best efforts of 50,000 people the building remained rooted to its spot. The novelist Tom Wolfe, in his *Kool-Aid Acid Test*, questioned Hippies' and Yippies' political nous.

Hippies and Yippies were of the late 1960s but they survived into the 1970s. Mary Quant thought their arrival marked the premature end of her 1960s, which she said 'sort of faded a bit when it became muddled with flower power'. Like her clothes, she thought, the 1960s should be crisp. But all through the overhyped and overexcited 1960s, as had been true in 200 years and more of interior decoration, 90% of the population saw no reason to abandon wallpaper, fitted carpets, three-piece suites and as many ornaments and portraits of green-faced Oriental women as they could squeeze in. Untroubled, they carried on with Victorians' tendency to accumulate but felt no need to buy original 19th-century pieces; they were not particularly concerned about authenticity. They liked the practicality of easily cleaned surfaces, as long as they had the benefit of colour and pattern. Victoriana was usually too dark and too bulky. When it came to period pieces they preferred Art Deco. Biba, the most fashionable women's boutique for the duration of the 1960s, had a Deco-esque logo and typeface. Not that the average householder cared. Deco was comprehensible.

Peter York said 'when asked about the sixties, there seems to be a qualitative difference in people's responses – they seem to be confused about what really happened (to them) and what the media said was happening'.[10] This may shed light on the excuse made by extant denizens of the decade: 'If you can remember the sixties you weren't there.' Or perhaps there was less of substance to remember that the myth suggests.

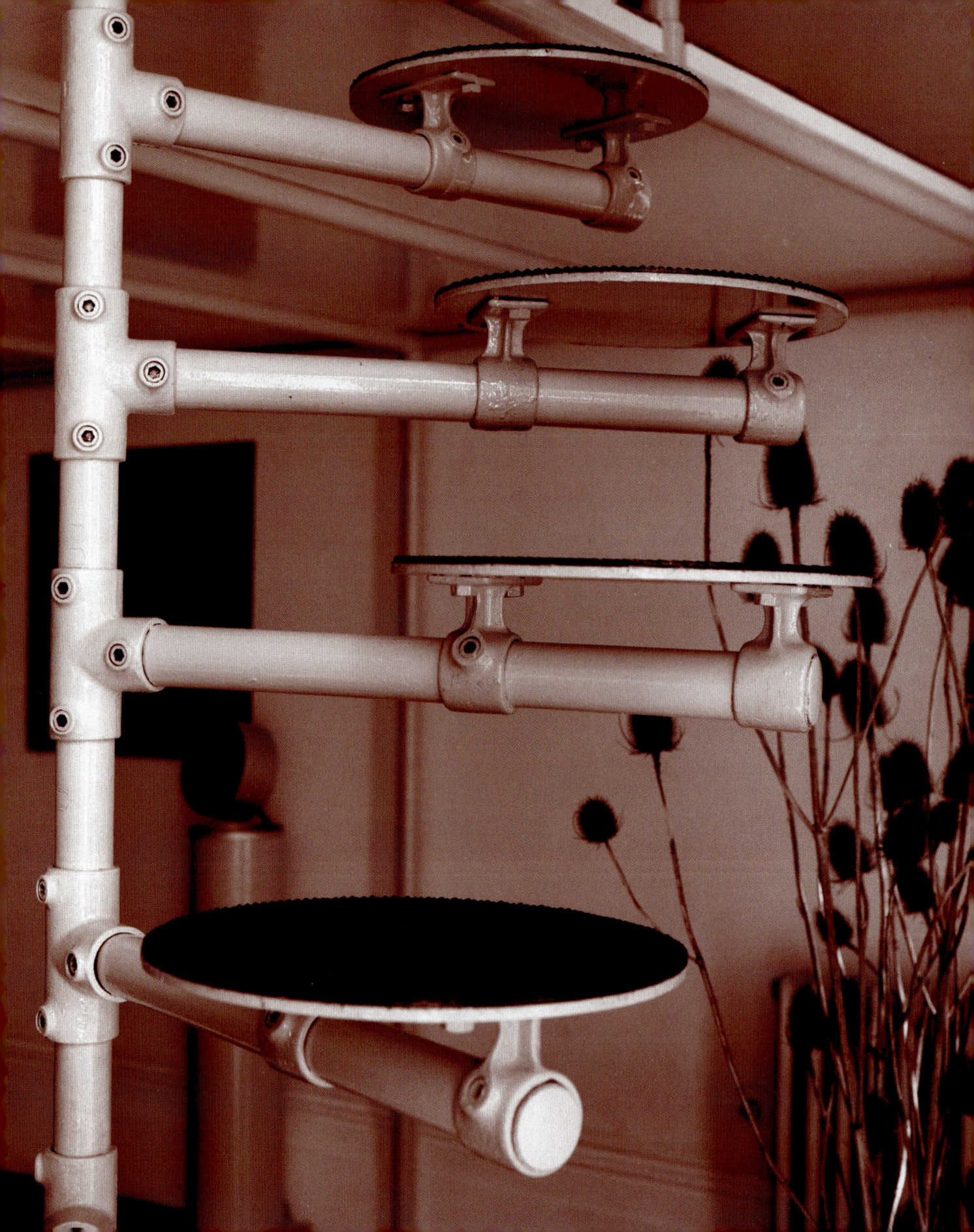

CHAPTER 8

Carrying on Regardless

'The story of the seventies was the story of everyone getting in on what a minority within a minority got in the sixties because they were around at the right time.'

Peter York, *Style Wars*, 1980[1]

Taste of the 1970s is maligned, considered grotesquely naive and condemned as an aesthetic absurdity. It could be so described but perhaps deserves to be assessed with generosity. There should be some gratitude for the way it exorcised the stylistic demons of the 1960s by indulging them to excess.

The decade began well. 1970 saw the First National Women's Liberation Conference, the formation of the Gay Liberation Front and the first issue of *The Ecologist* magazine. The idealism of the 1960s appeared to be marching on into the new decade but swinging sixties' dreams of a world made perfect by 'love, love, love', could only limp along until 1973 when idealism vanished in both Britain and the United States. Hedonism retained its popularity but, pleasant as love was, it did not deliver bare necessities. The careless rapture born in the 1960s began to look dangerously flippant.

In Britain, the real 1970s, the bleak 1970s, began when the lights went out – literally. Utopian fantasy confronted industrial inaction. Fuel shortages closed down power stations. The government introduced a three-day working week and Britain slithered down world economic league tables, was obliged to borrow from the International Monetary Fund and, in 1977, the pound was devalued. The country was hailed as the 'sick man of Europe'.

Industrial unrest reached a crescendo in the 1978/79 'Winter of Discontent' when further strikes by public sector unions shut down basic services. Countrywide squalor peaked in January and February of 1979 when in the deep midwinter strikes by refuse collectors meant that bags of rubbish were piled above head height in the streets of central London. Rats gorged themselves. Stoppages by hospital staff caused outrage and unofficial strikes by gravediggers in Liverpool and Manchester provoked fury as corpses accumulated in municipal morgues. Violence in Ulster escalated and the bombings then spread to English cities.

In the United States, Richard Nixon had become President in 1969. He finally extracted the country from the Vietnam War, brought back American prisoners of war and ended the draft. He laid the ground work for diplomatic relations with China and eased tensions with the USSR. He enforced desegregation in Southern schools, set up the Environmental Protection Agency and took the phone call from the first American astronauts to land on the Moon. He had, however, a reputation for deviousness, culminating in his resignation in 1974, following accusations of illegal activity by members of his staff. He had been nicknamed Tricky Dicky. He was succeeded by his amiable but languorous vice-president Gerald Ford who was, in turn, succeeded by Jimmy Carter – both presidents who were insufficiently Machiavellian to realise Nixon's idealistic ambitions.

Volte-face

The absurdities that Hippies and Yippies brought to politics seemed to mainstream architects to be matched by an American revolution in architectural theorising that confronted the problem of Modernism's unpopularity. The revolution, led by Robert Venturi, was crucial in changing attitudes to ornament within the profession. In his 1966 book,

Complexity and Contradiction in Architecture, Venturi had argued for 'the difficult whole' in architecture, and that included decoration. He wrote: *the main justification for honky-tonk elements in architectural order is their very existence. They are what we have. Architects can bemoan or try to ignore them or even try to abolish them but they will not go away for a long time because architects do not have the power to replace them (nor do they know what to replace them with).*[2] 'Honky-tonk' described the elements, out of tune with respectable rules of style and taste, that brought enjoyable discordances. He advocated 'messy vitality'. He counterpointed Mies van der Rohe's gnomic 'less is more' justification for his stripped back palette of form and materials with his own 'less is a bore'. To attack Modernism's core dogma required courage and wit was a useful shield.

Principal credit for the insurrection generally falls to Venturi, prompting frequent outbursts of outrage from his collaborator and wife Denise Scott Brown. When she objected to his receiving the Pritzker Prize in 1991 the jury dismissed her claim, with a hint of condescension: 'Ms. Scott Brown has a long and distinguished career of architectural accomplishment. It will be up to present and future juries to determine who among the many architects practicing throughout the world receives future awards.' Another undervalued female collaborator, or a recognition that Venturi had instigated the revolution?

Venturi and Scott Brown had taught at Yale School of Architecture in the late 1960s and had with a colleague, Steven Izenour, led students on a trip to contemplate architectural taste in Las Vegas. In 1977, the three published 'Learning From Las Vegas' in which they advocated a root and branch reassessment of Modernist presumptions, criticised the sterility of corporate architecture and drew conclusions about its strategic restructuring from Vegas's populist vigour. They argued that symbolism and decoration were crucial and that basic weatherproofing enclosures, which they called 'sheds', needed to be gratuitously elaborated, if they were to be loved by the laity. They suggested that inspiration for decoration might be found in pre-Modernist styles and wisely focused on Classicism, the most familiar, and gave forth Post-Modern Classicism, which wholly disconcerted Modernists.

Below left
A two-dimensional PoMo remodelling of a Classical Ionic column in painted chipboard, unpainted soft wood and MDF. London, 1982.

Below
A PoMo pediment interpreted in paint and wooden cubes.

Those who chose to dabble in it found it a creative purgative and it fascinated a public who, having been fed various dour strands of Modernism, found Venturi and Scott Brown's alternative bizarre but fascinating and fun.

The movement recognised that in public arenas, such as the hotels and casinos of Las Vegas, where they spoke with the authority of paying customers, non-architects had been validating ornament – and busily applying it in the privacy of their own homes. Post-Modern Classicism was primarily and quintessentially an American phenomenon. It was honky-tonk enough to earn itself the affectionate, and perhaps disparaging, abbreviation of PoMo.

Venturi and Scott Brown's 1977 cartoonish elevations for their 'Eclectic Houses' series seemed indebted to the pictograms of houses that made up Hollywood's cartoon townscapes. Those and the capital of their 'Ironic' column, in which the volutes of the classical Greek Ionic order were simplified to invite comparison with Mickey Mouse's ears, were the images that defined PoMo in Britain and caused angry anxiety amongst academics who had made comfortable livings contently proselytising on behalf of Modernism to generations of students.

In 1991 Venturi and Scott Brown's practice was commissioned to design an extension to the National Gallery in London, after an open competition failed to produce a satisfactory proposal. Their success confirmed that the wished-for alternative to Modernism had arrived and there was perhaps a semblance of the satisfaction in 1835 that had greeted Barry and Pugin's Neo-Gothic alternative to the predictable and tired Neo-Classical proposals for the rebuilding of the Houses of Parliament.

Below
Venturi, Scott Brown & Associates, National Gallery extension: A well-considered response; perhaps, too well-considered to excite the uninitiated.

The finished building infuriated Modernists who resented its collage of Classical pilasters and baffled traditionalists with its disregard of the finer points of Classical composition. Nor had it popular appeal; it had its honky-tonk elements but they were executed in monochromatic stone and were rather subdued. Perhaps the *enfants terribles* were too respectful of the institution and the site or perhaps too clever and too subtle. If it was the latter, they could be accused of failing to learn from Las Vegas.

Throughout the 1970s Britain had been indulging in its own untheorised reversion to tradition, which had something in common with J. M. Richards's advocation in 1940 of what he called 'tradition-rooted architecture' as a palliative in hard times.[3] Bricks, lead and zinc cladding panels, hanging tiles and appliquéd timber replaced concrete, tiled and slated pitched roofs replaced flat, houses became less like machines for living in and a little more like something that a child might conceive with coloured crayons. Even enormous social housing developments veered towards the picturesque and increasingly became collages of tactile materials.

In the 1950s, terraces of social housing had looked familiar but materials had not. At the beginning of the 1970s brick returned but buildings were becoming increasingly unfamiliar. A major development in London, Lillington Gardens in Pimlico, by Darbourne and Darke, created terraces but they did not mimic Pimlico's traditional stuccoed elevations in smooth concrete. Their walls were reassuringly brick but the irregular piling high of flats was more suggestive of terraces dug by farmers into mountain sides than London terraces. In the flats tenants still demonstrated their fondness for decoration.

Sentiment and ornament were insinuating themselves into the design vocabulary. In 1982 the architects and academics, Robert Jensen and Patricia Conway, published *Ornamentalism: The New Decorativeness in Architecture and Design*, a rapid retrospective appraisal of the revival of ornament in architecture. In the foreword the architectural critic Paul Goldberger described ornamenting as a radical act, committed in defiance of Modernist articles of faith imposed on architects and designers. He might have also mentioned society at large. To sweeten the pill for Modernists he suggested that Ornamentalism was not necessarily Post-Modern, or anti-Modern, and that ornament could be deployed in service of 'other Modern ideals'.[4] He was not specific about what these might be but was perhaps thinking that, given the movement's humanitarian aspirations, civilians might finally be given respite from mute brutality. Jensen and Conway made things clearer. They described the 'impulse to decorate' as fundamental to the human condition, a way of identifying buildings and the cultures that created them and proposed that ornament gave buildings a human scale.[5] They acknowledged early Modernists' good intentions but submitted that, in attempting to eliminate social inhumanities, they had eliminated architecture's capacity to give pleasure. They agreed with Goldberger that Ornamentalism remained broadly true to Modernist principles and in their support quoted the *New York Times's* revered critic Ada Louise Huxtable: 'But whatever comes next will be the product or inheritor of modernism, not the radical break that (Post-Modernism) is advertised to be. It will have at its heart the twentieth-century revolution that we call modern architecture.'[6]

Ornamentalism, they said, was 'the first serious attempt in fifty years to make Modernism keep its promise of projecting new possibilities …'.[7] And so it was: for when

Top left
The terraced slopes of Lillington Gardens, Pimlico, London, 1974.

Top right
A flat in Lillington Gardens offering further evidence of humankind's devotion to pattern, and compulsive desire to collect and display, 1972.

Below left
Byker Wall, a single structure containing 620 maisonettes behind a free-form wall of brick, tiles, timber and metal sheets. It had some of the romance of decay. Ralph Erskine Associates, Newcastle, UK, 1978.

Below right
An interpretation of the suburban London terrace house that accepts that most such houses have been subdivided to create several homes. Each 'house' contains two houses above a flat. The buildings adapt characteristics of the original model, particularly the projecting 'bay window' which adds depth to the street elevation in perspective. Jeremy and Fenella Dixon, St Mark's Road, London, 1979.

the appetite for appropriation of historicist motifs was satiated, enthusiasm for colour and complexity remained.

Squabbles about the nature, and worth, of Post-Modernism particularly when it chimed too tunefully with Classicism, agitated theorists and critics but for many practitioners such concerns were secondary to the dethroning of Modernism as the one true credo. Jensen and Conway suggested that, while ornament had historically been used to embellish buildings' essential elements, it was increasingly being used to deny or supersede them.

Ornamentation was no longer 'subservient to structure as dictated by the theories of the eighteenth and nineteenth centuries'.[8] It was in clear contravention of Pugin's principles and a reckless application of ornament for its own sake.

Venturi and Scott Brown's work freely strayed from strict Classical principles and could look Disney-fied, which was interesting because there were suggestions at the end of the 1970s that the design of cities and buildings should be handed over to the 'imagineers' of the Disney Studios; because people love visiting Disneyland and so should, he presumes, love living in a Disney World. Such worlds did come into being.

Seaside is a privately developed town in Florida, founded in 1961, not too far from Disneyland, designed to replicate an idealised seaside town of the early 20th century. Brightly painted wooden structures, public and private, are organised around a commercial core from which streets and lanes radiate to public open spaces. Individual buildings are required to be unique and they range in style from Victorian to Modern but all are made compatible by their designers' respecting the fundamental conceit. And it is obvious that taste demands that Seaside interiors should have white painted wooden floors, walls and ceilings with painted furniture on patterned rugs and copious subtle and unsubtle references to the sea.

Britain had its own urban replication. Poundbury is another private development, instigated by the Prince of Wales who, after a spat with Modern architects, undertook to build a prototype of how he thought planners and architects should create communities. It is modelled on a market town, with public and private buildings that draw on pre-Victorian models and are finished in brick or stucco under tiled pitched roofs. It had open spaces and narrow lanes. It was solidly built and irresistibly pretty, extremely popular and, for all its period references, a perfectly good place in which to carry on digital business. And it is perfectly obvious how the interiors should look. Walls and ceilings should be plastered

Below left
Housing in Poundbury: Eclectically mixed traditional forms and materials, Dorset, 2008.

———

Below
A commercial development in Poundbury, 2008.

and painted in pastel tones, floors should be wooden with large rugs with small patterns, furniture should be solid and unpainted, sofas and armchairs generously upholstered and a central pendant light should be augmented by lamps on small side tables. It should be mildly Georgian.

Venturi and Scott Brown had no qualms about guying tradition; their series of bent plywood chairs cut in simplified imitations of historic styles and designers, with brightly painted representations of decorative details, were cartoonish. All would have looked at home in 742 Evergreen Terrace in Springfield. When a replica of the Simpsons' house was built in Nevada as a prize in a 1997 competition, Manny Gonzalez, the architect responsible for translating the cartoon edifice into reality, said it was 90% normal. The competition winner chose not to live in the house; she lived in the east, had no wish to move and settled for a cash prize.

Shakespeare said 'if all the year were playing holidays; to sport would be as tedious as to work …'.[9] and it may be that, after frivolity has had its moment, something more serious must take its place: this does not mean there is no place for decoration but that excess of it may dull the taste buds.

Play time

In the UK it was a shopkeeper, Tommy Roberts, who saw crossover potential in the Disney canon. After trading in Victoriana and military wear in the 1960s he progressed to selling 'pop art' clothes in a shop he called Mr Freedom. Sniffing the mood of the 1970s, he licensed imagery from Disney to embellish further his offerings, which were already blatantly colourful, eccentrically cut, undoubtedly kitsch, and worryingly infantile. Surprising numbers of adults were happy to wear brightly coloured dungarees over brightly coloured striped sweaters and brightly coloured 'Kickers' shoes with thick soles and fat laces. They looked like big babies and their homes, decorated in the same vein, looked like nurseries. Roberts added 'pop art' furniture to his stock. He sold chairs that mimicked the colours and configurations of oversized Liquorice Allsorts sweets, and sofas inspired by the lower sets of dentures. They were all oversized, which added to the impression that their occupants were indeed infants. They had something in common with Claes Oldenburg's oversized and flaccid replicas of everyday objects that purported to be sculptures and were occupying public spaces in the United States.

Max Clendinning entered into the spirit and swung from white rooms to rooms that were wholly and exotically coloured. He performed the *volte-face* in 1973 in his living room. Ralph Adron painted the walls and ceiling. A red carpet matched the red upholstery on fat upholstered chairs with no visible structure.

Fantasies of American life continued to preoccupy Europeans. Increasingly affordable air tickets made New York a place of pilgrimage and, for the British, it was definitively glamorous compared to dowdy, failing London. Its frightening crime statistics added to its glamour. Its citizens were incarnations of self-confidence and self-obsession. *Flip*, a shop for

Opposite
Max Clendinning's dramatic move into colour. Alwyne Road, Islington, London, 1973.

Above
For a client, Clendinning took his new-found taste for colour to the extreme in his proposal for the living and dining areas. Old chairs, lacquered cabinets and raw floorboards add to the mixture. Knightsbridge, London, 1974.

Above right
Clendinning's 1970s palette was not simply about colour but also reflectivity and transparency. Knightsbridge, London, 1974.

second-hand American clothing, provided Londoners with the kind of garments they recognised from black and white films of the 1950s and which could now be further appreciated for their eccentricities of colours, patterns and cuts. Women could buy tight-waisted frocks with full skirts and males could snap up Hawaiian shirts and lurid sports jackets.

For all others there was denim, everywhere: 'By the late 1970s the Presley generation was in its forties and still expected style as of right. You saw it in the way the jeans markets moved, the way Levi's spent real money on developing the cut to deal with … *the older buttock*.'[10] Denim shops, with punny names like Jean Genie and Jean Junction crowded high streets but denim was not confined to jeans. Men could buy denim suits with extraordinarily flared legs and mammoth lapels. Esoteric dressing, according to tribal affiliations, remained a youthful preoccupation and in ten years' time those fashionistas would bring the same sort of enthusiasm to bear on their interiors.

Rodney Fitch, who had been managing director of the Conran Design Group, declined to become CEO of Habitat and instead set up his own multi-disciplinary design practice, specialising in retail design. He declared 'the purpose of life is shopping'. Just as Conran's Habitat had demonstrated a way of living to the comfortably prosperous middle class, Fitch's work with high street fashion shops made retail interiors that offered visions of modernity. Younger clothes shoppers had heard about, and sometimes seen, the boutiques of the 1960s and consequently expected clothes shops, however corporate, to cut a dash. Ideas that souped-up shops could transfer to homes.

American retailers, who had mastered the mechanics but not the excitement of selling, congregated in malls and competed to make the process undemanding and, by extension, unexciting. It was the American way. In Britain retailers were experimenting in a comparatively unfamiliar world of the affluent young. The big department stores acquired in-house 'boutiques'. Harrods had 'Way In' on its top floor and Selfridges spread Miss Selfridges across the country. The young were being introduced to 'lifestyle' which would increasingly incorporate the home. Americans' enormous department stores, even on Fifth Avenue, challenged little more than shoppers' bank accounts.

Britain continued to struggle economically throughout the 1970s and seemed to be becoming ungovernable as one indecisive election and one indecisive government followed another. The clouds of Imperial glory were floating away and citizens preferred not to notice and to enjoy themselves in what was beginning to seem like the last days of solvency. The 1960s had begun to change leisure as the flashing lights of discotheques supplanted the dull dancehalls in which a slowly revolving mirrorball was the nearest thing to a light show. In the 1970s cocktail bars with pastel-coloured drinks and decor appeared, glitzy with allusions to Deco and frequently with something tantamount to a cabaret. Pubs with heavy, dark wooden furniture, floral-patterned carpets sodden with spilt beer and pock-marked with cigarette burns seemed dreary and were usurped by wine bars, with stripped wooden floors and stripped wooden furniture, white walls with modernistic prints in thin black frames and no old men sitting in corners. They were the antithesis of pubs and opportunities for householders to try out the Habitat aesthetic.

The initial rush to parody historical motifs passed but PoMo offered a vocabulary that had moved beyond the accepted tropes of interwar Modernism. Diversity prevailed but, as Jensen and Conway were keen to imply, the impulse to make ornament remained stoutly Modernist at its hybrid heart. The modern American domestic interior remained uninhibited and its outrageous and undisputedly kitsch ingredients have now become irresistible to bloggers offering online design analysis. Outré 1970s images are easy targets for hindsightful humour. A caveat: statements made online come back to haunt and taste changes. Those who mock the 1970s will, in their turn, be mocked. In 2017 a freelance journalist Kellen Perry described, with a degree of restraint, the1970s American domestic interiors. On the *All That's Interesting* blog, under the heading *The Decade That Taste Forgot: Lavish and Luxe Interiors of the 1970s* he wrote on 6 July 2017: *The 1970s was an age of bold-but-earthy patterns, inspired by the nascent environmental movement; cartoonishly decadent and overwrought entertaining areas of marble, brass, fur, and shag (pile); and impossibly busy 'op-art' textiles and wallpaper.* James Lileks was a humourist working for the *Minneapolis Star Tribune*, the newspaper that had supported the Walker Center *Idea House* exhibitions in 1941 and 1947. In 2005, with less serious intent, he published *Interior Desecrations: Hideous Homes From The Horrible '70s* and offered an explanation for what he declared to be aberrations of taste: 'This is what happens when Dad drinks, Mom floats in a Valium haze, the kids slump down to the den with the bong and the decorator has such a desperate coke habit he simply must convince half the town to put up reflective wall paper.'[11] He offered his own précis of the style: 'Blazing plaid wallpaper. Vertigo-inducing matching patterns on walls, rugs, chairs, pillows, and blinds. Bathrooms straight out of "2001: A Space Odyssey".'[12] Un-professionals, unconstrained by dogma, had no difficulty dealing with melanges of the functional and the celebratory; it seemed the natural thing to do.

Up, up and away

On the evidence he saw around him in Britain, the design critic Bevis Hillier concluded that different styles were proliferating in the 1970s and tastes were polarising: for many, the difficulties of city life prompted a longing to retreat to handcrafted simplicities, whether they were found in rural isolation or, more conveniently, in an outer suburb.

Strikes in publicly owned utility companies made city living particularly unbearable for aspiring ruralists who dreamt of the country, and with it fantasies of self-sufficiency. John and Sally Seymour published *Self Sufficiency* in 1973 and explained how one could live with a degree of comfort on a modest smallholding. In 1975 the television comedy series *The Good Life* featured a 'delightfully' naive young couple who gave up proper jobs to be self-sufficient in their back garden in Surbiton, the most phonetically suburban enclave of Outer London. They grew vegetables, kept a pig and were sustained by handouts from the rich couple next door. Their self-sufficient existence seduced few, but the aesthetic trappings appealed to many.

In the wider world family life continued to be centred on the combined kitchen and dining room, a respectful facsimile of a farm kitchen. It was the era of pine furniture, stripped of paint, standing on stripped pine floorboards. Heavy wood grains and large knots were prized. In the mid-1970s the comedian Victoria Wood, performing in Islington, expressed her provincial astonishment at the proliferation of shops selling pine furniture and claimed to have seen a stripped pine fireguard. Islington, a well-treed Inner London Victorian suburb, was cheap enough in the 1970s to become the primary target for young left-leaning professional housebuyers keen to live in substantial late Georgian and Victorian terraced houses with decently sized back gardens where one might plant a few vegetables.

Remodelling strategies of the 1960s continued. Dividing walls in semi-basements were removed to make the combined kitchen and dining area essential to the proper nurturing of children. Tall 'Welsh' dressers, with open shelves to display floral patterned crockery, were prized. Kitchen units and heavy legged tables and chairs were stripped of paint. Small craft-based businesses emerged to make furniture from reclaimed floorboards, others flourished dipping painted wooden furniture and doors in acid baths to remove all traces of paint. Often the process would reveal not just knotty grains but thin cracks which were coveted for their authenticity.

On the ground floors the wall separating the front and back rooms was also removed and the new whole was kitted out with wooden sideboards and wooden bookshelves. Other furniture was generously upholstered and big sofas and big armchairs sat on 'ethnic rugs' in front of stone fireplaces, which often replaced originals that had been removed by Bucknellites. Heavy over-mantels bore large mirrors with carved gilt frames. Chandeliers were too urban and bourgeois, but plaster ceiling roses were prized for being 'original'. 'Original' became a favourite adjective of estate agents.

Books were considered the appropriate way to complete furnishings. Original green cover Penguins and blue cover Pelicans demonstrated praiseworthy bibliomania. Framed posters for ancient agricultural shows and faux-primitive portraits of farm animals, particularly enormously fat pigs, were preferred to landscapes. Bedroom floors were less thoroughly done over, and it was permissible for black cast iron or brass bed frames to replace wood, and enormous second-hand wardrobes were prized. The fashion designer Laura Ashley who specialised in long, romantic, floral-patterned dresses that suggested something ambiguously period and something to do with country living, began to produce furniture that was also distinctly retro, but its lines were simplified just enough for it not to be confused with the genuinely old with its dust-infused upholstery. Tweaks to traditional forms allowed them to sit easily in rooms dominated by televisions. Rural fantasies could also be woven in modest flats and kept alive by window boxes and dreams of a vegetable plot.

There were other city dwellers who relished city centre living and persevered with its inconveniences. They tended to be single males, typically designers or early adopters and practitioners of computer technologies. They favoured 'high-tech' interiors. They were perfectly satisfied with the one bedroom flats they could afford, deep in the romantic dereliction of city centres. Their walls and ceilings were white. Rough original timber floorboards were acceptable but floors covered in engineered timber flooring or plain light grey, plastic sheet were preferable since textures and unmodern materials were simply not 'tech'. Their artefacts had to smack of industrial origins. Office chairs with minimal upholstery and work stools from abandoned factories stood in for conventional armchairs and side chairs. Sofas needed metal legs to float upholstered seats and backs clear of floors. Metal tables were de rigueur and better if they had seen service in factories or workshops. Tableware was white ceramic or stainless steel. Food storage was in clear glass jars or metal tins openly displayed on metal shelves that were clipped to metal wall brackets. These and many minor pieces could be found in Habitat, which was simultaneously servicing the bucolic fantasists. Connoisseurs searched yacht chandlers for shiny chrome wires and tensioning devices.

High-tech aficionados tended not to own cars. They could not afford them, so they settled for lightweight sports bicycles and leant them casually against their empty walls. The bike was the emblem of their lifestyle; the more prized models were hung on brackets as objects of veneration, and were designated to be 'sculptural'. Paintings were displaced by black and white photographs or posters with a few primary colours, abstract patterns and obscure fonts. All were hung behind frameless glass. Wealthier High Tech adherents could take the principles further. In 1972 Pierre Botschi used off-the-shelf industrial components to build a bed platform under a high ceiling in his London flat.

Hillier also recognised that 'something else had entered 1970s design which was neither rural nor high-tech, but a calculated insult to both: 'kitsch'.[13] He wondered if the 'popularity of kitsch represented boredom with the po-faced worthiness of the Modern Movement'.[14] It is always satisfyingly simple to nominate as kitsch the mishmash of decorative devices that constitute high 1970s style. Colours were raw and relentlessly bright, patterns were frantic, plastics were the material of choice. Olivetti, the respectable office equipment company, produced the flimsy Valentin portable typewriter on which a kidult could pretend to be a writer. The bright red body, which slotted into a bright red plastic carrying case, easily outsold all other colourways and is now collected by connoisseurs of kitsch. Kidults keenly collected second-hand objects that had been challengingly modern in the 1950s and were reassuringly reminiscent of their childhood.

Aficionados of kitsch excused themselves, and still do, from making the effort and taking the risk of forming a judgement and getting it wrong in the company of their peers. It is easier to position oneself outside the debate and to shriek with laughter – admirers of kitsch are liable to shriek with laughter – at some something made or bought by someone innocent of sophisticated aesthetic perceptions. There are others who appreciate innocence, collect the same stuff with genuine appreciation and do not shriek.

Similar to enthusiasm for kitsch was that for vintage. Anything old but not old enough to be designated an antique could be categorised as 'vintage'. It was a means to make second-hand furniture respectable and to suggest that its buyers had an edgily independent connoisseur's eye. It excused one from having to risk an aesthetic judgement on something new. Collectors of kitsch also seek notoriety by outraging aesthetic conformists. They are the punks of interior decoration.

Anything outré, particularly after a brief passage of time, has potential to become kitsch and buying kitsch is about patronising naive taste. It declares superiority over those who make it and those who buy it.

Punks, the most offensive youth group to emerge since Teddy boys, with their ornamental safety pins and razor blades, excessive coiffuring and ripped clothing, may be declared *kitsch*. Leftish social commentators saw the benighted creatures as symptoms of working-class dissatisfaction with declining Britain but it would be closer to the truth to see them as a fruit of innovative capitalism, the creation of the alternative entrepreneur Malcolm McLaren who imported the idea of 'punk' from New York, reworked it and introduced it to disaffected youths who became the core customers for the torn and tattered outfits he sold them. Punks looked sinister but were fragile and more inclined to have damage inflicted on them by other aggressive collectives, including the few extant Teddy boys. Had they had a philosophy it would have been nihilistic. Their philosophy, such as it was, did influence a few of the younger interior designers, the best of whom were enlisted by McLaren, but punks were not the sort of people to concern themselves with homemaking.

Punk was superseded by an equally outrageous but diametrically different fashion cult, which was decidedly camp and probably *kitsch*. New Romanticism was the creation of a quite other kind of disaffected youth, those who wanted to move on from punk tattiness. Nor did they not want the shiny surfaces, plastic banquettes and spotlights of 1970s discotheques. They preferred the squalid interiors of failed boîtes. Decrepitude had its own glamour. They wanted the elegance of the past but not the past. They wanted to move on from the dreary 1970s and the rest of the country, although it did not yet realise it, felt the same. Root and branch political change was about to make it all happen.

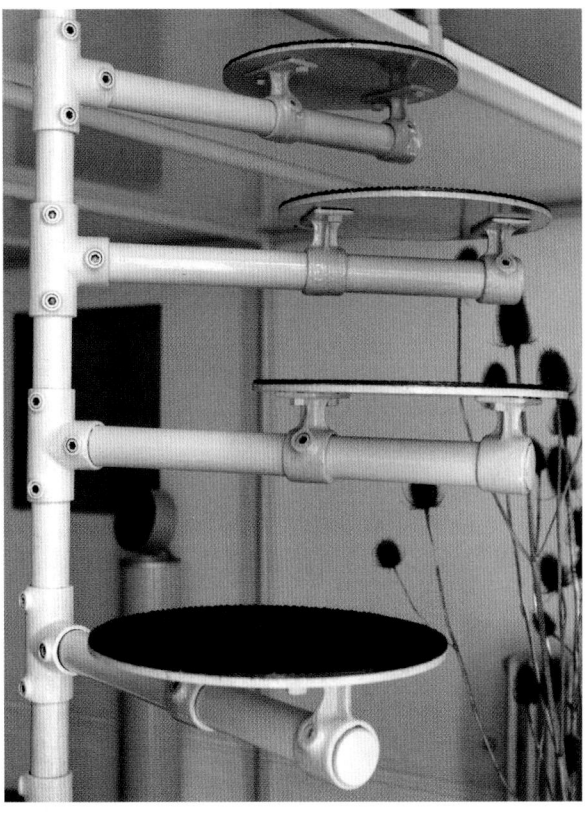

Opposite
The example of the Eames high-tech theory encouraged the ingenious assembly of elements from standard industrial components for Pierre Botschi's house. London, 1972.

Above
The visible nuts and bolts of the stair structure flaunted commitment to Eamesian redeployment of standard components. The expression of principle transcended practical consideration.

CHAPTER 9

Back to the Future

'Everyone wanted to go to the ball. Everyone wanted everything. And somewhere in London, the city that was once the capital of the world, two very different groups of people conspired to bring the ball to them: the Plotters and the Posers. The New Right and the New Romantics.'

Peter York[1]

The chaos that characterised British political activity throughout the 1970s culminated in the 1979 defeat of amiable James Callaghan's Labour government by implacable Margaret Thatcher's Conservatives. After a decade of centre left and centre right administrations being bullied by strong trade unions, Thatcher, with the backing of some formidable political strategists, introduced radical and contentious reforms that changed the mindset and infrastructure of the country. Alfred Sherman was chief strategist. A youthful Marxist who had converted to capitalism, his role was, he said, to 'think the unthinkable, question the unquestioned, say the unsayable'.[2] Perhaps that was what Modernists had been up to.

Thatcher had been seen as a stopgap leader of her party and her personal approval ratings were abysmal: she had a strange voice, a strange way of walking and she was a woman. Her tastes were definitively middle class; she was not a Modernist's cup of tea. Like Richard Nixon she was abhorred by aesthetics, liberals and leftists who, in the USA, had moved on to detesting Ronald Reagan who was elected President in 1980. He was presumed to be an incorrigible lightweight because he had been a Hollywood actor and was stubbornly good humoured. He and Thatcher formed a bond. Some thought he was smitten by her.

The military government in Argentina, judging Britain to be in decline on the evidence of the 1970s, invaded the Falkland Islands. Within three days Thatcher had dispatched a 'task force' on an 8,000-mile sortie and they defeated the occupying forces in a couple of months. The counter-invasion was decidedly more impressive than the USA's Vietnam venture. The country was getting back in the 20th-century's Great Game.

Trade unions were generally held responsible for the economic problems of the 1970s and the coal miners' union organised a strike in 1984 to protest against the closing of uneconomic pits. The government stockpiled coal to feed power stations and won a year-long conflict. Most Britons, even if overtly sympathetic to miners' individual predicaments, discreetly supported action; they remembered the strikes of the 1970s.

If violent confrontations boosted Thatcher's standing and the nation's self-regard it was two domestic policies that changed the national psyche. Since the post-war reforms of the 1940s state-owned, strike-ridden monopolies had controlled service industries. New legislation replaced the state providers of water, electricity, gas, telephones and public transport with competing phalanxes of privately owned companies, and a publicity campaign in the press and broadcasting encouraged the public to buy shares in the newly privatised services. Buying was made easy and soon shareholders outnumbered trade union members. Competition meant radically improved services. Waiting times for telephones were spectacularly reduced and customers were offered a heady choice of handsets. Choice required the exercising of taste.

The New Romantics' flame burned brightly, for a very short time. They aspired to be glamorous: art students led by a nucleus of astute and ambitious working-class youths had dressed exotically and abandoned punk's pogo dancing for more elegant moves. They were about visual extravagance, necessarily achieved on a tight budget spent in second-hand shops and theatrical costumiers. Robert Elms, explaining his New Romantic phase, said: 'there is no doubt that the ache for change … was also what drove us to don ridiculous outfits and preen and scheme for all our worth. Individualism as a response to class branding, me as a rejection of us, dressing up as an alternative to feeling down'.³

A considerable percentage of conventional citizens found themselves working for the newly privatised and glamorised utility providers, and in the expanding financial sector. They decided to dress accordingly. They no longer dressed as cogs in a nationalised industry but as likely candidates for promotion. Well-cut, well-pressed garments became the uniform. From that, it was a small step to worrying about one's home. The contagion spread across consumer culture and the 1980s were designated 'the decade of design'. The decade of denim was over.

Inside edge

Curious but influential experiments into Post-Modernism's potential were happening in interior design rather than architecture; ideas could be built faster and more fancifully in the shells of existing buildings, free from problems posed by weather, security and planning legislation. The groundswell of opinion against the routine destruction of old buildings, which did not have to be good to be protected, was flourishing. Planners routinely required that facades be retained which generally necessitated interior remodelling to accommodate new functions and designers were letting loose Post-Modern options. Workplaces were cheered up and when workers went home they took a taste for some of the new look with them. Even the architects who were putting up new buildings were beginning to make Post-Modernist forays: clients were choosing architects who would deliver Post-Modernism, which in its turn delivered tenants.

A legislative change in 1980 allowed tenants of council properties to buy their homes at severely discounted prices. Suddenly, householders who had been required to accept the exterior appearance of their homes as determined by their council landlords were free to indulge themselves. The results did not meet with the approval of arbiters of taste. Changes to exteriors became declarations of social class. Emancipated tenants rushed to replace flush front doors with panelled alternatives which frequently incorporated Deco-esque 'sun-rise' fanlights and they painted over the municipal colour in challenging hues. Modernistic aluminium door furniture was replaced by faux cast iron period novelties. Single window panes were subdivided by faux leaded lights and brickwork was clad in veneers of multicoloured reconstructed stone. None of the finished confections looked historically convincing but they were all unilateral declarations of independence and a preference for period detail and the status it inferred.

Building societies, founded in the late 18th century to help the deserving poor, remained the strict and cautious sources of borrowing for housebuyers. Applicants were scrupulously vetted. Government's re-trimming of financial regulations allowed banks to offer mortgages and the market became competitive. Loans were more available and easier to achieve. Former council tenants who had bought their leases were often keen to exploit their subsidised good fortune and to move from inner city terraces and tower block flats to new houses that flirted with the countryside. Speculative builders provided detached dwellings, often smaller and less well planned than public housing, which integrated the nods to period detail craved by buyers fleeing municipal stereotyping. Wanton expressions of individuality became less pressing when the house one bought marked membership of a like-minded community, but taste snobs still found much to disapprove off in the newly built streets which became 'avenues' and cul-de-sacs which became 'closes'.

Former council homes, which were cheaper because they retained some of their stigma, were bought by first time buyers who were almost invariably the aspiring young married couples whom mortgage providers considered better bets. They could do with their ex-council house what they wished: they could knock down dividing walls, add flashier kitchens and bathrooms and it was all a sound financial investment. When their children were born, they followed in the footsteps of former council tenants and decanted to the little British Levittowns, the proliferating suburbs that were ringing old town centres. Former council tenants tended to persevere, in moods of something approaching passive aggression, with the rawer tastes they had evolved behind the closed doors of their council housing. The second wave of buyers, who had come to home ownership at much younger ages, saw themselves as modern and were relaxed about shopping in Habitat. And Ikea was in the offing.

The idea that making, and spending, money was good built momentum throughout the decade. Thatcher negotiated the deregulation of financial markets and the introduction of electronic trading helped the Stock Exchange shed its ponderously traditional way of operating. It became more abrasively competitive; takeovers and mergers were simpler to achieve, and membership of the Exchange was opened to foreign bankers, who poured in. The lifestyle of London's stock market traders became part of 1980s mythology. The established denizens of the Exchange had recruited from public schools, but new banks looked for a different kind of dealer. Public school men were joined and jolted by aggressive, decidedly un-posh, products of state schools, a few of them women, who made enormous sums of money and were willing to flash their cash. Their suits were bespoke, their sports cars expensive, they gulped down expensive wines and bought expensive flats and, with the aid of interior decorators, who knew how to spend money, furnished them expensively and spent very little time in them. The tradesmen who serviced them, like the comedian Harry Enfield's plasterer alter ego, made 'loadsa money' and shared their enthusiasm for spending.

Bankers' lifestyle was emulated, with the necessary economies of scale, by the rapidly increasing numbers of workers in the lower echelons of banks and the privatised service industries. A great many people, of modest means, were beginning to feel rich, by osmosis. High street clothes shops, having stopped selling denim, began selling woollen suits, to both genders. The suits had hugely padded shoulders, the most salient manifestation of 'power dressing' and a sartorial declaration of status, however illusionary. *Dynasty,* an imported American television soap opera, provided weekly tutorials in oversized shoulder pads and camp interiors. People appeared no longer to know their place and appropriated the trappings of those they would formerly have acknowledged as their social superiors.

Shabby shabby chic chic

There was a long tradition of monthly magazines, *House and Garden*, *Homes and Gardens*, *Architectural Digest* et al. that deferentially recorded the perfectly presented homes of the very rich, upper classes. However, they were antiseptic and induced no more than respectful envy. Evidence of homes more appropriate to the mood of the 1980s was provided in 1981 when the publisher Kevin Kelly recruited Min Hogg to launch and edit *Interiors* magazine. The established magazines were well produced, in a politely traditional way but the colours were a little too raw and the layouts a little too fussy. *Interiors* was more dashing, with cleaner layouts and photographs with softer, deeper colours that concentrated on detail. It looked stylish. It carried on in interiors what New Romantics had done in clothing.

Readers were not confronted with comprehensive views of drawing rooms and ballrooms but with details in corners and crevices that they could imagine reinterpreting in their bedsits. It documented a distinctly louche lifestyle: that of posh people who were a bit short of cash and/or were indifferent to bourgeois anxieties about keeping up appearances. They were certainly not people who had bought their own furniture and were content to lounge on scuffed sofas in front of walls of peeling paint and faded curtains. It all looked effortlessly elegant (the heavy lifting having been done by one's ancestors) and vaguely affordable. Thus began shabby chic.

Hogg was a sociable young woman who, after attending the Central School of Art, had set up a photographic agency and then been fashion editor of *Harpers & Queen* from 1974 to 1979. When it and other magazines turned down her suggestions that they feature the kind of tired houses in which she was spending her country weekends she was delighted to do it herself. The magazine was launched in 1981 and so immediately successful that, in 1982, Condé Nast bought a half share and the name was changed to *World of Interiors* to avoid clashing with the American publication *Interiors*.

In an interview for a television programme, *Peter York's Eighties*, she explained why the time for the magazine was right, that the 'crumbling old houses' she published influenced the design of 'country house hotels' which in turn influenced the people who stayed in them, who could then find the materials to achieve a decent approximation to the look in the little decorating shops that were opening across the country, in market towns and pretty villages. She confirmed her lack of interest in the understated interior, with no curtains, no rugs, 'simple' new furniture and trophy hi-fi equipment. She sceptically listed elements which, as in clothing, were becoming desirable brand names, and could be trotted out to visitors and noted in estate agents' sales particulars. She complained that, as in clothing, fashionable suppliers had diffusion ranges. Czech & Speake were a desirable bathroom supplier and a soap dish, with their name prominently displayed in period font, offered less affluent aspirants the equivalents of a logoed tee-shirt. She disapprovingly listed desirable components for a 'Mayfair apartment' that were a fitted kitchen, preferably by Smallbone, 'fake Provencal tiles' for floors and 'amazing showers and baths'. A Mayfair flat was not the place to attempt *rus in urbe*. If an interior was not surrounded by acres of parkland it

Right
A good eye can simulate a convincing pedigree for a new interior with colour and an appetite for eclectic collecting. North Wales, 2016/17.

Below left
Second-hand pieces, slightly abraded and faded, if properly orchestrated suggest an interior brought together over extended time. North Wales, 2016/17.

Below right
Gentle mismatching of the age and provenance of major elements, augmented by astutely selected and precisely positioned accessories, suggest casual accumulation. North Wales, 2016/17.

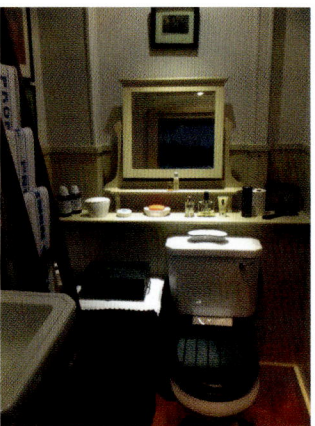

was not a natural candidate for *World of Interiors*, unless it was packed with esoterica and rubbed a little raw.

Hogg's appetite for the traditional could also be satisfied in a modest space. In the first edition of *Interiors* she featured a smallish studio flat, designed by Nicholas Haslam, for the singer Bryan Ferry. Ferry, a pop singer with an art school background, albeit in Newcastle, had established himself in the early 1970s as an exponent of eclectic fashion statements that avoided the pantomimic extremes favoured by members of his band and other 'glam' rockers. He was a traditionalist, inclined towards Savile Row tailoring rather than fancy dress. His fans were as interested in his stylistic manoeuvres as his music and were eager to emulate him. There was therefore excitement amongst the group, who were not habitual buyers of home decoration magazines, when they were offered the opportunity to see how he now chose to live. He would, they trusted, show them the way.

Some of Ferry's new friends were major and minor aristocrats and he spent enough time in their houses to recognise languid elegance when he saw it. Haslam, after a solid grounding at Eton, had drifted into interior design after lounging around the homes of his multitudinous collection of friends, of whom Hogg was an early member. He had not been formally burdened with Modernist theory. He could take it and he could leave it and he generally preferred to leave it. It was never going to give him the theatrical opportunities he wanted.

Hogg explained that his fans had expected Ferry 'to live somewhere with Mickey Mouse effigies and framed gold discs' but Haslam had provided something quite different, a 'miniature stately home in a small studio flat … every element was there, the pediments on the bookcases, the ruched blinds, the coffee table … two kinds of chintz on the curtains, blue and white china'.[4] A dentilled cornice separated the classical arrangements of classical furniture and pictures from the triangulated timber trusses that supported sloping ceilings. It was Post-Modern but free of the distortions that other designers felt obliged to include; to signal that they were not pasticheurs but wittily aware of what they were up to. Ferry's imprimatur gave validation to the look that was to characterise the yuppie interior. Yuppies (young upwardly mobile professionals), were very unlike hippies and yippies. They were the newly comparatively rich, the power dressers whose horizons had been changed by Thatcher's reformation.

Despite her decided preference for the authentically shabby Hogg did publish new projects and two of these were particularly important in the first years of the 1980s. The first was full-bloodedly New Romantic.

It was another small flat, this time for a New Romantic pop singer, the pseudonymous Adam Ant, whose manager was Malcolm McLaren who had moved on from selling clothes to punks to selling them to New Romantics. The flat was designed by David Connor who had collaborated with McLaren to design Seditionaries, his punk shop, in which images of a bombed Dresden covered the walls and naked light bulbs hung through holes punched in the false ceiling. The Ant flat was the diametric opposite of the shop, a precisely executed stage set in which a New Romantic could perform the routines of his daily life. Connor had toyed with the idea of becoming a set designer at art school and, despite three years on a quasi-architecture course at the Royal College of Art, retained some of those instincts. After graduating he worked briefly with the society decorator John Stefanides and learnt some un-architectural moves. The flat looked like a place in which Dickens's jilted Miss Havisham would have spent her lonely years. All wall and ceiling surfaces, all permanent elements, like the fireplace and door frames were marbled uniformly in blueish, greyish tones, by a specialist painter. The mundane functions of the marbled elements made their monolithic treatment the more extraordinary. The wing-backed armchairs were re-stuffed and over-stuffed and draped with bespoke grey printed fabrics, as if for protection in their owner's absence. The curtains, also grey and also specially printed, were long and spread across the grey painted floor. Fat concealed sausages of padding shaped and held their generous folds. An empty picture frame stood on the mantelpiece, another suggestion of abandonment. Melancholy was New Romantic.

Above
Adam Ant's flat, the universal marbling, the trailing curtains, the draped armchair and empty picture frame all contribute to a narrative than is implied rather than explained. It is a new romanticism. It suggests that designing an interior is not an objective activity. Camden, London, 1981.

Above centre
The truth of the universal marbling is revealed in the kitchen – where things get cooked up – as the steps of the process are revealed. Camden, London 1981.

Above right
Inspired by the Ant flat: draping gives a quite different character to a side table and revealing the feet adds detail. Belfast, 1983.

If Haslam had been content to deal with Ferry's period trappings in traditional fashion Connor was not. He demonstrated, in the little kitchen, that the marbling was *trompe-l'oeil* by serially revealing, on the end wall, the progression of paint layers that constituted the marbling process, right back to the flat base coat. It was a way to deal with the dilemma of fabricating ersatz traditional elements. His borrowing from the past was not a joke; it was witty.

Connor was a little embarrassed by the Ant flat, which, to a casual observer, looked like the work of a conventional decorator while he considered that his instincts were still Punkish. He was therefore pleased a year later when Marco Pirroni, who was Ant's guitarist and an ex-punk, asked him to deal with his flat. If Ant's flat had suggested a conventional stage set Pirroni's looked like a German Expressionist film set. Connor reprised textured grey walls but this time abandoned craft painting techniques and instructed an artist to reproduce, as far as could be done, the gestures incorporated in his sketches. He poured out *trompe-l'oeil* effects, twisting door frames and door leaves out of shape, tapering skirtings, hanging radiators at angles, cutting black and white plastic floor tiles to distort perspective. The furniture had no pretensions to grandeur. He covered metal-framed office chairs with paint-daubed plastics and what he called 'dog fur', which may not have been a strictly accurate description.

The Pirroni flat astonished but, unlike Ant's, it did not create a cult. It may have convinced clients that they did not want to follow Connor down that route and it may have partly exorcised his appetite for the anarchic.

Connor was not a lone trailblazer but his was the example that suggested anything was possible, if one had the nerve, and it inspired the increasing numbers of art school trained interior designers who were ready to experiment with Post-Modernisms. The general reluctance of their tutors to take the trouble to stray from Modernist orthodoxies only encouraged the more talented to push harder.

Connor's work was rarefied, and he needed rich and radical clients; specialist painters and bespoke fabrics were expensive. In the same year as the Ant flat, 1981, Jocasta Innes published *Paint Magic* and demonstrated how determined amateurs could achieve a comprehensive range of specialist paint effects. She had had an exotic childhood in China and by the age of 12 was thought to have lived in every continent except Antarctica. After working in journalism and short of money she had been inspired by the cookbooks of Elizabeth David, whose peripatetic background was similar to her own, to write *The Pauper's Cookbook* in 1971. She followed it five years later with *The Pauper's Homemaking Book*, a recognition that there was a popular emerging market amongst new homeowners with limited budgets but ambitions to decorate.

Top
The punk interior, wall painting that looks like graffiti and elements set askew to defy the dreary old rules of perspective.

Below left
The radiator hung at an angle to challenge the plumber, the skirting cut at an angle to challenge perspective, London, 1983.

Below centre
The triangular table defaced like the walls, the contorted chairs, the cacophonous floor – all very punkish.

Below
An imitation of the Pirroni flat by another hand, the free painting on the right hand wall, the markings on the found chair and the desk expediently knocked together from thin pieces of plywood, the rough painting of the rough floorboards, Glasgow, 1989.

Above
Strategic painting that breaks up flat walls and traditional mouldings and introduces the precise wiggle.

Above right
Loose daubing that breaks the flat surface and suggests a reflection of a window.

Five years later she launched *Paint Magic*, which followed a similar formula; an instruction manual for those not rich enough to employ specialist painters. The book explained with photographs the step-by-step processes of eliminating flat-painted walls. Amongst a battery of techniques she demonstrated stencilling, stippling and rag-rolling. The book sold over a million copies around the world. It gave practical means to those without financial means and democratised interior design. The techniques it promoted were not Post-Modern; they were certifiably Pre-Modern, ideal for the not-so-radical majority of amateurs. She also demonstrated how to apply grace notes, with trimmings of braids and embroideries, tassels and fringes. She established the Paint Magic company which sold ready-mixed decorative finishes and as design editor of *Cosmopolitan* magazine had a significant influence on the development of mainstream taste for the rest of the decade. Wallpaper companies followed her lead and began producing papers that replicated the effects of her specialist techniques and in 1986 Dulux launched its Colour Dimensions range which offered customers a huge range of colours that could be mixed on demand in do-it-yourself stores. Other paint manufacturers followed their example. Thereafter, colours became more subtle. Amateurs were being given every encouragement to get on with it.

Hard-edged cutting edge

Hard on the heels of the Ant flat *World of Interiors* did publish an interior that was distinctly at odds with Min Hogg's aversion to understatement. It was another small London flat, the first published work by John Pawson. It was as disconcerting as Connor's projects yet stripped of anything that might be construed as decoration, as far away aesthetically as could be imagined but it was possible to relish the work of both because both opened up unforeseen possibilities.

TASTE

The flat was on the first floor of a grand Victorian terraced house. High floor to lofty ceiling windows prompted him to remove a subdividing wall, to improve the proportions. The magazine images were riveting, particularly to eyes expecting *World of Interiors'* elegant excesses. Walls and ceiling were blaringly white but, in the most compelling image, a red-covered book lay open and face down on a black futon, edged with white tassels, on bare floorboards in front of a white painted period fireplace. In another image, pictures in thin black frames, rested on the floor and leant against a wall. Pawson explained that, if one took art seriously one should not hang it on a wall, where familiarity made one impervious to its merit, but should select one piece at a time for focused contemplation. It is as likely that he could not bring himself to defile a white surface.

He went on from this, by his later standards, unassuming start. He attracted a stream of very rich, artistically inclined, clients who 'collected' his interiors as they did conventional works of art. It was rumoured that owners of one kept a less demanding flat nearby to which they could retreat when the minimum became too much. His surfaces were not any old white, but a very specific hue, his walls were not just plastered. Plaster could be imperceptibly uneven so he preferred to use the perfect smoothness of MDF, to seal the joints with car body filler and spray paint the whole for a perfect smooth flatness. He augments his whitenesses with light stones and light woods and cuts his floorboards very wide to minimise the fuss caused by joints.

If those wallowing in shabby chic dreamt of life in a cottage those consorting with Minimalism aspired to live in a museum. It was a brave new design world in which such alien tastes co-existed.

Pawson defined Minimalism, which became the essential interior style for anyone with pretensions to be modern. It seemed a simple thing to replicate but no one, not even a dyed-in-the-wool Modernist, is as reductive as he; objects and fussy details creep in when the courage needed to leave well alone fails.

Imitators cannot control light as he does. He orchestrates artificial light and is prepared to block a view in the cause of diffusing a natural source. He is at his best in modest spaces, domestic interiors, which can be precisely dealt with and are occupied by respectful followers. Projects for private clients are rarely accessible to the curious, but those who have seen them confirm that, for once, reality transcends photographic image.

He became the public face of Minimalism (with a capital M). Modernism was minimalistic (small m) and relied on the old saw of a benevolent social agenda to validate its rejection of ornament. Its defenders insisted that it was not something as superficial as a style, although architectural historians identify strains within it that a neutral observer would recognise as sub-styles, none of which has the popular touch, with the exceptions of Art Deco and Contemporary, and no self-respecting Modernist saw those as anything other than fundamental betrayals of fundamental principles.

Pawson's Minimalism demonstrated how Modernism could be fine-tuned to satisfy visceral tastes, if a designer had the ability, and a priority, to make something that transcended objectivity. He made the basic components of Modernism stylish and that intrigued amateurs who liked the idea of joining the cult. His work receives extraordinary publicity. Journalists find him and his work easy to write about: they are intrigued by the apparent lack of objects in his home (they are all concealed in cupboards). He has an intriguing story. Pawson himself was another Old Etonian but could claim to have been bullied because of his accent and haircut, both of which betrayed northern origins. His family were wealthy but they were also Methodists and lived unostentatiously with no great inclination to accumulate possessions. After underperforming in the family textile producing business he retreated to Japan with the intention of becoming a monk. He did not enjoy performing a monk's menial tasks and retreated again, to teach English. A Japanese architect told him to go home and study architecture, which he did, persevering for three years at the Architectural Association school before, at 30, deciding he was too old for 'student stuff'.

Minimalism is an austere regime but has affinity with the Aesthetic movement's credo that one should own nothing that is not beautiful and it would seem to imply that not much is beautiful. It suggests that less can, after all, be more, if it appears to have mystical trappings. The extent to which taste is determined by myth is difficult to say but the apparent austerity of Minimalism gives it an ur-glamour.

Nuts and bolts and sentiment

Opposite
High Tech flat on the top floor of a warehouse; tension wires and tensioning devices, much made of the individual components of the stair and the methods of fixing them.

High Tech tends to be minimalistic. The architectural critic Hugh Pearman has paired it with Arts and Crafts because he considers both to be uniquely British styles. The stately towers of the leading British High Tech practitioners may be arty but they are not at all crafty. Pearman may be thinking of the decorative display of nuts and bolts, suspension wires and perforated metals.

The High Tech of the 1970s survived in spirit into the 1980s but succumbed to an infatuation with the rust and obsolescence of Industrial Chic, an extreme take on shabby chic for boys. It was driven by nostalgia and had the romanticism of Adam Ant's flat while scrupulously avoiding textiles. As in 1970s, metal office furniture was seconded to serve domestic needs, particularly if it showed signs of wear. Brickwork was exhumed from behind plaster and if it was poor quality so much the better. Unplastered concrete blocks, because they were so plainly utilitarian, were more desirable than brick for new walls. Abused floorboards were prized and, unless they were a threat to health and safety, were left as found. Rusted metal replaced timber, hybrid tables and shelves were welded together from recycled odds and ends of obsolete machinery. Welding was not refined, partly because it was carried out by inexperienced hands and partly to demonstrate its 'authenticity'.

Industrial Chic did not sit comfortably in suburban semi-detacheds. It really needed to be in an abandoned industrial building, in a decaying city centre. The precedent for recycling factories and warehouses began in New York in the 1960s, when building codes were slack. Artists of various disciplines began to populate redundant factory buildings south of Houston Street and clustered around Greenwich Village. Lofts had high windows and thick brick walls enclosing wide-open spaces that were punctuated by robust cast iron columns with picturesque patinas of rust, ceilings were high, often decorated by obsolete ductwork and conduit, wooden floors looked, and were, capable of supporting very heavy

Above
The kitchen – inevitably stainless steel, bought and bespoke.

machinery. The high, wide and open spaces lacked kitchens and bathrooms and sometimes running water but were viable places to paint and sculpt. Rents, if paid at all, were low.

If the amenities were poor the spaces had the cache mysteriously bestowed by artistic activity and began to appeal to those making huge amounts of money in the nearby financial district. Bankers could afford to domesticate them. The spaces lost some of their barely habitable romanticism, but owners still felt that they possessed the good old frontier spirit.

The huge spaces that remained, even after bedrooms and bathrooms had been carved out of them, had the proportions of a salon and something of the look of a furniture showroom that specialised in absurdly expensive 'modern classics' and contrived new pieces that their creators were happy to describe as 'sculptural'. Glamorous kitchens were in, or open to, this space and had ostentatious *batteries de cuisine*. Water pipes and electrical conduit were surface mounted, partly to flaunt the utilitarian aesthetic and partly out of expediency given that cutting chases for them into brick or concrete walls would

TASTE

degrade the desirable original surfaces. Bulky second-hand hot and cold taps were preferable to elegant chrome plated mixers and ovens and hobs were invariably stainless steel and sourced from suppliers of restaurant equipment. Bathrooms could be a little more refined.

As the upper floors of industrial behemoths became residential the bottom storeys became galleries and very expensive shops selling 'authentic' and 'upcycled' industrial pieces at a premium. The new inhabitants were, as a matter of honour, unfazed by high prices and enjoyed outspending one another.

London spawned its imitations. It did not begin with abandoned factories but with Thameside warehouses made redundant as the wharfs, once big enough for old cargo ships, were obliged to move downstream to accommodate container vessels. The transformation was slow. In 1973 a South African designer, Rae Hoffenberg, disillusioned with life in the fashionable brick terraces of west London, went east. Excited by hulking 19th-century brick shells and the expanses of river and sky that filled their windows, she bought her first dockland building. After three years of negotiation with planning authorities she was given permission to convert it.

Hoffenberg was so enamoured of the crumbling buildings around her and so fearful that they might be demolished that she began to buy and make structural repairs before selling them, as shells with service connection points, to those enthusiastic to emulate the gritty, bohemian NYC prototypes.

Tyro loft dwellers tended to be designers who wanted their own empty space to shape. In the beginning the whole movement was centred immediately downriver of Tower Bridge, on both banks. The South Bank had more glamorous buildings picturesquely served by narrow cobbled streets and riverside ground floors were appropriated by fashionable restaurateurs, including Terence Conran who, in 1989, made the area a 'destination' by opening his Design Museum in a former banana warehouse which, built in the 1940s, had a flat roof and visible concrete structure and, when painted white, looked distinctly Modernist.

The museum professed not to proselytise for any one perception of 'good' design but differences of opinion developed between the then director Alice Rawsthorn, Conran who continued to meet the institution's considerable financial shortfalls and the chairman of the trustees, James Dyson, best known for his radical vacuum cleaners. Rawsthorn cancelled a show proposed by Conran and substituted one about the flower arranger Constance Spry, which she said offered insights into domestic life in the 1950s. She then vetoed Dyson's unilateral promise of an exhibition to Issey Miyake and he was peeved by her alternative shows, of shoes by Manolo Blahnik and hats by Philip Treacy. He and Conran thought her programme frivolous and not celebratory of what they held to be 'serious' design. In his article on the fracas Deyan Sudjic suggested that Dyson with his purple plastic vacuum cleaners and Conran with Habitat's peasant wares and chesterfield suites felt '… uneasy at ignoring the message of form following function that they were schooled in'.[5] Dyson resigned and Rawsthorn followed 18 months later after further clashes with Conran.

The utilitarian austerity of the warehouse may have appealed more readily to male taste than to female and this was hinted at in 1987 when the Halifax Building Society chose to publicise its 'hole-in-the-wall' cash dispensers on television. Shot with impeccable taste the advertisement began with a handsome young man, who gave every outward indication

Top left
A derelict Thameside warehouse in 1930s London when only those most desperate for shelter would have considered living in them. Tooley Street, Southwark, London, 1930.

Top right
New Concordia Wharf: Converted to apartments in 1988 by Pollard Thomas Edwards and Associates. London, 1984.

Below
China Wharf apartments by Campbell Zogolovitch Wilkinson and Gough: One of the better attempts to recreate the majesty of the riverside warehouses, London, 1988.

of working in a 'creative industry', leaping from his bed in a loft filled with vintage industrial bric-a-brac and realising he had no milk for his cat's breakfast. He walked briskly down an empty cobbled street, waving in a socially inclusive way to the elderly newspaper vendor who had, unaccountably, set up his stall in that deserted spot. The young man found a Halifax dispenser and removed a large wad of money. The film ended as he poured the cat its milk and together they breakfasted contentedly on his balcony. Peeling paint above their heads said Metropolitan Wharf and that remains the building's name but the paint no longer peels and its management company describes it as containing 'creative work spaces (and) luxury loft apartments'. Romantic decay was only a phase on the way to a new form of gentrification, for the benefit of the new 'creative' gentry.

There were only so many riverside wharfs to satisfy the craving and, in 1992, the first inner city industrial buildings were converted. The evocatively named Manhattan Loft Corporation subdivided a small printing works in Clerkenwell, a working-class reserve in central London, and marketed it as Hoffenberg had done, as empty shells with service connection points. Creative clients snapped up the eight units.

'Loft living' became a 'lifestyle choice', synonymous with a kind of open planned spaces within former industrial buildings. Warehouses had picturesque shells, which an amateur could appreciate. And they had a clear connection to New York, which for Londoners of the late 20th century continued to have glamour. Britons, if they did not live in a house, lived in a flat and the infatuation with America was such that flats began to be marketed as 'apartments'. A 'flat' suddenly sounded flat. 'Apartment' became an estate agent's euphemism for

Below left
A good loft needed height, evidence of wear, mechanisms like sliding doors and utilitarian lights – and rooflights if possible.

Below
Furniture fit for lofts – reclaimed tubular steel framed work chairs with new blue plastic upholstery, and a new MDF table top on mild steel legs.

BACK TO THE FUTURE

an undersized but blatantly stylish flat. Americanisms were, as always, glamorous: lavatories became bathrooms. The old rules of U and non-U no longer held.

New-built 'apartment blocks' developed symbiotically with neighbourhood bars and restaurants and created an enthusiasm for city living. Architects put their energy into making attention-grabbing exteriors and, as adherence to strict Modernist principles faded, they drew on a more inclusive palette of materials which, sometimes, managed to meet customer taste halfway. The aim was to produce a 'landmark' building or, better still, an 'iconic' building, from which residents might enjoy reflected glory.

Amongst the singles and the childless couples enthusiasm for living in fashionable cities was strong. Couples became 'dinkys' (double income no kids) but even they struggled to buy a sliver of vintage warehouse. So developers built faux warehouses. The flats in them were cramped, with storage sacrificed in the cause of maximising the living area. Appearance out-punched practical considerations. Door handles were stylishly flashy because first impressions count. Kitchens were unnecessarily glossy. Two bedroom flats had two bathrooms, to insulate owners from embarrassing contact with the lodgers whose rent relieved the pain of mortgage repayments. Window were disproportionally large and opened onto a token balcony, not unlike those lampooned by Ozenfant but now assembled from steel and glass rather than poured-in concrete. They were not confined to London. They began to appear in the rehabilitated industrial cities of the north.

The dream never dies

City centre life is glamorous but speculative developers know that, sooner or later, every city dweller will aspire to live in the country and so they build faux country cottages, in suburbs and village peripheries. Magazine browsers may be titillated by the inclusion of an odd modernistic interior but majority taste continues to prefer the resoundingly traditional. Those who live in newly minted tradition are the sort who buy their own furniture; their chic is retro but not shabby. The home furnishing departments of the fashion chains provide economic alternatives to the little decorating shops in the pretty villages.

To generalise: in the 18th century the rich lived in the country, made money from their land and kept a 'town house' for formalised periods of social intercourse. In the 19th century the more prosperous members of the new middle class lived and made their money in towns and kept a country dwelling, house or cottage, for summer recreation. In the last decades of the 20th century as wealth and the sense of entitlement spread so did the urge to own a 'second home' in the country and faster cars and motorways made weekend commuting completely feasible. The weekend in the country remains the recreational ambition but rules of taste have to be observed.

Weekenders aspire to the Georgian rectory but will settle for a Victorian house and will make do with a cottage, especially a particularly old one. Rooms in houses are larger and foursquare with skirtings, cornices and mouldings around doors and windows. Rooms in cottages should be poky and walls thick and uneven and without mouldings, beams and rafters should be visible. Extant anachronisms are prized in both; bells that once summoned servants in houses and bread ovens set in the chimney breasts of cottages. *World of Interiors* illustrates basic rules of decoration.

'Cottage' curtains fall from window head to cill. 'House' curtains fall grandly to the floor, are of heavier fabric and lined. They do not hang listlessly; when drawn back they are gathered in theatrical sweeps and secured to the wall by tasselled cords. Blinds are a little too urban for both, except in the kitchen of the house.

Rough floorboards are essential in cottages and very old houses where upper floors that slope are desirable. Carpets are urban but reduce draughts that howl through gaps in floorboards: complaining about draughts is a tasteful way of boasting about the authenticity of one's cottage. Houses should have smooth tightly jointed, draught free floorboards. Draughts in houses enter through gaps in original sliding sash windows.

Rugs are preferable to carpets in both cottage and house although both cause anxiety when guests came back from brisk walks on muddy footpaths. Walks are brisk because the country can be cold and wet, and one field looks much like another.

Light finishes are favoured in both cottage and house as backgrounds for the dark brown furniture that consolidates impressions of age. Paints and wallpapers are primarily pastel although 'greenery-yallery' William Morris wallpapers bring the cache of certified

Below
The ideal country cottage, stone chimney breast, wood-burning stove, timber floor and decrepit armchair.

Below
Other desirables in an ideal country cottage: The vintage Aga to cook and heat and the stripped wooden table for food preparation and consumption.

Opposite
The formula for the converted cottage: White painted walls and black painted beams, exposed structural timber framing of an original wall; the change in level and the wooden boarded door are both desirable, the cream carpet is too genteel.

good taste. Stark white walls are the naive solution to small, heavily leaded cottage windows; sophisticates know that gloom is to be wallowed in. White walls are sometimes described as 'minimal' but only by the very naive. For some reason exposed structural timbers in cottages are invariably painted black. Textile and wallpaper patterns are small and predominantly floral, larger patterned floral chintzes are correct for upholstery fabrics although the larger houses can handle geometric patterns and velvets.

Neither country house nor country cottage lend themselves to open planning, either structurally or philosophically. Internal walls are almost invariably loadbearing and the formal composition of rooms around the fireplace in houses and the quaint miniaturisation of rooms in cottages are essentials of country living. An aberration in cottages that might justifiably be condemned as bad taste is the stripping away of plaster from internal walls to reveal the timbers that are structurally necessary to support upper floors. Decent solid walls become fences and destroy the integrity of the little rooms they once enclosed and prevent casual progression between the forcibly conjoined areas.

The converted barn is one option for a country dwelling that equates to the converted warehouse. A barn is utilitarian and monumental, built from indigenous materials by traditional techniques. Its lofty spaces offer opportunities for bravura gestures while its rural simplicity tends to curb the modernistic steel and glass excesses to which the metropolitan warehouse apartment is prone but quaint charm fosters and accommodates sentimental excess. Modernists took as their model the traditional artist's studio, the principal double height space with large windows and smaller rooms stacked off it to accommodate quotidian necessities. The barn potentially provides all that but discourages smooth white surfaces; it needs raw materials and it begs to be filled with all the rural knick-knacks and gewgaws that its habitants care to collect. A barn was, after all, made for storage, once for the wheat that made the bread that was the staff of life and now for the stuff of life, the thousand non-essentials that flesh is heir to.

CHAPTER 10

Having it and Having it More Abundantly

'Life is too important
to be taken seriously.'

Oscar Wilde

George Orwell took life seriously. In 1945 he predicted a nuclear stand-off between the USA and the USSR and coined the term 'Cold War' to describe it. In 1948 in his novel *1984* he described a dystopian future that would evolve as tensions and threats of war nurtured paranoias. He was not quite right and events proved once again the futility of making predictions.

1984 came and just before it went, Margaret Thatcher revealed in a television interview that the USSR's leader, Mikhail Gorbachev, was 'a man one could do business with'.[1]

This started a process that by the beginning of the next decade saw the end of the superpower stand-off. She used her good relationship with Ronald Reagan to persuade him to collaborate with Gorbachev. Reagan did and while it took a few years, and much internal machination within the Russian camp, they achieved rapprochement. In December 1991 the Soviet Union dissolved. It was a victory for capitalism but an ironic one, for the capitalist countries of the West were by then in the midst of a recession. The ending of the Cold War meant, of course, a sizeable reduction of jobs in the defence industries. The recession caused anxiety, but in fact only lasted a year. Eastern European countries, former members of the Soviet bloc, willingly provided cheap labour to produce, more abundantly, and more cheaply, the goods and services to which the West increasingly felt entitled.

Orwell may have got his details wrong but foretelling the future, whether by analysis or by runes, flourished. Faith Plotkin, a New Yorker, gave up her career in the law for marketing and changed her name to Faith Popcorn. In 1991, through her forecasting company BrainReserve, she published the *Popcorn Report*, and introduced the concept of 'Cocooning' or 'the impulse to stay inside when the outside gets too tough and scary'.[2] It might also have said that, as people became more interested in their homes, they were creating highly bespoke private environments. They had televisions and video players and were less inclined to look for entertainment in public places where anyone at all could enter one's metaphorical private space. Popcorn's accuracy was questioned when, in the five years following her prediction, social activities outside the home increased by 10%; but her business was forecasting and 30 years later she is right. People spend less time in shops and eat less in restaurants. Those needs are met online.

In the 1980s and 1990s, shopping thrived. Retailers were getting better at enticement. The UK clothes retailer Next was conceived by George Davies in 1982, with shops designed by David Davies Associates. Next provided the well-cut, well-tailored garments that people needed to settle into the 1980s lifestyle of owning shares and buying houses. The chain grew fast, and kept on growing. Its designers produced a formula for its interiors; white walls, timber floors, substantial looking wood and glass display furniture, a sprinkling of 'modern classic' furniture reproductions, all of which allowed customers to experience an elegant modernistic interior, a primer for how their homes might look. The shop design, and the clothing, offered affordable versions of the expensive 'designer' shops that were appearing in London, Milan and Tokyo with interiors by the most radical interior designers working with enormous budgets. It was a huge high street progression from the brash neon-lit, over-stocked shops of the 1970s. George Davies, abetted by the David Davies team, extended the repertoire of the chain's offers. Bigger stores had hairdressers, flower stalls and very chic cafes, with chrome and leather stools at a terrazzo counter on a terrazzo floor. Customers drank coffee from espresso machines and sparkling Perrier water at great cost. Gaudy cocktails belonged back in the 1970s.

The 1970s' leading retail designer, Rodney Fitch, explained Next's success, having zealously and perhaps jealously analysed its formula: *There was a sense of order, there was a sense of timelessness. Unlike most (designers') thinking, it wasn't a sort of hugely extravagant interior: it wasn't crowded, it was calm and the second aspect of that, of course, is the materials; simple woods, nice pleasant metals, calm colours and, of course, the ubiquitous low-voltage lighting.*[3] It was perhaps inevitable that Next would, in 1985, open its first 'home interiors range'. It was more conservative than the stores, and the cafe areas in particular, had led one to expect. It seemed to recognise that popular interior taste was still loitering around the country cottage model and so the range had a lot in common with the long dresses and floral prints with which Laura Ashley suggested the country rather than the boardroom. Upholstered armchairs prevailed. It was a recognition that Next customers, however radical their fashion buying, were not yet ready for radical home furnishings. It did not try to compete with Habitat, but it did encourage other high street fashion and departmental stores to dip their toes in the same water. The appetite for interior design was mysteriously mushrooming.

As always, changes in decor depended on what was in the shops. Shops supplying provocative modernistic options were few, small and expensive. Habitat continued to offer innovation and quality and its branches were expanding across the UK, but it was a little expensive for the expanding mass market. Designers had heard about Ikea and, because it was Swedish, their expectations of quality and style were high. Swedes were often puzzled when visiting British designers would ask that a visit to the nearest branch be put on their itinerary and the visitors were often perplexed when they got there. There were beautiful things but there were also things that were not – depending, of course, on one's taste.

Ikea, established in 1958, was expansionist. In 1985 it opened its first American store in Philadelphia and in 1987 its first British store in the Birmingham conurbation. That they did not open in New York or London may have been to do with caution about overheads or, equally, a suspicion that their best customers would be predominantly from the provincial suburbs, those who could best afford new houses and needed to fill them. To furniture-shopping Britons everything in Ikea seemed startlingly cheap and remarkably sturdy. The furniture designer and maker Sam Booth complained that he could not buy the materials he needed to make an object for the price that Ikea sold the finished piece. The process of assembling flat-pack pieces became a joke and stories of anxious moments deciphering the text-less instruction diagrams became bonding rituals amongst customers, and there were few citizens who lived within 50 miles of a branch who had not made the pilgrimage and could not share the experience. A minor service industry developed to serve those unwilling to tackle the challenge of assembling themselves.

Celebrating the 30th anniversary of its arrival in Britain, columnist India Knight wrote in the *Sunday Times Magazine* 'until relatively recently, taste was a luxury, a hobby for the upper-middle classes upwards. It was not democratic. You could have taste, of course, but you probably couldn't afford the things you liked …'[4] And Ikea caters for the gamut of taste. One can buy something mildly repro and one can buy something that touches the sharpest cutting edge. The enormous retailing sheds present crash courses in decorating options. All pieces are there to be poked and tested and room settings explain how they may be orchestrated. Mock-ups of tiny flats explain to young singles how they can have the home they long for in the most dreary of rented spaces and, when they move on, take it all with them or throw it away. Ikea will always be offering something new, better and affordable. For those who cannot make the pilgrimage to the sheds there are free catalogues, fat with photographs and, if not quite as elegant as Habitat's catalogues had been in their heyday, the images and the prices they list make mouths water. Like the room settings, they illustrate how collections of Ikea pieces may be composed and make it clear that, apart from a few white goods, there was no need to look further than Ikea.

Visiting an Ikea store is an educational and social experience. Ingvar Kamprad, Ikea's founder, was frustrated that customers to his first store abandoned their circumnavigation because they were hungry. So he opened a restaurant in every store with a signature dish of Swedish meatballs and a visit became a day out, sometimes for generations of one family. The food is palatable, inevitably cheap, and eaten while sitting on Ikea chairs at Ikea tables under Ikea light fittings. Customers leave through the 'marketplace' which offers those who have not succumbed to buying sofas, tables, chairs or kitchens an opportunity for impulse buying, some crockery, some cutlery, some glassware, something plastic: takeaways to freshen up the domestic rituals to which one returns. Paying at a supermarket checkout rules out the formalities of customer service that persist in traditional showrooms. Buying furniture as one buys groceries establishes home decoration as the stuff and staff of life.

Below
Blending in: The pattern of a wooden Ikea chair back rhymes with a chequered 1950s tiled floor.

Ikea operates across the world in about 300 stores and has begun its infiltration of Africa and South America, and 85% of its products are common to all stores. Television viewers across the world can spot their Ikea pieces in the backgrounds of American television sitcoms. It is the new International Style. Swedish Modern, with its bedrock of traditional values, has triumphed.

Ikea employs good designers and allows them to experiment, in a market-driven way. It develops popular taste by respecting popular taste. There are those who think it too pervasive and will pay a premium for products for no better reason than their not being from Ikea. There are sometimes better made, better looking products in more expensive shops, depending on one's taste, and they deserve to be bought by those who can afford them or are prepared to make sacrifices to afford them. Such shops are the delicatessens of furniture and fittings, offering ingredients for those wishing to cook up more esoteric interiors. The occasional piece, whether antique or bewilderingly modern, set amongst Ikea pieces proclaims an independent mind. Habitat customers did the same.

Ikea provides a common decorating language: its products are the vocabulary and people are judged by the words they use and the sentences they form. Just as there were U and non-U words so there are U and non-U products. But they are less of a gauge of class and more of an indicator of taste, if the two can ever be separated. It may, however, now be safe to suggest that Ikea has levelled the playing field; money can't buy you taste, but it will buy the services of an interior decorator. And a minor service industry has emerged to provide bespoke doors for the carcasses of Ikea kitchen cupboards, which look, and are, more expensive, but not necessarily better.

Learning experiences

World of Interiors demonstrated that a market existed for magazines with elegant photographs of sumptuous interiors and imitators followed. While tabloid newspapers conscientiously focused on celebrity scandals and topless models the broadsheets and their Sunday supplement magazines, saw profits in 'property porn'. If *World of Interiors* had a particular taste for the well-worn period interior the new publications tended to favour the neat and new and gently helped to adjust the antennae of taste. Of the newer magazines *Elle Decoration*, launched in 1989, came closest to matching *World of Interiors* production values and steered a slightly different editorial policy, favouring modernistic projects and information about new products. Newsagents dedicated shelves to magazines dedicated to domestic interiors. The public were receiving the primers they needed to hone their taste and take their homes beyond mundane.

The appetite for magazines did not go unnoticed beyond publishing. In 1996, the television programme *Changing Rooms* became cult viewing. Conceived by Peter Bazalgette, the great-great-grandson of Sir Joseph, the creator and builder of London's sewage system, it ran until 2004 and featured interior designers transforming shabby homes into something extraordinary in a very short time on a very small budget. Given project times, budgets and the need to entertain a broad television audience the solutions were not refined or scrupulously executed. Most were tacky but usually provoking. They excited those unfamiliar with interior design and, of course, were ritualistically scorned by practitioners and persons of taste. When they were revealed on camera to their owners, some were appalled, some wept and denounced the end result. It was a matter of taste but shock, and occasionally horror, was 'good television' and there were enough palatable proposals to convince viewers that they could match the standards and do it themselves. The programme's success owed a lot to its most popular designer, Laurence Llewelyn-Bowen. Despite his self-parodying flamboyance on *Changing Rooms*, in other programmes he displayed a serious understanding of design. He was the *fin de siècle* Barry Bucknell and the differences between the two men, Bucknell's honest hands-on toil in the service of practical home improvement against Llewelyn-Bowen's louche hands-off confecting of 'lifestyle', confirmed that priorities and expectations had evolved in 40 years.

Modern times, modern tastes

Since 2010 and the proliferation of apps and app-literates online, the selling of furniture, household objects and finishes has become increasingly important and delivers a cornucopia of options. One may buy one's furniture from Australia with no more effort than buying it a street away. Online retailing is not confined to the modernistic market but while it is unlikely that the appetite for reproduction period interiors will melt away even the most stubborn conventions appear to be eroding.

Digital tools have changed how people buy and they have also changed the way they see themselves. With home computers, tablets and smart phones technophobes suddenly find themselves owning very slick modernistic objects: there were no half-timbered computer casings, although there are some very kitsch phone sleeves. Whether they were aware of it or not, or whether they like it or not, people are beginning to feel and to be modern. Nuclear families sitting on reproduction period furniture sharing a communal activity are becoming abnormal.

On 13 March 2019 Kate Morley, the Consumer Affairs Editor of *The Telegraph* asked 'Is this the end of the three-piece suite?'[5] She suggested that two armchairs and a sofa, all identically styled and upholstered and once indispensable, were no longer a 'staple in living rooms' and cited the decision of the John Lewis department store chain to stop selling them, although they will continue to be available as bespoke items. The article was prompted by the British Office For National Statistics announcing that it was no longer including the price of three-piece suites in its calculation of inflation. It also dropped envelopes and hi-fi systems, two more obvious casualties of digitality.

Three-piece suites have been replaced by what John Marsh, a John Lewis buyer, called 'statement sofas and accent chairs', which may be sales-speak for 'big and peculiar'. Other than in start-up restaurants there has, so far, been no evidence of a trend for mismatched dining chairs. Marsh also reported that sales of modular sofas had increased, because they were useful for adapting to open planned spaces. The traditional formal configurations of well-stuffed sofa and chairs organised around a fireplace confirmed that householders could afford to conform to the prevailing convention and had the good taste to do so. When central heating became ubiquitous and fireplaces disappeared new seating models evolved.

Ikea and online retailers continue to offer chairs and sofas in matching styles and finishes but not as composite units. Only 2% of searches on the John Lewis website are for three-piece suites. This may reflect reluctance to choose between a number of tempting pieces, when one can have one of each, or may be a consequence of the divergent tastes of co-habiting individuals.

And there is a new genre of reproduction furniture. Copyrights lapse on 'Modern Classic' furniture and pieces nominally 'inspired by' Le Corbusier and Mies van der Rohe are reproduced and sold at a fraction of the price of the same models made under franchise agreements. Plastic chairs by the Eameses are particularly popular, and particularly cheap; moulded plastic components are easily reproduced and cheaply transported. Bucket seats stack together and legs bundle up to make a neat parcel for shipping. If one looks carefully

and has done the research the differences between original and repro may be spotted but they are insignificant and only the anally retentive will be disconcerted. Plastic also allows more colour options; the original can be titivated for a broader market.

The Eames DSM chair with its tapering timber dowel undercarriage has become ubiquitous. The DAR version, with the same bucket seat on a web of skeletal chrome legs, is decidedly less ubiquitous. It would seem that a natural material continues to score over the man-made. Taught taste is likely to admire the conjunction of two man-made materials and the ingenuity of the metal structure but untaught taste goes with its instinct.

The replica trade has made 'modern classics' affordable. Those who originally created them declared their work to have a social function, to improve the physiological and psychological well-being of the poor, but the mechanics of the market meant that niche manufacturers made them and the wealthy owned them. They were not to be found where workers shopped. Interestingly a stacking chair with a plastic bucket seat, broadly similar to the Eames, and black metal legs, designed by Robin Day in 1963, became standard issue and ubiquitous in schools and community meeting places across the world. The seat was available in light grey, charcoal or orange, the last a particularly fashionable colour in the 1960s but while the whole was a clever solution to lightweight stackability the more conventional profiles of the seat and the legs determined by the practicalities of stacking made it admired by the taught but unloved by the untaught. It survives but although cheaper than the most basic Eames replica it tempts only local government officials squeezing what they can out of tight budgets. It does not appear in living rooms.

Above left
The Eames DSM chair – a copy 'inspired by' the original that in appearance is indistinguishable from the original.

Above
An 'inspired' copy of the Eames EA208 allows the home office to enjoy corporate office luxury.

Soft Modern

For 100 years, the purest principles of Modernist pioneers have been eroded and untaught eyes have become accustomed to a milder aesthetic that is distinctly modernistic. It took 60 years, and a cultural shift in popular taste, to see virtue in Victorian furniture. Post-Modernism's breaking of Modernism's taboos and the abundance of its stylistic options have encouraged homeowners to follow not rules but their instincts. The collective aesthetic might be described as Soft Modern, physically softer in that it has no inhibitions about cushions and curtains and intellectually softer in that it had no inflexible doctrine to burden it. It is the anonymous and unsung style that is embraced by the young householders who want to prettify but have no taste for brown furniture.

Decorators' modern

It is a visually rich style, for the rich, offered by interior decorators to those who recognise that they do not know enough about the ingredients, the furniture, fabrics, complementary

Below
A decorator's modernisation of a small flat in Mayfair: The new finishes respectfully complement the dominant elements of the original room with a muted colour palette, London, 2019.

Above
The same decorator's work – integrating informal dining and sitting areas in a mews house; a balanced transition from the practical kitchen to the richness of the chairs by the fireplace. Kensington, London, 2018.

objects that need to be confected into something they want without knowing quite what that may be. A good decorator extrapolates coherence from the clues they offer and gives them what they want but adds something they could not envisage. Decorators' interiors tend to remain intact because clients lack empathy with the solution delivered and do not know how to go about personalising it.

In contrast, no matter how informative or how interesting a taxonomy of styles may be, those interiors created autonomously by their occupants exist in a state of continuous evolution. If coherence did exist when the empty room was first decorated it will be eroded as new ideas and new acquisitions seduce and are added to the mix. The aesthetic will change superficially but a core taste will shape a hybridised collection that is more powerful than the sum of its parts.

Minimalism-lite

The cult of minimalism flourishes after many fashions. Self-denial, however mild, implies discernment and a virtuous disdain for wanton acquisition but its rules are understood superficially and systematically broken: austerity is diluted, pictures are hung on walls and objects begin to gather dust on flat surfaces. The trope that persists is whiteness and that is not unique to minimalism for white walls are also excellent backdrops for knick-knacks, the accumulation of which is a temptation few humans can resist.

Minimalism-lite has become the new suburban chic, but the committed amateur must observe some principles. Walls and ceilings should be white – but matt and not too bright. Mouldings should be eliminated but, if listed on grounds of historic merit, must never be painted anything other than white; they must fuse. Floors and furniture should be of light-coloured woods, upholstery should be avoided, a woven rush seat is acceptable, and leather tolerated. Curves and curtains are unacceptable. Roller blinds, with central pull cords, are acceptable but must be white, to filter natural light. Hanging things on walls is just wrong. Art is frivolous and pictures should be avoided, or at most set on the floor and leant against a wall, as should mirrors. Crockery should be white, and utensils should be stainless steel and stored from sight in cupboards to be brought out when needed. If one saves a considerable sum of money one can buy crockery and cooking implements designed by Pawson, which are exquisitely elegant. Alternatively, kitchen and dining necessities – and they should be considered necessities – may be bought more economically from commercial catering suppliers. Acquiring decorative objects, even if ostensibly useful, should not be contemplated.

Opposite
White *objets* against a white wall, Scotland, 2014.

Above left
As open fires become redundant a handsome fireplace (painted white) does not stray too far from the rules of Minimalism-lite and provides a useful shelf on which to concentrate decorative pieces. The visual pun of chess board squares and black tiles is a good one. Belfast, 1990.

Above
Minimalism-lite – the white walls, the wooden floor, the diffused natural light, the furniture and fittings have character but keep a low profile, London, 2005.

Neo-Scandinavian

Those who find universal white too stark but are wary of brash colours and who enjoy the well-considered and well-placed object, will drift towards something best categorised as neo-Scandinavian. Their interiors will show restraint but they will choose textiles that have more texture and pattern, and colour – bright colour – will be acceptable. They will enjoy detail that is both functional, and quasi-functional. They will enjoy the well-turned length of wood but will be chary of heavy grain and mouldings. They will hanker after walls clad in vertical, or horizontal, timber boarding.

Right
An embroidered fabric in a woven basket, heavy stonewear jars on bare floorboards in front of horizontal grey-painted wooden boarding are distinctly neo-Scandinavian.

Far right
Unpainted wood in any form is neo-Scandinavian (the chair back in the foreground is from Ikea).

Below left
A simple 'country' antique chair in front of a grey-green painted wall is neo-Scandinavian.

Below right
Preserved fruit in glass jars on a knotty kitchen table in front of grey-painted vertical boarding is neo-Scandinavian.

TASTE

Above
In neo-pagan times, well-shaped and well-marked stones can act as animistic objects.

The impulse to be Minimalist pre-dates modernity and those who find the aesthetic theory a little dry can find directions in more spiritual antecedents.

The Shakers are a Christian sect who left behind the laxities of 18th-century England and retreated to live with uncompromised simplicity in New England. Their communal habitations were built with great precision and skill and their interiors had a particular austerity. All furniture was wooden and upholstery was eschewed. They had something approaching a decorative language that displayed a wit born of practical good sense or perhaps a perverse unbending logic. Wooden side chairs, when not required, were hung on wooden dowels that projected from wooden rails that ran round rooms at picture rail height. There were, of course, no pictures. Round wooden knobs on the flat fronts of drawers stacked from floor to ceiling for the length of a wall made the simplest of patterns. The principles of denial appeals to jaded consumers but few can afford furniture that is made so perfectly by hand and even fewer would acclimatise to the rigours of the lifestyle. The austere forms may be adapted with minimal compromise to make dining tables and chairs and dinner parties, if they avoid excess, can have some affinity with the cult's communal eating habits. The Shakers' predilection for well-organised cupboards with simple wooden doors has unfortunately led to their name being appropriated by manufacturers of the simpler fronted kitchen units.

Westerners, dissuaded of their own religious traditions, are inclined to dabble in Buddhism. The traditional Japanese interior is ostensibly minimal but in a decidedly tactile way with a rich mix of lacquered wood, straw tatami mats, sliding partitions of white paper panels set in delicate timber grids and paper lanterns. Both interior and garden are held to embody the abstract truths of Zen philosophy, whatever those may be. The interiors may be imitated to varying degrees of authenticity and for most enthusiasts, white walls, a straw mat, a painted paper scroll hung on a wall, a paper lantern and a thoughtfully placed bonsai will do. Householders with outdoor space will occasionally attempt to replicate the Japanese gardens of rocks, raked sand and tinkling water, which look satisfyingly austere when compared to the densely planted colours and complexities of the English country garden. The aesthetic is more satisfactorily realised in the set piece of a garden than in an interior where prosaic activities must be accommodated and loadbearing walls lack ethereality. It is best attempted in an open-plan flat and it helps if one lives alone.

Images of Japanese and Shaker interiors have colonised contemporary imaginations. Books of their exquisitely photographed interiors pile up on coffee tables and bookshelves in artistically inclined households. The aesthetics are impossible to replicate convincingly in a contemporary dwelling but they give the minimal glamour.

Travel broadens home decorators' minds and sources. It can provide the ethnic products that undermine the integrity of many a *soi-disant* minimalist interior. Destinations for mass tourism tend to have been reconnoitred by the rich with time and the means to investigate the picturesque and the mysterious. When they write their books the mass market follows. The romanticised self-sufficiency of Mediterranean peasantry continues to hold the imaginations of northern tourists who dream of lofty rooms with tiled floors and uneven white walls, sparsely furnished with heavy wooden furniture banged together long ago by a carpenter rather than a cabinet maker. Other than influencing paint colours, none of those tropes are readily available but ceramics, textiles and indigenous crafts that can be carried in overhead lockers on planes or a spare corner of a crowded car are enough to satisfy nostalgic longings. Since holidaymakers tend to return to favourite destinations, collections grow and have a visual coherence that defines the style.

As long haul holidays have become more affordable tourists venture further and the more exotic the destination the greater the enthusiasm to bring back evidence of having been there. Morocco is long established, first as a safe place for wealthy debauchees, then as a destination for hippies interested in hashish and then as an exotic holiday foothold in Africa for travellers en masse who flocked to bargain in souks for garish lanterns of coloured glass set in intricate metal frames, ceramics with lavish patterns, leathers that seemed to have been very recently removed from the animal, silver trinkets and Berber rugs, produced by 40 tribes each of them weaving their traditional pattern which may be tastefully slung across a worn sofa.

Many homes will have, amongst their old furniture, a smattering of relics, brought back by British administrators from India and Far Eastern colonies and protectorates, as proof of former status and exotic adventure. When the Empire melted away and imperialists retreated they were followed by hippies in search of swamis and gurus, and drugs. Plane-borne tourists followed to snap up souvenirs, brightly coloured textiles and objects in dark woods and beaten metals. Perhaps concerns about cultural appropriation by the benign plundering of other people's marketplaces, will prevail and collecting objects from cultures other than one's own will become *verboten*. Demands that museums return marble friezes from the Parthenon to Greece and Benin Bronzes to Nigeria are longstanding; whether holiday souvenirs bought with empathy will become contraband remains to be seen.

To collect is human and for some to become an obsessive collector is inevitable. It begins in childhood and may evolve into no more than a habit or become an obsession. Obsessives' rooms are devoted to curated displays of esoterica. The collector's eye will in all likelihood make even divergent collections coherent and together they will amount to something comprehensible. The result may be classifiable as a branch of minimalism because a good collection, precisely displayed leaves no room for alien introductions. Objects can be allowed to accumulate until the existence of one is lost in the haze of all and the whole becomes more than the sum of its parts. This may be classified as baroque abstraction. Both methodologies represent variations on the same psychosis.

Top left
Fish made at the end of a working day from superfluous raw material by workers at the Murano glass factories.

———

Below left
Compulsive collecting.

Top right
Lighthouse models turned from Serpentine rock for the Victorian Cornish tourist trade.

———

Below
Less compulsive collecting.

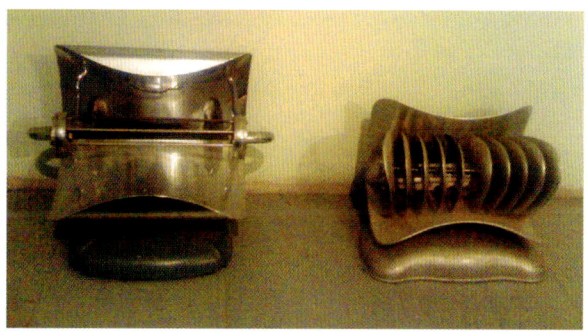

Collections can be specialist or eclectic. Specialist collectors are at the mercy of their obsession and must flaunt their trophies; the rooms that contain them are styled by default and may have curiosity rather than aesthetic merit. Some collections work better than others. Displays of 18th-century embroidered samplers, products of a female sensibility, will enhance. Displays of brightly painted pressed tin toys, collected primarily by grown-up boys, will probably not. The interior remains a feminine domain.

Eclectic collectors are likely to make more beautiful interiors by assembling a collection of disparate objects that are united because they caught the eye and the fancy. The criterion for such collecting is primarily a visual one and the objects are likely to share an aesthetic.

The new International Style

When in the 1930s Modernism was appropriated by American businesses and their architects as the style that best expressed their corporate identity and became the International Style, borrowing its label from MoMA's exhibition of 1932. The rigid formula of steel and glass towers with vast marble clad entrance halls, empty but for a few chrome and leather chairs, was doled out across the world wherever large businesses congregated and the contagion spread downwards, and components of the style became accepted by default as inevitable. But a new International Style has emerged that no longer attempts to impose a homogenous aesthetic across an increasingly homogenous world but takes cues from disappearing local vernaculars. In a time of mass travel and mass communication mushrooming middle-class consumers increasingly identify with their local traditions and retain symbolic vestiges of them in their homes. It is a phenomenon particularly to be found in post-imperial territories that look for identity in their pre-imperial past.

Even as it seems that the world has agreed to be modern a rear guard of anti-modernists fights on, their courage sustained by the presumption that the Modern and the modernistic are novelties and that, with maturity, those who admire them will come to their senses. The passage of time suggests they are wrong but their antipathy towards modernity is therefore visceral.

For some antis the artefacts that are their weapons of choice need to be old but not excessively so. Art Deco is the least venerable of the periods that many can embrace. The 1950s' Contemporary has decorative intent but there is something disturbingly modern about it; it is too fond of plastics and abstractions and too devoid of dignity.

More serious reactionaries who commit to a particular period will search for its artefacts and are likely to become implacable connoisseurs. Others may be more inclusive and value artefacts either for their age or for their appearance of age and are undisturbed by reproductions but yearn for hand crafting. Casual modernity-phobes will settle for reproductions and will become beneficiaries of developing technology. Digital cutting can effortlessly produce delicate patterns in two dimensions and digital 3D modelling can perfectly replicate mouldings. Perhaps the wish, occasionally expressed by Modernists, that a new form of decoration will evolve will be realised. It will not be Modernist but it will be unarguably modern. Technology constantly invents the future. Art rushes to keep up.

To infinity and beyond

Websites and blogs devoted to the home proliferate, from the fairly serious Dezeen, which toes a broadly Modernist line and is the first reference source for most professional architects and designers, to the spontaneously effervescent work of amateurs, the enthusiasts and the 'influencers'.

The domestic interior has inspired a free-to-play computer game. *Homescapes* invites players to act as designers for an appreciative client called Austin and his cat and to choose between furniture and fittings from a collection that does not begin to dabble with elegance or modernity. The avatar is charming and the cute cat wanders randomly and unbidden across the screen. More serious games may be in development.

At the risk of repeating Orwell's mistake by speculating about a future, one might cautiously suggest that a virtual home may represent the future. One might need no more than a comfortable chair and a virtual reality headset with haptic accessories to immerse oneself in one's ideal habitat or habitats. Money and the realities of building will be irrelevant. One might live in homes in a swathe of styles and on several continents and share the experience with connected guests. Opinions on taste would be as pertinent as ever and perhaps more damning since there could be no mitigating financial or practical excuse, for what guests might presume to call bad taste.

Epilogue

'We do not always choose our preferences: instead tastes, fashions and opinions ebb and flow through the population by a kind of contagion.'

Rory Sutherland[1]

Humankind caught the contagion for home decoration when it moved into caves and daubed the walls and it seems that we have never shaken off that decorating bug. Those of us for whom domestic life has become undemanding and incomes disposable have time to consider the prettification of our homes and how to achieve it in the way that best suits us. It is our pleasure shaped by the evidence, in print and online, which becomes increasingly un-ignorable of the homes of our peers and our decorating betters.

In 19th-century Britain, amateur and architectural tastes were harmonious. Aesthetic arguments were conducted on high moral ground and ornament was considered next to godliness. Amateurs respected architects who respected the wishes of the clients who paid their fees and produced ornament on an industrial scale for the factories that generated the amateur wealth that bought the ornament that kept the factories that generated … etc.

Those virtuous circles were broken when a few Modernist visionaries pronounced on matters of architectural taste and blighted the lives of the many. Trainee architects who had once been apprenticed to established practitioners were increasingly taught in the aesthetic ghettoes of schools of art and architecture. Theorising was rarefied and one-sided and pleasure was sacrificed to principles of no particular coherence. For 100 years amateurs have struggled to wriggle free of professional diktats. Taught and untaught have skirmished on the home front; high brows against gut instincts. Professionals have taken it upon themselves to diagnose and offer a remedy to contagious decoration but amateurs had no wish to be cured.

One may question the divine right of professionals to impose rules of taste, but it can be conceded that they are equipped to explore options and offer possibilities. It was perfectly acceptable that they speculate about a new way to house the lumpen masses but something else to expect the unfortunates to live in it. It is the innovation that adapts to broader tastes that prevails. Speculative builders understand the pleasure principle. But making architecture is a reductive process designed to bring order to disorder and in so doing it eliminates the impractical and the irrational and with them the ornamental.

Amateurs absorb their taste from what they see and what they hear. It evolves cautiously, uninterested in and resistant to the new. It is messy, mixing nostalgia and whimsy with the occasional strange new thing that it occasionally finds, for some reason, irresistible.

Professionals are taught a singular taste that values the rational above the intuitive. They are unlikely to find approval for their works amongst the untaught and so they seek it from those who have been similarly taught and together they drift into groupthink. Pedigree professional taste shrinks from mongrelised amateur taste.

In 19th-century Britain the prosperous and proliferating urban middle class found its identity and values validated by the country's pre-eminent place in the world. Its tastemakers were however preoccupied by its long history, took their cues from the past and lost sight of the future it was creating. In the United States former colonials and a miscellany of new immigrants began to evolve their national identity. They were unburdened by their own short history and, by the beginning of the 20th century, found themselves with a new way of living that seduced the world. Tom Wolfe wondered why they had produced so little of aesthetic merit and complained that 'the whole rest of the world loves American junk'.[2] It was beguiling and too easy to love.

Below
Taste changes but ducks endure as arch and ironic, Post-Modern references to a decorative staple. We move on but we find it hard to forget.

Halfway through the 20th century, Britain, confused about its past and unsure of its future, unexpectedly embraced frivolity and led the world in pursuit of it. For no obvious reason its interests and its tastes became distinctly juvenile. It presented the world with a hybrid of its own and America's youth culture. Eccentric clothes defined waves of young fashionistas who became interioristas and brought their enthusiasm for quirks of taste to the decoration of their homes. They understood lifestyle and, in the decades that followed, consumed furnishings, fittings and finishes with the commitment they had brought to buying clothes. Their diversely decorated homes were the places in which the children who have become the new professionals grew up. Those children rebelled – of course – and presently choose to live in the Brutalist tower blocks, loathed by the proles for whom they were made, but they will begin to dream, if they do not already, of a country cottage with a perfect broadband connection.

Taste must always be a puzzle. It belongs to its time and it can't stay still.

Notes

Prologue

Louis H. Sullivan, *Kindergarten Chats: On Architecture, Education and Democracy*, Scarab Fraternity Press, 1892.

Chapter 1

1. Simon Heffer, *High Minds: The Victorians and the Birth of Modern Britain,* Random House Books, London, 2013, p 81.
2. Ibid.
3. Henry Mayhew, *London Labour and the London Poor*, Wordsworth Classics of World Literature, London, 2008, p 380.
4. Clive Edwards, *Turning Houses Into Homes,* Routledge, Abingdon, 2017, p 4.
5. Matthew, *The Bible*, chapter 6, verse 28.
6. Clive Edwards, *Turning Houses Into Homes,* Routledge, Abingdon, 2017.
7. Ibid, p 86.
8. Ibid, p 87.
9. Mark Girouard in his Introduction to: Sarah Lasdun, *Victorians at Home*, Weidenfeld & Nicolson, London, 1981, p 19.
10. Simon Heffer, *High Minds: The Victorians and the Birth of Modern Britain,* Random House Books, London, 2013, p 81.
11. Clive Aslet, *The English House*, Bloomsbury, London, 2008, p 4.
12. Ibid, p 4.
13. Anthony Trollope, *The Small House at Allington* vol.1, British Library, London, p 165.
14. Anthony Trollope, *The Small House at Allington* vol. 2, British Library, London, p 98.
15. Augustus Pugin, *The True Principles of Christian or Pointed Architecture*, J. Weale, London, 1841.
16. Simon Heffer, *High Minds: The Victorians and the Birth of Modern Britain,* Random House Books, London, 2013, Preface, p xiii.
17. Richard Redgrave, *Supplementary Reports on Design, Great Exhibition of 1851*, Clowes, London, 1852, p 1589.
18. Sarah Lasdun, *Victorians at Home*, Weidenfeld & Nicolson, London, 1981, p 12.
19. Simon Heffer, *High Minds: The Victorians and the Birth of Modern Britain*, Random House Books, London, 2013, p 757.
20. Augustus Pugin, *The True Principles of Christian or Pointed Architecture,* J. Weale, London,1841.
21. Ibid.
22. John Ruskin, *The Stones of Venice*, Smith, Elder & Co., London, 1851.
23. Owen Jones, *Grammar of Ornament*, Day and Son Ltd., London, 1856.
24. Simon Heffer, *High Minds: The Victorians and the Birth of Modern Britain*, Random House Books, London, 2013.
25. Osbert Lancaster, *Homes Sweet Homes*, John Murray, London, 1939, p 36.

Chapter 2

1. *The Quarterly Review* July 1867, p 61, cited in Simon Heffer, *High Minds: The Victorians and the Birth of Modern Britain*, Random House, London, 2013, p 757.
2. Clive Edwards, *Turning Houses Into Homes*, Ashgate Publishing, Farnham, 2005, p 8.
3. Ibid, p 89.
4. Ibid, p 81.
5. Ibid, p 81.
6. Geoffrey Beard, *The National Trust Book of the English House*, Penguin, London, 1991, p 238.
7. Augustus Hare, *The Years With Mother*, 1896, cited in Geoffrey Beard, *The National Trust Book of the English House*, Penguin, London, 1991, p 244.
8. Ibid, p 245.
9. Ibid, p 244.
10. Ibid, p 258.
11. Ibid, p 261.
12. Ibid, p 263.
13. Ibid p 82.
14. Ibid, p 104.
15. Ibid, p 144.
16. Ibid, p 105.
17. Ibid, p 62.
18. Ibid, p 75.
19. Ibid, p 116.
20. Ibid, p 117.
21. Ibid, p 117.
22. Ibid, p 107.
23. Ibid, p 111.
24. Ibid, p 104.
25. Ibid, p 127.
26. Ibid, p 139.
27. Le Corbusier, *Towards a New Architecture*, G. Crès, Paris, 1927, p 114.
28. Henry Mayhew, cited in Clive Edwards, *Turning Houses Into Homes*, Ashgate Publishing, Farnham, 2005, p 153.
29. J. Ginswick, cited in Clive Edwards, *Turning Houses Into Homes*, Ashgate Publishing, Farnham, 2005, p 154.
30. Ibid, p 154.
31. Osbert Lancaster, *Homes Sweet Homes*, John Murray, London, 1939, p 36.
32. Ibid, p 36.

33. Sarah Lasdun, *Victorians at Home*, Weidenfeld & Nicolson, London, 1981, p 16.

34. Ibid, p 16.

35. R. Kerr (1865), cited in Clive Edwards, *Turning Houses Into Homes*, Ashgate Publishing, Farnham, 2005, p 164.

36. Benjamin Disraeli, cited in Ibid, p 164.

37. Mrs Panton, cited in Ibid, p 138.

38. Osbert Lancaster, *Homes Sweet Homes*, John Murray, London, 1939, p 42.

39. Ibid, p 42.

40. E. F. Benson, *As We Were*, Penguin Classic Biography, London, 2001, p 16.

41. M. T. Saler, *The Avant-Garde in Interwar England: Medieval Modernism and the London Underground*, Oxford University Press, Oxford, 1999, p 156.

42. Sarah Lasdun, *Victorians at* Home, Weidenfeld & Nicolson, London, 1981.

43. Ibid, p 121.

44. Osbert Lancaster, *Homes Sweet Homes*, John Murray, London, 1939, p 44.

45. Ibid, p 121.

46. Osbert Lancaster, *Homes Sweet Homes,* John Murray, London, 1939, p 44.

47. Ibid, p 54.

48. Peter York, *Authenticity is a Con*, Biteback Publishing Ltd, London, 2014, p 108.

Chapter 3

1. Bevis Hillier, *The Style Of The Century*, The Herbert Press, New York, 1998, p 19.

2. Osbert Lancaster, *Homes Sweet Homes*, John Murray, London, 1939, p 56.

3. Ibid, p 56.

4. E. F. Benson, *As We Were*, Penguin Classic Biography, London, 2001, p 331.

5. F. T. Marinetti, *Manifesto of Futurism*, Sackville Gallery, London, 1912, p 5 (British Library General Reference Collection RF.2008.a.33).

6. Le Corbusier, *Vers une Architecture* (1923), translated by Frederick Etchells, *Towards a New Architecture* (1927), Dover Publications, New York, 1986, p 1.

7. Adolf Loos, *Architektur*, cited by Karel Teige, *Modern Architecture in Czechoslovakia and Other Writings*, Getty Research Institute, Los Angeles, 2000, p 155.

8. Adolf Loos, *Ornament and Crime*, cited in Nicholas Pevsner, *Pioneers of the Modern Movement*, Faber & Faber, London, 1936, p 21.

9. Ibid, p 21.

10. Louis H. Sullivan, *Kindergarten Chats: On Architecture, Education and Democracy*, Scarab Fraternity Press, Chicago, 1892, p 187.

11. Ibid, p 187.

12. Getty Research Institute, *Art & Architecture Thesaurus*. www.getty.edu/page/aat/300021472 (accessed 7 October 2019).

13. Jacob Bronowski, *The Ascent of Man*, BBC, London, 1976, p 251.

14. Frank Lloyd Wright, *The Natural House*, Penguin Reissue, London, 1991.

15. Amédéé Ozenfant, *Foundations of Modern Art*, Dover Publications, New York, 1931 p 144.

16. Osbert Lancaster, *Homes Sweet Homes*, John Murray, London, 1939, p 76.

17. Ibid, p 76.

18. Ibid, p 76.

19. Evelyn Waugh, *Decline and Fall*, Penguin Modern Classics, London, p 157.

20. Ibid, p 157.

21. Ibid, p 157.

22. Ibid, p 158.

23. Ibid, p 159.

24. Ibid, p 159.

25. Ibid, p 64.

26. Ibid, p 58.

27. Louis H. Sullivan, *The Tall Office Building Artistically Considered*, Getty Research Institute, Los Angeles, 1896.

28. Recorded in the archive of the Association of Women Industrial Designers, 29 March 2013.

29. Anthony Flint, *Modern Man: The Life of Le Corbusier*, New Harvest, New York, 2014.

30. David Arkin, cited by Jean-Louis Cohen, *Le Corbusier and the Mystique of the USSR: Theories and Projects for Moscow 1928–1936*, Books on Demand. 1992, p 40.

Chapter 4

1. *Homes Sweet Homes*, John Murray, London, 1939, p 60.

2. Osbert Lancaster

3. Ibid, p 60.

4. James Agee, *Night of the Hunter*, screenplay, 1955.

5. Gustav Stickley, cited by Paul Duchscherer and Douglas Keister, *Inside the Bungalow: America's Arts and Crafts Interior*, Penguin Studio, November 1997. p 4.

6. Ibid, p 4.

7. Deborah Sugg Ryan, *Ideal Homes 1918–39*, Manchester University Press, Manchester, 2018, p 51.

8. Alison Light, cited by Deborah Sugg Ryan, *Ideal Homes 1918–39*, Manchester University Press, Manchester, 2018, p 59.

9. Deborah Sugg Ryan, *Ideal Homes 1918–39*, Manchester University Press, Manchester, 2018, p 60.

10. Ibid, p 51.
11. Ibid, p 159.
12. Ibid, p 60.
13. Ibid, p 60.
14. Ibid, p 161.
15. Ibid, p 60.
16. Paul Follot cited by Alastair Duncan, *Art Deco*, Thames & Hudson, London, 1988.
17. Osbert Lancaster, *Homes Sweet Homes*, John Murray, London, 1939, p 72.
18. Ibid, p 72.
19. Ibid, p 72.
20. Design & Industries Association, cited by Deborah Suggs Ryan, *Ideal Homes 1919–39*, Manchester University Press, Manchester, 2018, p 15.
21. H. J. Birnstingl, cited by Deborah Sugg Ryan, *Ideal Homes 1918–39*, Manchester University Press, Manchester, 2018, p 75.
22. Osbert Lancaster, *Homes Sweet Homes*, John Murray, London, 1939, p 72.
23. Walter Gropius, *The New Architecture and the Bauhaus*, The MIT Press, Cambridge, MA, 1965, p 66.
24. Kenneth Clark, Ornament in Modern Architecture, *Architectural Review*, December 1943, p 149.
25. Ibid, p 150.
26. Ibid.
27. Deborah Sugg Ryan, *Ideal Homes 1918–39*, Manchester University Press, Manchester, 2018, p 10.

Chapter 5

1. Dominic Bradbury, *Mid-century Modern Complete*, Thames & Hudson, London, 2014, p 6.
2. Osbert Lancaster, *Homes Sweet Homes*, John Murray, London, 1939, p 78.
3. Ibid, p 78.
4. Ibid, p 78.
5. Harry Hopkins, *The New Look: A Social History of the Forties and Fifties*, Secker and Warburg, London, 1964, p 165.
6. Stephen Calloway, *Twentieth-century Decoration: The Domestic Interior from 1900 to the Present Day*, Weidenfeld & Nicolson, London, 1988, p 288.
7. W. D. Wetherell, *The Man Who Loved Levittown*, cited by Colin Marshall, www.theguardian.com/cities/2015/apr/28/levittown-america-prototypical-suburb-history-cities (accessed 7 October 2019).
8. Daniel S. Defenbacher, cited by Alexandra Griffith Winton, *The Modern Period Home*, Routledge, Abingdon, 2006, p 91.
9. Alexandra Griffith Winton, *The Modern Period Home*, Routledge, Abingdon, 2006, p100.
10. Lois Miller, Helen Tully and Dorothy Vine letter to D. S. Defenbacher, cited by Alexandra Griffith Winton, *The Modern Period Home*, Routledge, Abingdon, 2006, p 102.
11. Judith Gura, *The Guide to Period Styles*, Bloomsbury, London, 2016, p 312.
12. Ibid, p 332.

Chapter 6

1. Bill Bryson, *The Life and Times of the Thunderbolt Kid: Travels Through my Childhood*, Black Swan, London, 2008, p 1.
2. Richard Yates, *Revolution Road*, cited by Colin Marshall, www.theguardian.com/cities/2015/apr/28/levittown-america-prototypical-suburb-history-cities (accessed 7 October 2019).
3. William Levitt cited by Colin Marshall, www.theguardian.com/cities/2015/apr/28/levittown-america-prototypical-suburb-history-cities (accessed 7 October 2019).
4. Anne Fogarty, *Wife Dressing: The Fine Art of Being a Well-dressed Wife*, Julian Messner Inc., New York, 1959.
5. Harry Hopkins, *The New Look: A Social History of the Forties and Fifties*, Secker and Warburg, London, 1964, p 271.
6. Ibid, p 271.
7. William Feaver, *A Tonic to the Nation: Festival of Britain 1951*, eds. M. Banham and B. Hillier, Thames & Hudson, London, 1976, p 54.
8. Harry Hopkins, *The New Look: A Social History of the Forties and Fifties*, Secker and Warburg, London, 1964, p 477.
9. Hugh Casson, 'Twenty Years On', *Designers Journal*, issue 37, 1988, p 52.
10. Harry Hopkins, *The New Look: A Social History of the Forties and Fifties*, Secker and Warburg, London, 1964, p 477.
11. Robert Elms, *The Way We Wore*, Picador, London, 2005, p 17.
12. Marghanita Laski, 'Espresso', *The Architectural Review*, vol. 118, issue 705, 1955, p 165.
13. Ibid, p 165.
14. Nancy Mitford, *Noblesse Oblige*, New Edition, Oxford University Press, Oxford, 2002.
15. Richard Hoggart, *The Uses of Literacy: Aspects of Working-Class Life*, New Impression Edition, Penguin, London, 1973.
16. Michael Billington, *State of the Nation: British Theatre Since 1945*, Faber & Faber, London, 2009.

Chapter 7

1. Roger Miller, *England Swings (like a pendulum do)*, pop/country song, 1965.
2. Mary Quant, 'Mary Quant Interview', *Time Out*, 2008, www.timeout.com/london/things-to-do/mary-quant-interview (accessed 9 October 2019).

3. Philip Larkin, *High Windows*, Faber and Faber, 1974, https://allpoetry.com/Annus-Mirabilis (accessed 9 October 2019).
4. Christopher Brooker, *The Neophiliacs* (1969) cited in James Delingpole, *The Spectator*, 3 March 2019.
5. Paul Johnson, 'Beatlism', *New Statesman*, February 1964, www.newstatesman.com/culture/2014/08/archive-menace-beatlism (accessed 9 October 2019).
6. Hunter Davies, *Sunday Times Magazine*, 4 March 2019, p 61.
7. Yvonne Roberts, 'So Farewell Habitat. You Made Us Modern', *Guardian Online*, 26 June 2011, www.theguardian.com/commentisfree/2011/jun/26/yvonne-roberts-habitat (accessed 9 October 2019).
8. Stephen Bayley, Mr Habitat, *Architectural Review*, vol. 160, issue 969, 1977, p 287.
9. Sir Edward Elgar at Birmingham University, 1905 cited by John Bratby, *The Spectator*, 11 August 2018.
10. Peter York, *Style Wars*, Sidgwick and Jackson, London, 1991, p 182.

Chapter 8

1. Peter York, *Style Wars*, Sidgwick and Jackson, London, 1991.
2. Robert Venturi, *Complexity and Contradiction in Architecture*, Museum of Modern Art, New York, 1984.
3. J. M. Richards, *The Castles on the Ground* (1946), cited in Deborah Sugg Ryan, *Ideal Homes 1918–39*. Manchester University Press, Manchester, 2018, p 161.
4. Paul Goldberger, *Ornamentalism: The New Decorativeness in Architecture and Design*, Allen Lane, London, 1982, foreword.
5. Jensen and Conway, *Ornamentalism: The New Decorativeness in Architecture and Design*, Allen Lane, London, 1982, p 17.
6. Ada Louise Huxtable, *Ornamentalism: The New Decorativeness in Architecture and Design*, Allen Lane, London, 1982, p 17.
7. Jensen and Conway, *Ornamentalism: The New Decorativeness in Architecture and Design*, Allen Lane, London, 1982, p 18.
8. Ibid.
9. William Shakespeare, *Henry IV, Part 1*.
10. Peter York, *Style Wars*, Sidgwick and Jackson, London, 1991, p 11.
11. James Lileks, *Desecrations: Hideous Homes From The Horrible 70s*, Crown, New York, 2005.
12. Ibid.
13. Bevis Hillier, *The Style of the Century*, Herbert Press, New York, 1998.
14. Ibid.

Chapter 9

1. Peter York and Charles Jennings, *Peter York's Eighties*, BBC Books, London, 1995, p 9.
2. Alfred Sherman cited in Peter York, *Peter York's Eighties*, BBC Books, London, 1996, p 12.
3. Robert Elms, *The Way We Wore*, Picador, London, 2005, p.184
4. Min Hogg cited in Peter York, *Peter York's Eighties*, BBC Books, London, 1996, p 93.
5. Deyan Sudjic, 'How a flower arrangement caused fear and loathing', *The Observer*, 3 October, 2004, www.theguardian.com/artanddesign/2004/oct/03/art3 (accessed 10 October 2019).

Chapter 10

1. Dr Juliette Desplat, 'A man one could do business with', 11 March 2015, https://blog.nationalarchives.gov.uk/man-one-business/ (accessed 10 October 2010).
2. https://en.wikipedia.org/wiki/Faith_Popcorn (accessed 10 October 2010).
3. Peter York and Charles Jennings, 'Rodney Fitch Interview', *Peter York's Eighties*, BBC Books, London, 1996, p 61.
4. India Knight, 'Happy 30th Birthday Ikea', *Sunday Times Magazine*, 15 October 2017, p 5, www.thetimes.co.uk/article/india-knight-happy-30th-birthday-ikea-you-democratised-good-taste-hppvv609c (accessed 10 October 2010).
5. Kate Morley, 'Is this the end of the three-piece suite?', *The Telegraph*, 13 March 2019.

Epilogue

1. Rory Sutherland, 'The Wiki Man', *The Spectator*, 21 July 2018, p 61.
2. Peter York, *Style Wars*, Sidgwick and Jackson, London, 1991, p 223.

Index

Page numbers in **bold** indicate figures.

78 Derngate, Northampton **56**, 57
2001: A Space Odyssey (film) 145

A

Aalto, Alvar 107
Adron, Ralph 142, **143**, 156
Aesthetic movement 32, 40–41
Aghion House, Alexandria **53**
Albert, Prince 16–18, 19
Alberti, Leon Battista 47
Ant, Adam 171–172, **172**
Aram, Zeev 136
Architectural Association 77
Architectural Review 77–78
Arkwright, John 26
Art and Architecture 102, 103
Art Deco **56**, 57, **58**, 78–81, **78**, **79**, **80**, **81**, 88, 202
Art Moderne 80–81, 88, 94
Art Nouveau 41, 44, 47, 88, 107
Arts and Crafts 19, 27, 33–41, **34**, **36**, **37**, **38**, 50, 55–57, 71, 77, **83**, 88, 107
Arts and Crafts Exhibition Society 37
Ashbee, C. R. 37–38
Aslet, Clive 6
Attlee, Clement 93

B

Badovici, Jean 63
Bakelite 59, 81
Barbarella (film) 145
Barbican, London 121, **122**
Barcelona Pavilion **62**
Barker, Thomas Jones 3
barns, converted 184
Barry, Gerald 110
Barry, Sir Charles 7
Bassett-Lowke, Wenham Joseph 57
Bauhaus 46, **47**, 61, 66
Bayard-Condict Building, New York **50**
Bayley, Stephen 140

Bazalgette, Peter 191
Beatles 130, 134, 135
Behrens, Peter 47, 51, **56**, 57
Belfast Modern Architecture Exhibition 112
Belgravia, London 6–7
Bennett, Alan 127
Benson, E. F. 32–33
Berry, Chuck 135
Betjeman, John 55, 78, 125, 127
Beyond the Fringe 127
Billington, Michael 127
Birnstingl, Harry Joseph 77, 86
Bon Marche (retailer) 28–29, **29**
Booth, Sam 189
Botschi, Pierre 161, **162**, **163**
Boudin, Stephane 136
Bradbury, Dominic 91
Breuer, Marcel 59, 103, 136
Bright Young Things 55, 73, 78, 125–127
Bronowski, Jacob 52
Brooker, Christopher 134
Brutalism 121–124
Bryson, Bill 109
Bucknell, Barry 119, 191
Buddhist influences 199–200
bungalows 71, 84
Burges, William 24, **24**, 25
Burne-Jones, Edward 35, 37
Byker Wall, Newcastle **154**

C

Cardiff Castle 24, **24**
Carlyle, Thomas 11
Carpenter Gothic 72
Casson, Hugh 110–112, 117
Castell Coch 24
Changing Rooms (television programme) 191
Chicago Tribune tower competition 49, **49**
China Wharf, London **180**

Christie, Agatha 59
Chrysler Building 72
Churchill, Winston 93, 95, 116
Clark, Kenneth 88–89
Classicism
  Neo-Classicism 2, 21, 47, 66, **66**, 67, 92, 107
  Post-Modern Classicism 150–153, **151**, **152**, 155
Clendinning, Max 140–142, **141**, **142**, **143**, **144**, 156, **157**, **158**
Coates, Wells 59, **59**, **60**
coffee bars 125, **125**, 126
Cole, Henry 17–19
collecting 4, 103, **105**, 200–202, **201**
Colonial Revival 72
Connell, Amyas 57, **57**, **58**
Connor, David 171–173, **172**, **173**
Conran, Terence 136–140, 179
Contemporary style 113–114, **113**, **114**, **115**, 119–121, **120**, **121**, **123**, 125, 131, 138, 202
Conway, Patricia 153–155, 159
Council of Industrial Design 95
country cottage, ideal 74, 75, **75**, 86, 182–184, **183**, **184**, **185**
Crystal Palace 17, **18**, 19–21
Culliford, Leonard 76

D

Daily Mail 73
Daily Mirror 74
David, Elizabeth 138, 173
Davies, George 188
Davies, Hunter 140
Day, Lucienne 114, **114**, **115**
Day, Robin 114, **114**, 193
De Stijl group 45, **45**, **46**, 51
de Wolff, Elsie 61
Defenbacher, Daniel S. 100–102, 103
Defoe, Daniel 25
department stores 28–29, **29**, 30, **48**, 49, 159, 192

Design and Industries Association 82
Design Museum, London 179
Dickens, Charles 11
Dior, Christian 93
Disraeli, Benjamin 32
DIY 119
Dolmetsch, Heinrich 16
Dom-Ino House design 47, 49
Dromore Castle, Limerick **40**
Dupont, Henry 136
Dutch Colonial 72
Dvorak, Max 49
Dyce, William 19
Dyson, James 179

E
E1027 house, Côte d'Azur 63–64, **64**, **65**
Eames, Charles 102, 103–104, **104**, **105**, 192–193, **193**
Eames, Ray 102, 103–104, **104**, **105**, 192–193, **193**
Eastlake, Charles 27
Edgeworth, Maria 30
Edwards, Clive 3–4, 25, 28, 29
Elgar, Sir Edward 145
Elms, Robert 124, 166–167
Empire State Building 72
Entwhistle, Clive **79**
Epstein, Brian 130
Esavian furniture 94, **94**, 119–120
Exposition des Arts Decoratifs, Paris 53, 54, 78

F
Faulkner, Charles 35
Feaver, William 113
Ferry, Bryan 170–171, 172
Festival of Britain 110–114, **111**, **112**, **113**
Fitch, Rodney 158, 189
Flint, Anthony 63–64
Fogarty, Anne 110
Follot, Paul 79
Ford, Ford Maddox 35
Franz Joseph, Emperor of Austria **48**, 49, 145

Freud, Ernst Ludwig **80**
Futurism 45

G
Getty Research Institute 50
Gillows (retailer) 29
Girouard, Mark 4, 14, 32, 39
Godwin, Edward 39, **40**
Goldberger, Paul 153
Gonzalez, Manny 156
Goodwin, Philip L. 103
Gorbachev, Mikhail 188
Gore, Catherine 26
Gorton, Asheton 145
Gothic Revival 2–3, 4–13, **7**, **8**, **12**, **13**, 14–15, 19–21, **20**, 24, **24**, 35
Gray, Eileen 63–64, **64**, **65**
Great Exhibition 17–18, **18**, 19–21, **20**, 24
Gropius, Walter 46, **47**, 59, 88
Guild and School of Handicraft 37–38
Gura, Judith 103–104
Guthrie, Woody 72

H
Habitat (retailer) 136–140, **137**, **139**, 158, 189, 190
Hampstead Garden Suburb **83**
Hare, Augustus 26
Harvey, Marshall **83**
Haslam, Nicholas 170, 171, 172
Heals (retailer) 120, **120**
Heffer, Simon 1, 2, 11, 13, 14
Heseltine, Michael 30
High and Over, Amersham 57, **57**, **58**
High Tech 176, **177**
Hillier, Bevis 43, 160, 161
hippies 145–147
Hitler, Adolf 66, 92
Hoffenberg, Rae 179
Hoffman, Josef 63
Hogg, Min 169–170, 171, 174
Hoggart, Richard 127, 130–131
Holly Mount, Buckinghamshire **37**
Homescapes (computer game) 203
Hopkins, Harry 94, 113, 116

House of the Future (1928) 73
House of the Future (1956) 122–124, **123**
Houses of Parliament 7, **7**
Huxtable, Ada Louise 153

I
Idea House project 100–102
Ideal Home exhibition 73, 77, **115**, 122
Ikea (retailer) 189–191, **190**, 192
Industrial Chic 176–182, **177**, **178**, **180**, **181**
Innes, Jocasta 173–174
International Style 50–51, 202
Izenour, Steven 151

J
Japanese influences 39, 199–200
Jeanneret, Charles-Edouard *see* Le Corbusier
Jensen, Robert 153–155, 159
John Lewis (retailer) 192
Johnson, Paul 134
Johnson, Philip 103
Jones, Owen 15–16, **15**

K
Kamprad, Ingvar 190
Kelly, Kevin 169
Kennedy, Jacqueline 135–136
Kennedy, John F. 135
kitsch 84–86, 159, 161–163
Knack … and How To Get It, The (film) 142–145
Knight, India 189
Kubrick, Stanley 145

L
Lancaster, Osbert 21, 31–32, 39, 41, 44, 53–54, 55, 70, 78, 79–80, 87, 92
Larkin, Philip 130
Lasdun, Denys **78**
Laski, Marghanita 125
The Lawn, Harlow 116, **117**
Lawn Road flats, Hampstead 59, **59**
Le Corbusier 31, 47, 49, 52–53, 54, 59, 61, 63–64, 66, 78, 79, 92, 117, 136, 140, 192

Lein, Malcolm 100
Lein, Miriam 100
Lester, Dick 145
Levitt, William 98, 110
Levittown houses 98–99, 110
Light, Alison 75–76
Lileks, James 159
Lillington Gardens, Pimlico 153, **154**
Llewelyn-Bowen, Laurence 191
loft living 176–182, **177**, **178**, **180**, **181**
Lonsdale, Horatio 24
Loos, Adolf 16, 48–49, **48**, **49**, **50**, 67
Lovell Health House, Los Angeles **55**

M

McCarthy, Joseph 110
Macdonald, Margaret 41, 60
Mackintosh, Charles Rennie 41, **56**, 57, 60
McLaren, Malcolm 163, 171
Macmillan, Harold 131
Mahony, Marion 62, 63, 64
Mann, Thomas 30
Marsh, John 192
Marshall, Peter Paul 35
Matthews, W. P. 119
Maugham, Syrie 61, **61**
Mayhew, Henry 3, 11, 31
Mayorcas, Elie **75**
Mencken, H. L. 16
Merchants' National Bank, Grinnell, Iowa **67**
Mies van der Rohe, Ludwig 46, 50, **62**, 63, 66, 136, 151, 192
Miller, Roger 129
Minimalism 174–176
minimalism 199–200, **199**, 201
Minimalism-lite **196**, 197, **197**
minimum house 98, 100
Minneapolis Star Tribune 102, 159
Mission Revival 72
Mitford, Nancy 125–127
Modernism 14–15, 45–67, 80, 88–89, 194, 202, 205
    in Britain 55–59, **56**, **57**, **58**, **59**, **60**, 93–94, 116–118, **117**, **118**
    critiques of 52–54, 75–76, 77–78, 92
    in Europe 45–49, **45**, **46**, **47**, **48**, **50**, 51, 66–67, **66**
    International Style 50–51, 202
    in United States 49–51, **50**, **51**, 54–55, **55**, **67**, 72, 103–104
    white interiors 60–61, **61**, 142–145, **142**
    women in 60–61, **61**, 62–64, **62**, **64**, 65
    see also Minimalism; Post-Modernism
Moore, Dudley 127
Moore, Henry **118**
Morgue, Oliver 145
Morley, Kate 192
Morris, William 33–37, **34**, **36**, 38–39, 52
Mount-Temple, Lady 35
Mulberry House, Smith Square, London **78**
Museum of Modern Art (MoMA) 50, 51, 72, 103, 202
Mussolini, Benito 55, **66**, 67
Muthesius, Hermann 55–57

N

National Gallery extension, London 152–153, **152**
Nelson, George 102
Neo-Classicism 2, 21, 47, 66, **66**, 67, 92, 107
Neo-Gothic 2–3, 4–13, **7**, **8**, **12**, **13**, 14–15, 19–21, **20**, 24, **24**, 35
neo-Scandinavian 198, **198**
Nessen, Walter von 102
Neutra, Richard 54, **55**
New Brutalism 121–124, **122**, **123**
New Concordia Wharf, London **180**
New Romanticism 163, 166–167, 171, **172**
new towns 117–118, **118**
New Ways, Northampton **56**, 57
Next (retailer) 188–189
Nicholls, Thomas 24
Nixon, Richard 135, 150, 166

O

Oaklands Estate, Clapham Park, London **80**
Old Barn, Stanmore, London **87**
Oldenburg, Claes 156
online retailers 192
Ornamentalism 153–155
Orwell, George 188
Ozenfant, Amédée 52, 53, 78, 89

P

Palazzo della Civiltà Italiana, Rome **66**
Parrish, Dorothy Mae 'Sister' 136
Pavillion de L'Esprit Nouveau 53, 78
Pawson, John 174–176, 197
Paxton, Joseph 17
Pearman, Hugh 176
Perret, Auguste 52, **53**, 89
Perriand, Charlotte 63, 64
Perry, Kellen 159
Pfeiffer, Albert 63
Phillips, George 16
Pimlico, London 4–7, **5**, 153, **154**
Pirroni, Marco 172, **173**
Popcorn, Faith 188
Post-Modernism 150–156, 159, 194, **206**
    interior design 167, 169–174
    Ornamentalism 153–155
    Post-Modern Classicism 150–153, **151**, **152**, 155
Poundbury, Dorset 155–156, **155**
Prairie houses 50, 51, **51**, 62
prefabricated houses 95–97, **95**, **96**, **97**, 98–99
Pre-Raphaelite Brotherhood 11, 24, 35
public housing 53, 76, **76**, 93, 121–122, **122**, 134, 153, **154**, 167–168
Pugin, Augustus 7–11, **7**, **8**, **9**, **10**, 14–15, 19–21, **20**, 33, 35, 52
punk 163

Q

Quant, Mary 130, 136, 147
Quarterly Review, The 23

R

Race, Ernest **113**

Racinet, Albert 16
raumplan strategy 49, **50**
Rawsthorn, Alice 179
Reagan, Ronald 166, 188
Red House, Bexleyheath **9**, **34**, 35
Redgrave, Richard 14
Reich, Lilly **62**, 63, 64
residential towers 53, 116–117, **117**, 121, **122**, 134
retailers 25, 27–31, 131, 156–159, 188
    department stores 28–29, **29**, 30, **48**, 49, 159, 192
    Habitat 136–140, **137**, **139**, 158, 189, 190
    Ikea 189–191, **190**, 192
    Next 188–189
    online 192
Reynolds, Malvine 99
Richards, J. M. 59, 77–78, 89, 153
Rietveld, Gerrit **45**, **46**
Roberts, Isabel 62
Roberts, Tommy 156
Roberts, Yvonne 140
Robertson, Howard 77
Robie House, Chicago **51**
Robin Hood Gardens, London 121–122, **122**
Ronan Point, London 134
Ross, Alan 125, 127
Rossetti, Dante Gabriel 35
Roth, Alfred 61
Royal Festival Hall, London 112
Ruskin, John 11, 15, 27–28, 33, 41, 52

S
Saarinen, Eero 102, 103
Saler, M. T. 33
Salon des Artistes Decorateurs **65**
Scandinavian design 103, 104–107, **106**, **107**, 114
    neo-Scandinavian 198, **198**
    see also Ikea (retailer)
Schindler, Rudolph 54, **55**
Schröder House, Utrecht **45**, **46**
Scott, Gilbert 35

Scott Brown, Denise 151–153, **152**, 155, 156
Seaside, Florida 155
Seven Sisters, Moscow **66**, 67
Shakers 199, 200
Sheraton, Thomas 4
Sherman, Alfred 166
shops *see* retailers
Smith, Adam 25, 28
Smithson, Alison 121–124, **122**, **123**
Smithson, Peter 121–124, **122**, **123**
social housing 53, 76, **76**, 93, 121–122, **122**, 134, 153, **154**, 167–168
Soft Modern 194–195, **194**, **195**
Spanish Colonial 72
Speer, Albert 66, 92
Stalin, Joseph 46, 66, **66**, 67
Stefanides, John 171
Stein, Gertrude 54–55
Stein, Leo 54–55
Stickley, Gustav 71
Stokes, J. 27
Strasser House, Vienna **50**
Strawberry Hill, London 11–13, **12**, **13**
Streamline style 80–81, 94
suburbia 71–78, **74**, **75**, **76**, 82–88, **82**, **83**, **84**, **85**, 98–103, 131
Sudjic, Deyan 179
Sugg Ryan, Deborah 69, 75, 76, 77, 89
Sullivan, Louis 49–50, **50**, 51, 59, 67, **67**
Sunday Times Magazine 131, 189
Sutherland, Rory 204

T
Taylor, Bill 119–121
Taylor, Lindsay 119–121
Teddy boys 124–125, 163
Temple of Rubies, Madhya Pradesh, India **79**
Thackeray, W. M. 28
Thatcher, Margaret 166, 188
The Grange, Ramsgate 8, **9**
tourism 200, **201**
tower blocks of flats 53, 116–117, **117**, 121, **122**, 134

Tower House, Kensington, London **25**
Trollope, Anthony 6
Tudor Walters Report 76
Tudorbethan style 74, 76, **87**, 88

U
Utility furniture 95

V
Vadim, Roger 145
Venturi, Robert 150–153, **152**, 155, 156
Victoria and Albert Museum 19
Vitruvius, Marcus 47
Voysey, Charles 27, **37**, 38, **38**

W
Waldegrave, Frances, Lady 13, **13**
Walker Arts Center, Minneapolis 100–102, 104
Walpole, Horace 11–13, **12**
Wasmuth, Ernst 51
Waugh, Evelyn 54, 55, 78, 125, 127
Webb, Philip **9**, 35
Wegner, Hans 107
Weissenhof exhibition, Stuttgart 77
Wells Coates circular radio 81, **81**
Wetherell, W. D. 99
Whistler, James Abbott McNeill 39
White House 135–136
white interiors 60–61, **61**, 142–145, **142**, **196**, 197, **197**
Whiteleys (retailer) 29, **29**
Wilde, Oscar 39, 40
Wolfe, Tom 147, 205
Wood, Victoria 160
Woolworth Building 72
World of Interiors 169–171, **170**, 174–175, 183, 191
World's Fair, New York 100
Wright, Frank Lloyd 49, 50, 51, **51**, 52, 54, 62–63

Y
Yerbury, F. R. 77
yippies 146–147
York, Peter 41, 147, 149, 165

Image credits

i	RIBA Collections
iii	RIBA Collections
viii	Architectural Press Archive / RIBA Collections
5	Architectural Press Archive / RIBA Collections
7	*Left* Eric de Mare / RIBA Collections
7	*Right* RIBA Collections
8	RIBA Collections
9	*Top* RIBA Collections
9	*Bottom* Janet Hall / RIBA Collections
10	RIBA Collections
12	*Top* Martin Charles / RIBA Collections
12	*Bottom* Bernard Cox / RIBA Collections
13	*Left* Architectural Press Archive / RIBA Collections
13	*Right* Architectural Press Archive / RIBA Collections
15	*All* RIBA Collections
18	*Top* RIBA Collections
18	*Bottom* RIBA Collections
20	RIBA Collections
22	Edwin Smith / RIBA Collections
24	*Both* Edwin Smith / RIBA Collections
25	RIBA Collections
29	*Left* RIBA Collections
29	*Right* Edwin Smith / RIBA Collections
34	*Both* Janet Hall / RIBA Collections
36	RIBA Collections
37	*All* RIBA Collections
38	*Both* RIBA Collections
40	*Both* RIBA Collections
42	RIBA Collections
45	Hans Jan Durr / RIBA Collections
46	Tim Benton / RIBA Collections
47	RIBA Collections
48	Keith Collie / RIBA Collections
49	RIBA Collections
50	*Left* ORCH Chemollo / RIBA Collections
50	*Right* Tim Benton / RIBA Collections
51	Bernard Cox / RIBA Collections
53	RIBA Collections
55	*Top* Damien Blower / RIBA Collections
55	*Bottom* RIBA Collections
56	*Top right* RIBA Collections
56	*Middle right* RIBA Collections
56	*Bottom left* Morley von Sternberg / RIBA Collections
56	*Bottom right* Morley von Sternberg / RIBA Collections
57	Morley von Sternberg / RIBA Collections
58	Morley von Sternberg / RIBA Collections
59	RIBA Collections
60	*Top left* Architectural Press Archive / RIBA Collections
60	*Top right* Architectural Press Archive / RIBA Collections
60	*Bottom left* Architectural Press Archive / RIBA Collections
61	RIBA Collections
62	Robert Elwall / RIBA Collections
64	RIBA Collections
65	*All* RIBA Collections
66	*Left* Bernard Cox / RIBA Collections
66	*Right* Edwin Smith / RIBA Collections
67	*Top* Damien Blower / RIBA Collections
67	*Bottom* Damien Blower / RIBA Collections
68	Architectural Press Archive / RIBA Collections
74	RIBA Collections
75	Architectural Press Archive / RIBA Collections
76	RIBA Collections
78	*Left* Architectural Press Archive / RIBA Collections
78	*Right* Architectural Press Archive / RIBA Collections
79	*Left* Architectural Press Archive / RIBA Collections
79	*Right* RIBA Collections
80	*Left* Architectural Press Archive / RIBA Collections
80	*Top right* RIBA Collections
80	*Top right* RIBA Collections
81	Architectural Press Archive / RIBA Collections
82	John Maltby / RIBA Collections
83	*Top left* RIBA Collections
83	*Top right* Architectural Press Archive / RIBA Collections
83	*Bottom* Martin Charles /RIBA Collections
84	Architectural Press Archive / RIBA Collections
85	Architectural Press Archive / RIBA Collections
86	Drew Plunkett
86	Drew Plunkett
86	Drew Plunkett
87	RIBA Collections
90	Henk Snoek / RIBA Collections
94	*Both* Drew Plunkett
95	Architectural Press Archive / RIBA Collections
96	*Top* Architectural Press Archive / RIBA Collections
96	*Bottom left* Architectural Press Archive / RIBA Collections
96	*Bottom right* Architectural Press Archive / RIBA Collections

97 *Top* Architectural Press Archive / RIBA Collections	123 *Top* John McCann / RIBA Collections	164 Julian Powell-Tuck
97 *Bottom* Architectural Press Archive / RIBA Collections	123 *Bottom left* Architectural Press Archive / RIBA Collections	170 *All* Nigel Hurlstone
104 RIBA Collections	123 *Bottom right* John Maltby / RIBA Collections	172 *Top left* David Connor
105 RIBA Collections	125 John McCann / RIBA Collections	172 *Top middle* David Connor
106 Henk Snoek / RIBA Collections	126 Architectural Press Archive / RIBA Collections	172 *Top right* Joyce Porte
107 RIBA Collections	128 RIBA Collections	173 *Top* Julian Powell-Tuck
108 John Maltby / RIBA Collections	132 John Donat / RIBA Collections	173 *Bottom left* Julian Powell-Tuck
111 RIBA Collections	133 John Donat / RIBA Collections	173 *Bottom middle* Julian Powell-Tuck
112 *Left* Architectural Press Archive / RIBA Collections	137 John Maltby / RIBA Collections	173 *Bottom right* Drew Plunkett
112 *Right* Architectural Press Archive / RIBA Collections	139 *Top* John Donat / RIBA Collections	174 *Left* Lindsay Taylor
113 *Top left* Architectural Press Archive / RIBA Collections	139 *Bottom* John Donat / RIBA Collections	174 *Right* Drew Plunkett
113 *Top right* Architectural Press Archive / RIBA Collections	141 RIBA Collections	177 John Donat / RIBA Collections
113 *Bottom* Drew Plunkett	142 *Top* RIBA Collections	178 John Donat / RIBA Collections
114 *Top* Drew Plunkett	142 *Bottom* John Donat / RIBA Collections	180 *Top left* RIBA Collections
114 *Bottom left* Drew Plunkett	143 *Top left* RIBA Collections	180 *Top right* Ken Kay / RIBA Collections
114 *Bottom right* Drew Plunkett	143 *Top right* RIBA Collections	180 *Bottom* Reid & Peck / RIBA Collections
115 *Top left* Architectural Press Archive / RIBA Collections	143 *Bottom* RIBA Collections	181 *Left* Drew Plunkett
115 *Top right* John Maltby / RIBA Collections	144 RIBA Collections	181 *Right* Drew Plunkett
115 *Bottom left* Drew Plunkett	148 John Donat / RIBA Collections	183 Drew Plunkett
115 *Bottom right* Drew Plunkett	151 *Left* Drew Plunkett	184 Drew Plunkett
117 John McCann / RIBA Collections	151 *Right* Drew Plunkett	185 Drew Plunkett
118 *Top* RIBA Collections	152 Janet Hall / RIBA Collections	186 Natalie Gibson
118 *Bottom left* Henk Snoek / RIBA Collections	154 *Top left* Architectural Press Archive / RIBA Collections	190 Drew Plunkett
118 *Bottom right* Henk Snoek / RIBA Collections	154 *Top right* RIBA Collections	193 *Left* Drew Plunkett
120 Lindsay taylor	154 *Bottom left* RIBA Collections	193 *Right* Drew Plunkett
121 *Top left* Edwin Smith / RIBA Collections	154 *Bottom right* Martin Charles / RIBA Collections	194 Josephine Cicero
121 *Top right* Architectural Press Archive / RIBA Collections	155 *Both* Christopher Hope-Fitch / RIBA Collections	195 Josephine Cicero
122 *Top* Danilo Leonardi / RIBA Collections	157 RIBA Collections	196 Drew Plunkett
122 *Bottom* Christopher Hope-Fitch / RIBA Collections	158 *Left* RIBA Collections	197 *Left* Joyce Porte
	158 *Right* RIBA Collections	197 *Right* Drew Plunkett
	162 John Donat / RIBA Collections	198 *All* Drew Plunkett
	163 John Donat / RIBA Collections	199 *Both* Drew Plunkett
		201 *Top left* Drew Plunkett
		201 *Bottom left* Natalie Gibson
		201 *Top right* Drew Plunkett
		201 *Bottom right* Drew Plunkett
		206 Lindsay Taylor